EARTHSHIP

HOW TO BUILD YOUR OWN

Michael E. Reynolds

First Printing   August 1990
Second Printing   April 1991
Third Printing   November 1991
Fourth Printing   April 1992
Fifth Printing   February 1993

SOLAR SURVIVAL ARCHITECTURE
P.O. Box 1041
Taos, New Mexico 87571
EARTH

Special Thanks

to

Dennis and Gerry Weaver
    for helping to bring the Earthship into the public eye.

Christa Rybczynski
Lawrence Grown
Claire Blanchard
Duane Davis
Peter Kolshorn
    for helping to put the book together.

Dirk Sullivan
Justin Simpson
Jonah Reynolds
    for helping me with Solar Survival Architecture while I put the book together.

Pat Habicht
    who bought the first Earthship and has continued to sail with us.

Paul O'Conner
    for most of the photography.

My wife Chris
    for the name Earthship, for support and inspiration and for making me write this book.

Front Cover Photo - **Justin Simpson**
Back Cover Photo - **Jerry Jameson**

CONTENTS

INTRODUCTION

Noah was told by God to build an ark. Just exactly how God told Noah is left up to the imagination. The fact remains that the clouds on the horizon were revealed to Noah and even though he lived nowhere near water, he was inspired to build a ship. He must have experienced much ridicule for wasting time, energy, and materials on this ship. **Inspiration,** however, **is more powerful than ridicule.** Noah saw the clouds on the horizon and the coming flood, so he built a ship to float on the seas, for there was a time coming when there would be no land.

Today, it doesn't take a prophet to see the clouds on the horizon. There are many signs of the "coming flood". The overall abuse of the earth by humanity is about to leave our ever growing population "flooded" with survival emergencies, on many levels. This will affect water, air, food, shelter, energy, etc. All factors of human survival, as we know it, are immediately threatened by the rapidly deteriorating condition of the planet Earth. The media is full of emergencies regarding polluted oceans, rivers and streams, vanishing wildlife, air quality, radioactive waste, garbage, homeless families, etc. The situation is escalating and in many cases irreparable damage (relative to human life span) is done. This is no special awareness available only to one person. All of us can see the clouds on the horizon.

Just as Noah needed a life supporting ship that would float independently without access to land, we are in need of life supporting ships that will "float" independently without access to various archaic self-destructive systems upon which we have grown dependent. These systems include centralized energy systems which give us acid rain, radioactive waste and power lines lacing the earth like spider webs. We have heating and cooling systems for our living spaces that totally depend upon these centralized energy systems. Most housing today would be totally nonfunctional in terms of comfort, water, toilets, electricity, etc. without massive inputs of energy from centralized sources. There is also food, another basic living need, which also comes mostly from centalized production systems. The quality of this food is, at best, questionable, and it requires energy consuming transportation systems for distribution. All of this is available only through money, which itself is another system between us and our sustanence. Due to the fact that these systems have evolved within a certain narrowness of vision, they have begun to reach points where they do more harm than good. They are literally destroying the planet as they precariously sustain our rather incomplete concept of human life. Our ability to evolve beyond these systems is becoming increasingly necessary, and has a twofold impetus.

1. If we learn to live without these systems, we could radically slow down destruction of the planet and possibly reverse certain aspects of the deterioration.

2. If it is already too late, we will need, in the near future, living units to sustain us via direct contact with existing natural phenomena.

We need to evolve self-sufficient living units that <u>are</u> their own systems. These units must energize themselves, heat and cool themselves, grow food and deal with their own waste. The current concept of housing, in general, supported by massive centralized systems, is no longer appropriate, safe, or reliable. We are now in need of **<u>Earthships</u> — independent vessels — to sail on the seas of tomorrow.**

1. CONCEPT

THE DETERMINING FACTORS OF THE EARTHSHIP IDEA

- What it means to interface
- Why we should do so

This chapter will elaborate on and develop the "independent vessel" concept as a necessary spark toward the evolution of habitat on this planet. There will be discussion of what the vessel must be capable of in order to independently support human existence. Idealistic visions will be digested into realistic possibilities.

A VIEW FROM THE STARS

Some light beings from Alcyone once sent a representative to Earth to analyze the situation there. The light being came, spent some time on Earth and went back to Alcyone and made the following report:

"Basically there were three kinds of creatures there. One type of creature was rooted in the ground. It was very evolved, relative to its host planet. It must have been very intelligent. Without moving from place to place, it took what it needed from the air, the sun, and the ground to sustain a very long and low stress life. It dropped its by-products on the ground around it and they entered the ground and were recycled back into the creature itself. When it died, it entered the ground and became food for its offspring. It was more than a creature; it was a system. It had totally <u>interfaced</u> with its host planet."

The next kind of creature was also very evolved, but it had to move around to sustain itself. It also took what it needed from the air, the sun and the ground. Some of them took each other. Its by-products entered the ground. When this creature died, it also entered the ground, and all became food for the creatures discussed above. These creatures also took some of the above creatures into them for food. There seemed to be a physical exchange between both of these creatures in terms of both food and air. They each inhaled what the other exhaled. They had interfaced with the planet and with each other."

"The last kind of creature was not very well adapted to this planet. As a matter of fact, this creature may have been an alien. It took from both of the other creatures as well as the planet, and gave nothing back except by-products which made it difficult for itself and the others to continue living. It seemed to be taking over the planet like some kind of malignant growth. These creatures prolifically multiply, fight each other, ruthlessly slaughter the other two types of creatures, and ruthlessly abuse the host planet. They do not seem to understand their environment, their chemistry, or themselves. Possibly, they should be contained in some intergalactic corral to keep them from harming other creatures and planets, as well as themselves. In general, this planet was very beautiful and serene until this third creature began to multiply into such numbers that its effect has become a serious threat to the planet itself."

The situation was examined and the light beings from Alcyone decided to enter these creatures and evolve them from the inside out and awaken them to the system of which they are a part. They have the potential to interface with the planet and make it even more beautiful and wonderful than it was before they came. So it was and the project began...

A LOOK AT THE EXISTING CONCEPT OF HOUSING

It was early fall in Cincinnati, Ohio and the trees still had all their leaves. A freak early snowstorm came and the leaves on the trees caught too much of the snow and weighed them down with more weight than the branches were designed to hold. Consequently, many branches broke and they took down power lines with them. This happened in so many places around the city that large numbers of homes and commercial districts were without power. For a couple of days, people could not even buy food because the stores could not operate without power. Many people, thinking they were well prepared for such an emergency, got out their stored canned goods, laid away for just such an occasion. Unfortunately, the majority of the people in the city had electric can openers and they could not get into their emergency stash of food!

The concept of housing really has not changed much in centuries. We started with compartments to shelter us from the elements. Soon, we began to do things in these compartments that required light, fire and water and a reasonable level of comfort. To achieve this we began to bring energy and water to the compartments first by hand, and later by systems. The systems have evolved from carrying wood for a fire pit to nuclear power plants making huge quantities of power that is fed through wires to various compartments all over the planet. The systems have radically evolved; <u>the compartment is still a compartment</u>.

The systems, which are now centralized, have grown to be more important aspects of housing than the compartment itself. We are now dependent upon and vulnerable without these systems. When the systems fail due to some catastrophe, such as a hurricane, tornado or earthquake, people gather together in community facilities such as gymnasiums, with emergency systems. **Existing housing is nonfunctional without systems.** We build all kinds of compartments out of wood, concrete, steel, and glass. We even put them on wheels, but they are still just compartments that we pump life support into. One can easily imagine the limitations, dependency, and vulnerability of being on a life support system in a hospital. What if you found that you had to stay on a life support system for the rest of your life? Many people would rather die than live this way. <u>*We are living this way.*</u>

We are also dying this way. The systems give us power in one hand and poison in the other. Acid rain, radioactive waste, spider webs of power lines, polluted rivers and oceans, vanishing wildlife are all part of the "price" for the life support systems necessary to make the current concept of housing functional.

A person on a life support system in a hospital has to be always within reach and "plugged in" to the various systems that keep him/her alive. So it is with our current concept of housing. This need to be plugged in keeps us from using thousands of acres of dynamic and beautiful land . Some of the most beautiful places on the planet are rendered useless for human habitation because the systems that support housing do not go there. The limitations, the dependency, the vulnerability, and the poison give us many reasons to question the existing concept of housing and ask ourselves, *"Is this really something that we want to attempt to go into the future with?"*

THE SYSTEMS OF EXISTING HOUSING

The systems that render the existing housing compartments habitable are as follows:

Electrical energy production and distribution systems:
These systems provide the electrical energy for lights and appliances and, in many cases, heating and air conditioning. Also, in some cases, the water pumping for the living compartment is dependent upon these systems. In order for these systems to keep up with the demand, they are producing seriously hazardous by-products and effects, as well as lacing the planet with a web of wires.

The price for this power, in terms of money, is high and is getting higher. These systems are owned by corporations whose aims are not always in the best interest of the people or the planet. The price for this power, in terms of ecology, is the depletion of resources which took millions of years to produce and the pollution of the delicate environment that sustains life. It is no longer safe for us to keep using systems, and their reliability is questionable as we voyage into the future.

Water systems:
Centralized water systems always involve electricity in some way, so the water systems are dependent on the electrical systems. This, in addition to questionable purification and treatment processes, leaves many cities with water that is undrinkable and dependent upon the power grid. In rural situations, pumped well water is almost always dependent upon the power grid and in many areas is already undrinkable due to sewage, cattle urine, or radioactive waste.

Sewage systems:
In cities, all waste water goes to the sewage systems and in rural areas, it goes to smaller sewage treatment plants. In very rural areas, it all goes into septic systems. *80% of this water could be reusable as grey water.* In most cases, this is not even considered, so we are left with massive amounts of sewage to treat. The result is extreme pollution in and

around the water near cities, and a waste of very rich irrigation water in rural areas. Again, most sewage systems depend in some way upon electrical systems to function.

Gas systems:
The natural gas systems are the cleanest and the least destructive to the planet. However, in times of catastrophe, they go out (gas lines break) quite often. The distribution of this gas is potentially dangerous and unreliable in times of disaster, and will continue to get more expensive. If the complete functioning of a home depended upon gas, this home would be just as vulnerable as those using any other system. Of course, gas must be shipped by vehicle in rural areas, which is an obvious vulnerability in times of disaster.

Food systems:
Food has become just as much of a system as anything else. The centralized food production system is definitely one of the major support systems for human habitat on this planet. The existing housing compartments do nothing toward dealing with the food needs of the human inhabitants. Food is mass produced, not with human health in mind, but with profits in mind. **Money is, unfortunately, the major objective of all systems.** The various chemicals used to produce more food, faster, have radically affected the quality of fruits, vegetables, dairy products and meats. (Read <u>Diet for a New America</u>, by John

Robbins). The quality of the global waters is also beginning to affect fish. Distribution of food is dependent upon vehicles which may or may not run during economic, natural, or human-made disasters. The existing food system is, therefore, unreliable as well as unhealthy. In addition, it is so wrapped up in the monetary system, that it almost ceases to be food. Speaking of wrapped, it is also wrapped in various plastics and packaging which are a serious disposal problem. Trees and animals don't have to wrap their food; why should we? Is it because we are intelligent?

Materials Systems:
The major materials presently used for housing compartments have many factors that warrant some rethinking.
1. Too much wood is used and although this is a renewable source, trees need time to grow.
2. Many materials are made in centralized areas and have to be shipped all over the country. This is an economic and an energy factor.
3. Most materials require specific skills to use them. This renders them out of the reach of unskilled people to use.
4. There is much energy involved in the manufacturing of materials and consequently much pollution is the result of this.
5. Many new materials are unhealthy to be around. Unfortunately, this is not discovered until they have been used for years.
6. Manufactured materials tend to dictate the nature of housing. It should be vice versa.

Monetary systems:

This system obviously supports the living compartment because all other systems are made available only through this system. If one has no money, the other systems are shut off, regardless of need. People have actually died because their utilities had been shut off during the winter, due to their inability to pay bills. This puts our very survival dependent on a rather shaky and hollow economic system. Thus, the living compartment is in a very vulnerable place. **Not only do we have to deal with the potential unreliability of the various support systems, but we have to deal with the unreliability of the system which gives us access to the support systems.**

DEVELOPING THE NEW CONCEPT OF HOUSING

The above systems, plus a slap dash compartment, make up existing human habitat on this planet. A new concept for habitat must also deal with systems as well as a compartment. Since there are so many problems with the centralized nature of existing systems, and since no one really knows what our voyage into the future will bring, (relative to their continued feasibility and reliability), **we would be much better off and have more control over our lives if our new concept for housing inherently, within its own nature, provided the systems to which we have grown accustomed.**

It would help if we could meet the redesign effort halfway by reevaluating our needs. This is very similar to designing a vehicle to make a voyage into space for five years. The vessel must be self-contained so our usual amount of needs must be reduced.

When one buys a house today, he/she is essentially going on a voyage on planet Earth for the next thirty or forty years. Considering the condition of the planet, (due to years and years of abuse), our vessels must now be self-contained. **Our numbers are too great for us to continue taking from the planet — we must now stand with it.**

The future must see a self-contained vessel capable of sustaining an environment for human habitat on its own, through its own interfacing with natural phenomena. This would allow the vessel to be taken anywhere — to the top of a mountain, out in the desert, to an island, anywhere.

<u>It would be an **Earthship**</u>.

One very important aspect of this new concept for housing is that it must be available to the masses. That is to say, it cannot be a multimillion dollar vessel that only the rich can afford. Everyone is entitled to voyage into the future. The concept, design, and actual method of manifestation of an Earthship must be developed with this in mind. **In addition to interfacing with natural phenomena, this concept must interface with the nature of the common person.**

THE SYSTEMS OF THE EARTHSHIP

The Earthship must, by virtue of the way it interfaces with the existing natural phenomena, provide a compartment that maintains its own levels of comfort. **The Earthship itself must be a heating and cooling system.**

Heating and Cooling system

The sun is a source of heat. The Earth itself is a battery to store heat. Earthships, therefore, must begin relating to both of these phenomena in their design.

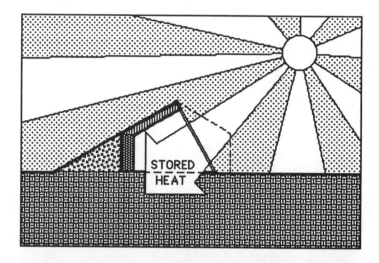

"We" is a more appropriate concept for the future than "I"

House as Battery

Put a cast iron skillet and a tin pan on a stove and heat them both. Then turn off the stove. The tin pan will cool off in a couple of minutes; fifteen minutes later, the skillet will still burn your hand to touch it. This is because it is thicker and has more mass than the tin pan. It is a better 'battery' for holding heat.

Housing evolved on this planet out of a physical and emotional need for shelter. Early on, shelter began to involve the use of energy. Fires were used inside shelters for warmth and cooking. Then electric lights and various appliances appeared. We now have a multitude of appliances, as well as elaborate heating and cooling systems, all of which have become necessities of housing. **The current result is that now energy is as much a factor of housing as shelter.**

No one would really think of building a house that did not provide shelter. For example, can you imagine a beautiful floor plan built on the ground without a roof? This would be absurd. At this point in our evolution, we must accept the fact that energy is essential to housing; it **is just as absurd to build a house with no provision for energy as it is to build a house without a roof.**

The energy factor can be broken into two categories - appliances and temperature. As will be discussed later, the electrical energy requirements of appliances can be met with immediately available technology, collected from the sun or wind, and stored in batteries for later use. Temperature can be collected and stored much the same way as electrical energy. A glass wall on the south face of a house will transmit heat to the space and the mass behind it. That space and mass, potentially the entire house, can serve as a battery to store the heat. This concept is known as thermal mass, and works well anywhere there is exposure to any source of heat.

Thermal mass has been utilized for centuries by animals and ancient civilizations, but has been given up for more 'modern', 'economical' construction methods which make no provision for storage of heat.

The idea that we call a battery is really a reflection of a pattern or phenomenon upon which the entire universe is based. This is the relationship between energy and matter. All matter is actually stored energy, while all energy is actually 'evaporated' matter. **Matter itself is essentially a battery.**

In much the same way that matter stores energy, dense mass stores temperature. The more dense the mass is, the more temperature it stores. Therefore, a house or shelter made of dense mass is much better for storing temperature than a house made of thin pieces of wood. This is true regardless of the original source of temperature be it heat or cooling.

A good analogy can be made to the way a barrel stores water. If the water storing capacity of a barrel were compared to the temperature storing capacity of most houses, the 'barrel' would be 1" deep, rather than 3'-0" deep. Most houses have little or no dense mass, therefore they store no temperature.

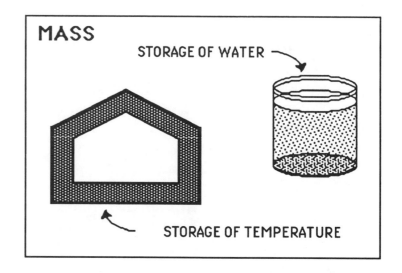

MASS

STORAGE OF WATER

STORAGE OF TEMPERATURE

Consequently, energy must continually be brought in via wires and pipes from outside sources to control inside temperature.

Today's better insulation helps keep this heated air from escaping, but insulation does not absorb or store heat. If houses could store heat from any source, as a barrel stores water, they would require much less energy to stay 'full.' Instead of using mass, we usually continuously heat or cool the air in our houses to control their temperature. **Air does not hold temperature.** This is like trying to collect water on a flat surface – it just runs away. Just as we must collect water in a barrel if we want to save it, we must collect temperature in mass if we want to save it.

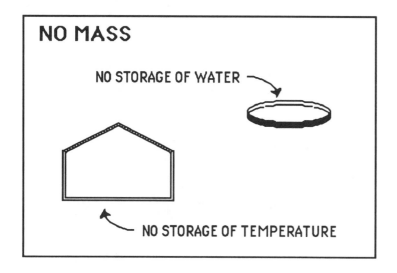

NO MASS

NO STORAGE OF WATER

NO STORAGE OF TEMPERATURE

Since we go to the trouble and expense of putting heat into a house, we should do what we can to make the house hold that heat. **Houses should be built with mass surrounding every space to allow them to truly act as batteries.**

Our bodies, being 96% water – which is mass, function similarly. A certain amount of energy is put into our bodies, via food, etc. Some of this energy results in heat, which is stored in the built-in mass of our bodies; our bodies are batteries. Thus we can maintain 98° F. when the air around us is 50° F. and we consume food only occasionally. If our bodies held no heat, we would have to eat all the time, putting energy in constantly to maintain our body temperature. We would run out of food, wear out our digestive systems and have time for nothing but eating.

Housing is similar. Without mass, we are running out of fuel, taxing our energy systems, and wasting most of our time making and paying for fuel. This payment is suffered both economically and ecologically. If our houses are to hold heat as our bodies do, they must be made of mass. The more dense the mass, the more temperature it stores. The Earthship provides for this storage by wrapping every room with 3'-0" thick dense walls. It is interfacing with the earth, by aligning with the phenomenon of thermal mass.

The concept of house as battery is appropriate anywhere, regardless of solar availability. **No matter what the heating or cooling source, the battery will retain the temperature.**

<u>**Food system:**</u>
An Earthship should encounter the Earth in such a way that it provides space and environment for year round growing of edible plants, fruits, and nuts. Diets could be leaned toward what is easily produced in the environment provided by the Earthship, as the Earthship's food production capabilities are slowly evolved toward the desires of the inhabitant.

<u>House as Greenhouse</u>
For the inhabitants of Earthships to be independent, they will have to produce food. What will this mean in the design of the vessel?

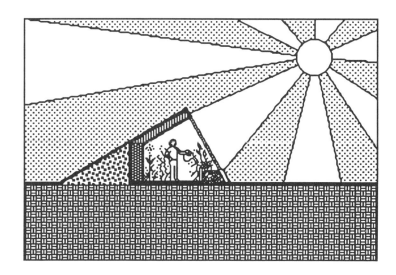

Obviously, we need dirt; there will need to be areas with dirt floors. Current Earthships provide planters, but entire rooms and spaces will be needed to grow reasonable quantities of various types of food. For example, we will need height for growing citrus and nut trees. Major requirements of a garden must be provided within the vessel, so food production can occur year round, protected from temperature extremes and potentially bad air and acid rain. This means that a certain amount of space will be for plants, not for people. These factors are all design determinants for the vessel. **As important as a bedroom, there must be a garden.**

Electrical system:
The Earthship must provide enough electricity to light itself and to run various appliances to which humans have grown accustomed. Obviously, the cost of the components that provide this electricity would be regulated by a more efficient approach, on the part of the owners, to the overall use of electricity. The simple admission of sunlight reduces the need for daytime lighting.

House as Power Plant
The vessel must be a small, independent power station. Through wind and/or sun, it must capture enough energy to meet the electrical demands of the inhabitants in a clean way. Currently, this can be done by collecting energy from windmills and photovoltaic panels

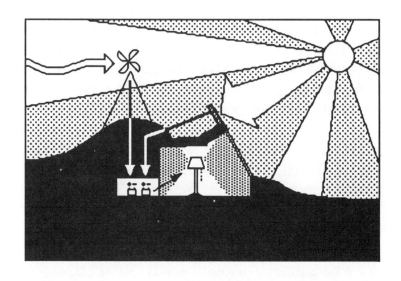

- storing the energy in batteries, and using the energy as needed from the batteries. Photovoltaic cells have been developed to convert light energy from the sun into electricity. They have become more reliable in more areas than windmills; however, it is important to note that windmills can be made with less technology. This energy is stored in conventional electric vehicle type (golf cart) batteries. This method has already proven itself in the 'sun belt' to be an adequate solution for the requirements of home appliances. Based on what has been learned there, this method will soon be sensitive enough to provide for energy requirements in other areas where the sun must come through clouds. In the future, there may be other ways to collect and store energy; soon we will be taking it right out of the air, out of the atoms.

(Read <u>Tapping Zero Point Energy</u>, by Moray B. King) Our specific use of energy may evolve; but, today, we need energy which comes to us through wall sockets. This cannot be changed overnight. The concept of the energy producing vessel can be evolved in many ways; but, **the immediate application must start with that to which we are accustomed, and lead us to that which is more appropriate.**

Just as a generator is designed as an integral part of a car, a power generating system must be integral in the design of Earthships. The aesthetic of the Earthship is a result of the systems' requirements. Current Earthships are built and finished with earthy materials, and are buried with earth. They feel good, but their appearance is subject to performance. It will be difficult, if not impossible, to design an English Colonial Earthship. An empty wood box can be decorated as an English Colonial, but it would need power lines and systems. An Earthship cannot have these connections to the power grid. The days of preconceived ideas about what Architecture must look like are over. **Buildings, housing especially, must become interfacing vessels, evolving the preconceived ideas of style and appearance to independence and performance. Emotionally, this is another way <u>we</u> must change to meet the Earthship halfway.**

Water system:

The Earthship must, within its own electrical system have provision for pumping water with existing conventional methods, as well as catching rain and snow melt. An Earthship must provide its own water.

House as Water Provider

Currently, we bring water systems to houses. An Earthship can have a well that is pumped from the Earthship's independent power system. Vessels can also catch water. These systems can be built into the nature of the vessel itself, eliminating the need for an outside water system. In the future, we may discover ways to take water from the air, by condensing it; but, even now, we can pump water with power produced by the vessel. Soon it will be important to distill water for human consumption. Distillers will have to be built into the vessel. Hot water will also have to be provided by the vessel itself. Various solar hot water heaters work in many areas with current technology. Earthships must eventually produce, distill, and heat their own water.

Sewage system:

An Earthship must divide its water waste into grey water and black water, reusing both and/or delivering both to the Earth in a form which is totally acceptable to existing natural processes.

House as Septic System

Black water comes from the toilet; grey water comes from everywhere else, (lavatories, tubs, sinks, etc.). Current systems put all grey and black water together underground in a septic tank or sewer; all of this water must be chemically treated and ends up polluting our rivers, streams, oceans, and underground, largely because of sheer volume. Then we buy chemical fertilizers for our plants. Instead, we could be using the grey water, which is right in front of us to feed our plants. There are food particles in the kitchen sink; there is protein in the bath water. Plants thrive on these things. The waste system for grey water can be tied into the garden. This can be done in many ways, but direct flow is the easiest.

When the grey water is reused, the septic tank or sewer needs become minimal because only black water from the toilet is sent to it. Current septic tanks and sewer systems are so large because they have to deal with the shower, dishwasher, clothes washer, etc... altogether. A much smaller septic tank for black water only may even be contained, or at least have a minimal effect on surrounding areas. Sewer systems for cities would also be much more manageable with only black water. The reuse of grey water would, of course, mean watching what you put down your drain - no Drano or harmful chemicals.

Gas system:

Since gas is the least offensive system in conventional housing, early Earthships that do not quite make it all the way to total independence should use gas as a back-up. This should still be for as few needs as possible.

House as Methane Plant:

Gas (methane) can be made from sewage and compost. Ideally, Earthships could produce enough gas from their compost and black water septic tanks to deal with their own gas needs. At this point, gas is only required for cooking and backup hot water. Domestic methane could easily meet this demand.

Materials system:

The shape and fabric of an Earthship must grow out of the "natural" resources of our age. This includes anything that appears on the planet in large quantities and in many areas. These materials and the techniques for using them must be accessible to the common person in terms of price and skill required to use them. The less energy required to turn a found object into a usable building material the better. Designs for Earthships must relate to the direct use (with little or no modification) of natural resources of the 21st century.

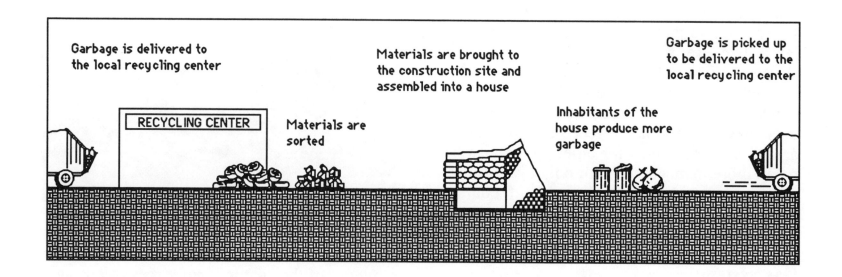

Garbage is delivered to the local recycling center

RECYCLING CENTER

Materials are sorted

Materials are brought to the construction site and assembled into a house

Inhabitants of the house produce more garbage

Garbage is picked up to be delivered to the local recycling center

House as Assemblage of By-products

An Earthship of the future should make use of indigenous materials, those occurring naturally in an area. For centuries, housing has been built from found materials such as rock, earth, reeds, and logs. Now, there are mountains of by-products of our civilization that are already made and delivered to all areas. *These are the natural resources of the twenty-first century.* An Earthship must make use of these via techniques available to the common person. In a time when mortgage payments take up 75% of monthly income, homelessness is an epidemic, and the stress is becoming a disease, **housing must return to the grasp of the individual.**

Monetary system:

Because the Earthship itself provides all of the systems upon which the inhabitant would be spending much money , and the fact that the Earthship, inherently in its concept and design, is very accessible to the common person, the dependence upon the existing monetary system would be greatly reduced, thus reducing stress to both people and the planet.

House as a Method for Survival, (Money):

The ideal vision of the Earthship would therefore be — a vessel that provides both space and systems for humans and edible plants, independently, through its own interfacing with natural phenomena. This would reduce and ultimately remove the stress involved with living on this planet, both to humans and the rest of the planet. This concept of living, (independent voyage vs. dependent trap), could change the nature of the human mind itself. It could provide a basis and a direction for conscious evolution on the Earth.

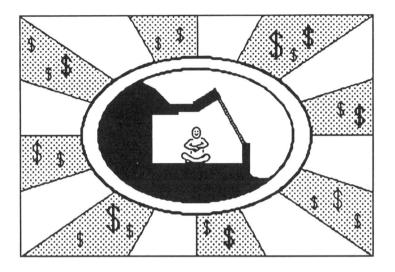

This is a vision for tomorrow to inspire us. Now, what can we _do_ today?

TODAY

The bummer factors of existing housing are:

- it is continually increasing the need for the monstrous systems which are failing and flailing and destroying the planet
- its location is limited relative to the availability of systems
- it is non-functional without systems
- its method of manifestation contributes to the stress level of both people and the planet

19

An independent vessel must:
- be able to function anywhere
- decrease and ultimately dispense with
  the need for the outside systems
  which currently support the
  living compartment
- be accessible to common people
- grow food
- deal with its own waste and by-
  products
- make its own energy
- make its own temperate climate
  inside
- make use of the by-products of the
  twenty-first century

All of this must be done by interfacing with natural phenomena, without any connection to outside sources.

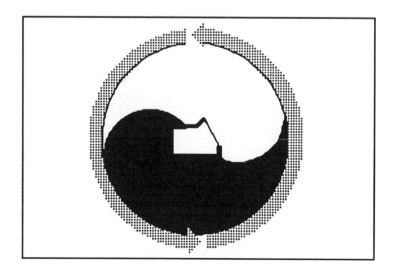

WHAT IS MEANT BY INTERFACING

"Interfacing" is a word which is used a lot these days. When a solar electric system or a wind powered electric system is hooked up to the existing power grid, and more power is needed than can be provided by the solar or wind electric system, it is provided by the power grid. When there is an excess of solar or wind generated electricity, it goes back to the power grid. This is called 'interfacing with the existing power grid.'

Interfacing is a dance between two systems. In the example above, the solar/wind system interfaces with the existing system and they give and take, back and forth. It is a dance, a wave, a pulse, an alignment, as opposed to merely taking from the existing power system.

Animals and trees interface with the natural phenomena of the planet. A tree grows out of the planet, feeds from the planet, dies, rots back into the planet, and its offspring feed from the rot that the tree became. It breathes the carbon dioxide given off by animals, and provides oxygen for animals to breathe. Trees and animals are active participants in the processes of the planet and each other.

Humans' lifestyle, including housing, is not interfacing with the planet. We are getting further and further away from the processes of the planet. Currently, we are basically taking from the planet, while we are not returning anything useful to the planet. Our life is <u>on</u> the planet, but not <u>of</u> the planet.

Interface: A point at which relative systems interact.

Deface: To mar or spoil the surface or appearance of; disfigure.[1]

Existing houses, due to the fact that they are totally supported by destructive out-of-control systems, contribute to the <u>defacing</u> of the planet. A new concept of housing must <u>interface</u> with the planet. By interfacing with the planet, it supports us as humans while supporting the planet as an organism. This recognizes both the planet and the relative systems. This requires aligning ourselves with the processes of the planet and reevaluating our concept of living. Housing <u>is</u> how we live; we may have to begin to reevaluate how we live in order to relate to a new concept of housing.

There are many existing natural phenomena which result in temperature, energy, food production, and all things we need to sustain life. We must learn to align ourselves with these phenomena - to <u>interface</u> with them. We must create a vessel which helps us to do this. Through interfacing with existing phenomena on site, the vessel must provide an environment which will sustain human life. This is a visionary concept, which cannot be achieved overnight. We will only be able to create a facsimile of this ultimate interfacing vessel - the Earthship. However this is the first step toward the <u>vision</u> of the ultimate interfacing vehicle. The facsimile interfaces with the Sun and the Earth and begins to take care of us; but we must accept the fact that it is not nearly as evolved as the vision. It is simply a step in the direction of the vision.

Our minds can move toward the truth more swiftly than our bodies and emotions.

---

[1]Webster's II, New Riverside Dictionary, Berkeley Books, New York, 1984.

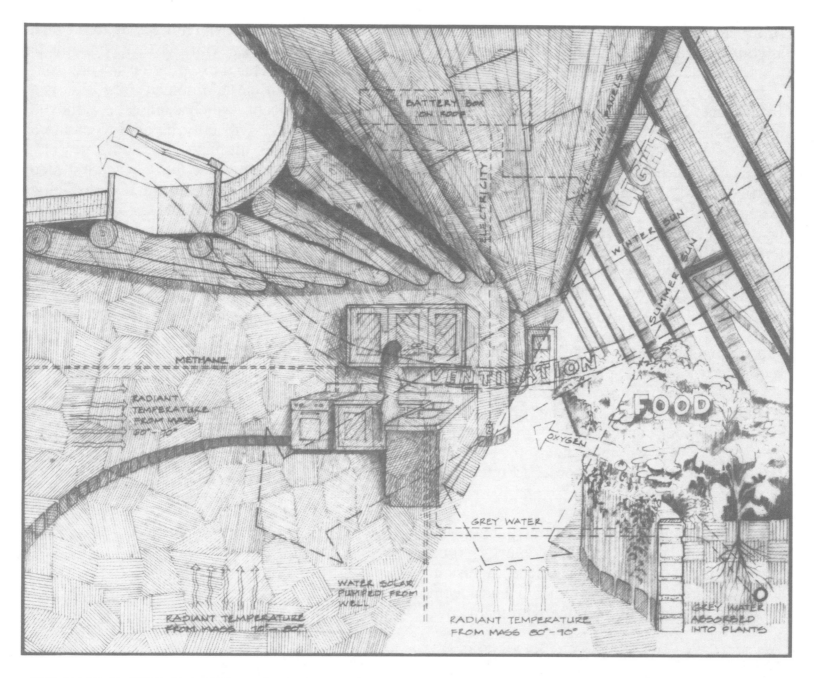

WE CAN ALIGN OURSELVES WITH NATURAL PHENOMENA AND INTERFACE WITH THEM

22

THE EARTHSHIP AND ITS RELATIONSHIP TO THE CAR

The inventors of the automobile perhaps had visions of faster, smoother vehicles rolling on wheels, such as the cars we have today; however, the best they could produce with their current industry and technology was the Model T. Likewise, our current technology today makes Earthships barely functional, perhaps even crude, relative to the <u>vision</u> of the concept. It is only a step away from the dependent house, but it is a significant step. Future Earthships will keep evolving toward that vision, as a Model T evolved into a 1990 Porsche.

The automobile was an invention and a vision; however, this vision was limited. The inventors did not envision the planet filled with millions of cars emitting carbon monoxide, or cities filled with traffic jams, making life so unhealthy one could barely walk down the sidewalk. The car has evolved to the point where it could be the wrong thing now, due to fumes, noise, pollution, the dependency on oil, and the stress it puts on the planet. The concept of moving along in a capsule may be fine, but there needs to be a new kind of vessel. The concept of a gasoline fueled vessel must be evolved beyond the dependency on gasoline, the emission of pollutants and the noise.

Likewise, the house must be developed into a new kind of vessel. It is merely a package now - an empty box. If there were only a few of these houses scattered around the planet, there wouldn't be a problem. But, when an idea or vision is taken relative to people, who keep multiplying, it too must be multiplied. Simply multiply each invention times 1 billion. If Henry Ford had taken the Model T times 1 billion, he would have thought of the pollutants, and the gasoline dependency as problems. Existing housing has similar problems - it requires a massive amount of energy and sewage systems which in turn pollute the environment. This housing times 1 billion is going to kill all of us and make our planet uninhabitable.

Next, consider the concept of the Earthship times 1 billion. It is interfacing with the planet, not stressing it. Compare this to multiplying a tree times 1 billion; there is no real problem. If we are going to interface, we must look to trees, animals, rivers, etc. to see the rules of interfacing. If we are to design a vessel which won't backfire in the future, it must be looked at on a mass scale. We must envision what it would be like to live in the midst of Earthships, which emit no pollutants, deal with their own waste, are partially covered with earth, and require no outside systems. This is like standing amongst 1 billion trees, instead of 1 billion cars. Our current housing and automobile situation shows the shortsightedness of our vision. The concept of the Earthship is prepared to evolve; it has a broader vision. The way in which a tree interfaces with the earth is the format for how the independent vessel should evolve. We must begin *leaning toward this vision. (*See A Coming of Wizards, Chapter 6, Michael Reynolds) It cannot be done overnight; but, **if we lean in that direction, we are participating in our own evolution and giving ourselves a chance for survival.**

EVOLUTION OF OUR LIFESTYLES RELATIVE TO THE VESSEL

It is probable that, even if we did have the ultimate interfacing vessel available to us now, we wouldn't be able to survive in it. We would have to evolve our living habits toward what the vessel could provide. For instance, our diets would change. The vessel could not produce packaged microwave dinners and other processed foods, so we would have to lean our diets toward what it could produce - fruits, vegetables, and grains. The Earthship will continue to evolve to be able to produce more foods, as we continue to lean toward a new diet. Current Earthships do provide growing spaces for plants, with the living spaces for people. These growing spaces are easy to care for because they are in the "path of everyday living". But because they cannot

supply everything, we must supplement the vessels with grocery stores. Ultimately, as both we and the Earthship evolve, we will be able to grow all of our own food, and reduce or dissolve our need for packaged foods. This is true of all needs. As we "lean" our lifestyles toward what the Earthship can provide, we evolve the Earthship toward what we need. Someday we will meet.

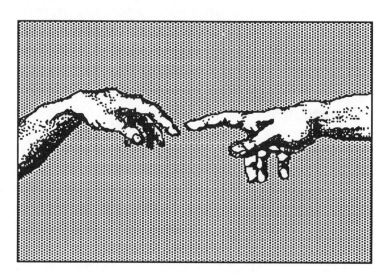

The evolution of our lifestyles will affect all aspects of living. It is already affecting the lives of people who live in Earthships. These people have discovered that we usually use a tremendous amount of electricity. To match that existing 'need,' a very large solar power system would be needed. Rather than spend the extra $300 for each extra solar panel, most Earthship owners try to evolve their electricity consumption to meet the capacity provided in a reasonably sized and priced system. This is not a radical change; it usually means turning off unnecessary lights, using less appliances, staggering the use of the appliances one does use, and generally being aware that the supply of electricity is limited. We tend to think of our electrical energy as being unlimited, but the truth is that our consumption is taking from the planet in a radical way. In the Earthship, we will constantly be evolving toward lowering our consumption, while the vessel continues to be able to provide more.

The purpose of this book is to develop a vision based on a revised concept of housing on this planet. The Earthship is an immediately available step in that direction. It is becoming more and more evident that we need a revised concept for living. We are facing crises in energy, water, air, and food quality. We must respond with the design of the human habitat. **It must now be a vessel, that will float on the seas of tomorrow.**

JUST AS MOSS GROWS ON THE NORTH SIDE OF TREES,
PEOPLE WILL FLOURISH ON THE SOUTH SIDE OF MOUNTAINS

2. <u>LOCATION</u>

INTERFACING WITH LOCAL PHENOMENA

- **With what can we interface?**
- **How do these phenomena work?**
- **How is an Earthship placed on a site?**

In the Northern Hemisphere, moss grows on the north side of trees and snow melts on the south side of mountains. If you want a log to float downstream, you must place it in the current, not near the shore in an eddy. Earthships must also be placed for optimum interaction with natural phenomena. This chapter explores the natural phenomena of the planet and explains how to interface an Earthship into the existing phenomena of the area.

THE PHENOMENA

The Earthship was developed at 37 degrees North latitude and at an altitude of 7000 feet. The winters get as low as 30° below zero and the summers as high as 100° F. In this climate of extremes, the Earthship (through interfacing with natural phenomena) maintains a temperature of 65°- 75° F with no backup heating or cooling systems. These extremes have demanded evolution of the Earthship's performance, both in terms of heating and cooling itself. The phenomena have been studied in theory and reality, and the interfacing methods have evolved through testing and experimentation, so that at this point, the Earthship can be taken almost anywhere.

We will first explain how these phenomena determine the design of the Earthship in Northern New Mexico. This will provide an understanding of how to relate to these phenomena as design determinants. At the end of the chapter, we will discuss how the interfacing with these same phenomena varies in different climates.

The phenomena with which the Earthship interfaces are all related to the four elements, FIRE, EARTH, AIR and WATER.

FIRE

Fire provides HEAT, LIGHT and ENERGY. The SUN is unarguably our major source of the above. The sun is a natural phenomenon.

Conventional housing compartments shield the living spaces from the sun, thus disregarding it as a potential source of heat, light, and energy.

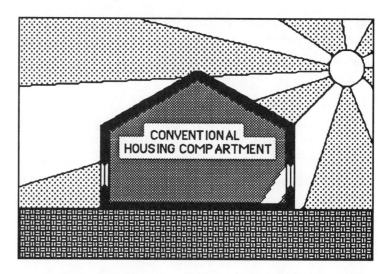

An Earthship must **encounter** the sun and interface with it to gather this limitless heat, light and energy. This suggests a different shape for the compartment, and an orientation toward the sun.

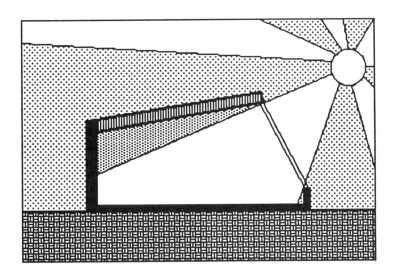

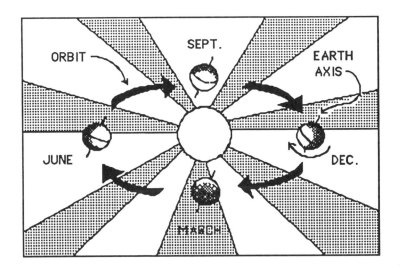

This in turn suggests an analysis and understanding of this phenomenon called sun. We must understand this fire in order to interface with it.

Sun / Earth Relationships

Orbit
The Earth orbits around the sun once a year, in an elliptical path (the shape of an oval), and at an average distance of about 93 million miles (150 million kilometers).

Earth Axis
The Earth also spins about its own axis, which accounts for the apparent rising and setting of the sun.

Tilt
The tilt of the Earth is 23 1/2° from the plane of its solar orbit, which is why (in the Northern Hemisphere) the sun appears lower in the sky in the winter and higher in the sky in the summer.

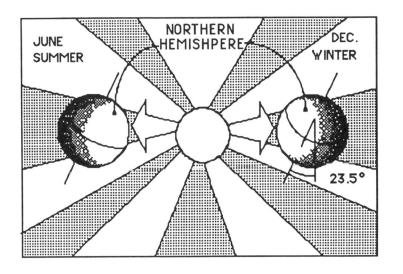

The opposite is true in the Southern Hemisphere. Due to this tilt, the sun comes to Northern New Mexico at about 30°, relative to the surface of the earth, in the winter,

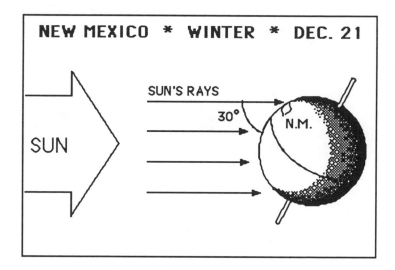

and about 77°, relative to the surface of the earth, in the summer.

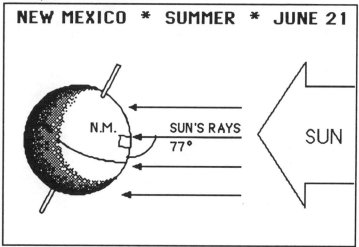

Solstice / Equinox

The sun will appear at different angles in the sky from different locations on the globe. Relative to the Northern Hemisphere, it is always at its lowest point in the sky on the day called the *winter solstice*, and at its highest on the *summer solstice*.

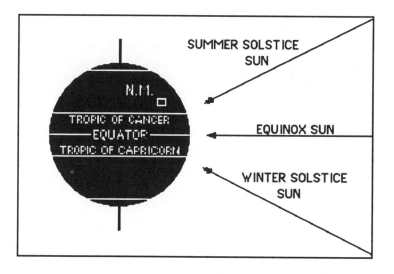

These dates are December 21 and June 21, respectively. In the Southern Hemisphere, it is the opposite. Midway between these points are the two *equinoxes*, March 21 and September 21, on which days the sun is in the midpoint between its solstice positions, i.e. straight above the equator.

Altitude

The apparent height of the sun can be measured as its angle above the horizon plane of the earth. This is called its *altitude*.

There is a difference of 47 degrees between its summer and winter altitudes, as seen from New Mexico at noon.

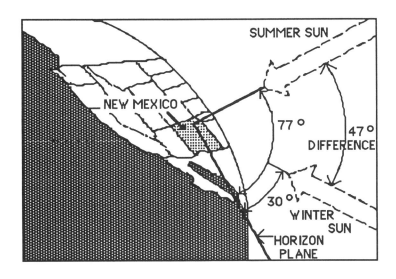

LOCATION – ORIENTATION

IN NORTHERN NEW MEXICO, AND ANYWHERE AT ABOUT 37° NORTH LATITUDE, THE SUN IS AT A 30° ALTITUDE AT NOON ON THE COLDEST DAY OF THE YEAR. THE MOST IMPORTANT THERMAL PRIORITY FOR THIS AREA IS GETTING ENOUGH HEAT THROUGH THE WINTER. THEREFORE, WE FACE THE GLAZING OF THE EARTHSHIP TO THE SOUTH, AND TILT THE GLASS AT 60° TO BE PERPENDICULAR TO THE SUN AT ITS LOW POINT. THIS REDUCES REFLECTION TO A MINIMUM IN WINTER WHEN HEAT IS NEEDED.

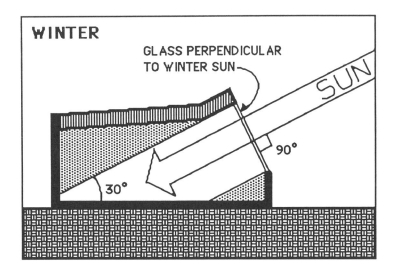

THIS SLOPE ALSO RESULTS IN CONSIDERABLE REFLECTION IN THE SUMMER, WHEN HEAT IS NOT WANTED.

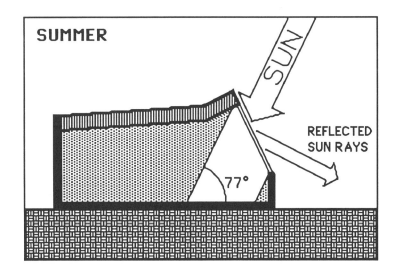

Azimuth

These same phenomena also account for the change in length of days between summer and winter. The sun is not only higher in the sky in the summer, but also goes through a wider plan arc, or *azimuth*. In northern New Mexico, the summer azimuth is about 240° while the winter azimuth angle is about 120°. This means that the <u>winter</u> sun rises 60° east of south and sets at 60° west of south. When heating is and issue, these winter angles must be related to in the front glass face configuration.

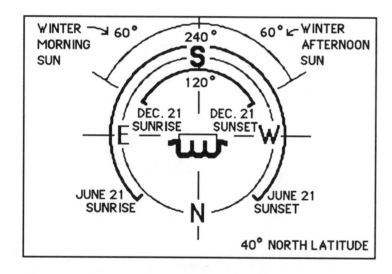

LOCATION – CONFIGURATION

AN EARTHSHIP IN NORTHERN NEW MEXICO SHOULD HAVE A FLAT FRONT FACE. IF THERE ARE TO BE ANY PARTS THAT ARE PULLED FORWARD OF OTHER SEGMENTS, THEY SHOULD RELATE TO THE WINTER AZIMUTH ANGLE OF 60°, SO AS NOT TO CREATE ANY SHADOWS THAT WOULD BLOCK SOLAR GAIN.

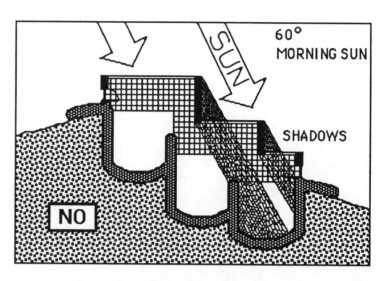

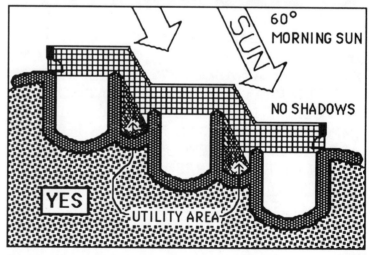

Solar Arc

In combination, (altitude and azimuth changes) the sun appears to move through our sky in a 3-dimensional *solar arc*, as the earth rotates.

This path changes every day from shortest and lowest on the winter solstice to longest and highest on the summer solstice. It is always symmetrical about its high point (its zenith) at noon, which also points to true south.

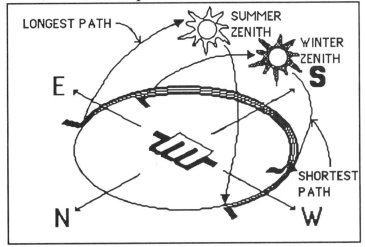

LOCATION-STRATEGIC AIM

EARTHSHIPS IN NORTHERN NEW MEXICO ARE POSITIONED SO THAT THEIR NORTH-SOUTH

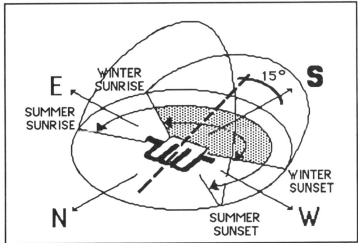

AXIS IS SLIGHTLY (10-15 DEGREES) EAST OF

TRUE SOUTH. THIS ALLOWS THEM TO CATCH THE HEAT OF THE SUN A LITTLE EARLIER IN THE WINTER MORNINGS.

Percent Solar Possible

Different points on the globe get different amounts of sunshine, but places along the <u>same</u> latitude lines see the same number of sun hours on any given day. Also places along the same latitude, will see the sun at the same altitudes. This means the solar orientation for an Earthship will be the same on any given latitude assuming the elevation above sea level is the same. Climate obviously varies with elevation difference.

Places that are on the same latitude may not get the same amount of actual sunshine, due to clouds, smog, haze or any other conditions that might block out the sun.

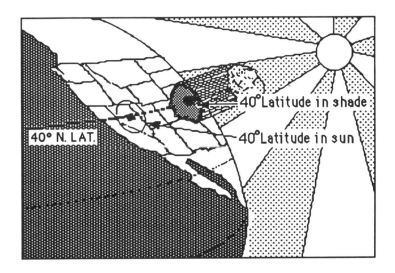

LOCATION – SOUTHERN EXPOSURE

ON DECEMBER 21, WHEN THE SUN IS AT ITS LOWEST POINT IN THE SKY, IT IS ONLY 30 DEGREES ABOVE THE HORIZON AT NOON. AN EARTHSHIP IN NORTHERN NEW MEXICO MUST BE LOCATED WHERE THERE WILL BE NO OBSTRUCTIONS THAT MIGHT BLOCK THIS LOW WINTER SUN. A FEW DECIDUOUS TREES (THOSE THAT WILL LOSE THEIR LEAVES IN THE WINTER, THEREFORE LETTING SUN THROUGH WHEN IT IS MOST NEEDED) ARE OKAY.

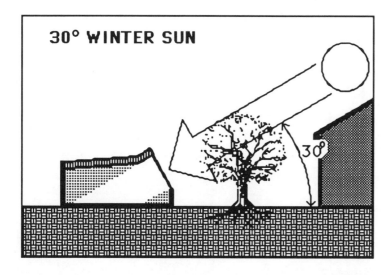

EARTH

The earth receives, stores and refines the heat, energy, and light from the sun. There are many earthly phenomena involved in these processes. Since the Earthship receives the sun much the same as the earth itself does, it would obviously employ the same processes of interfacing with the sun that the earth itself uses.

Heat

A brief discussion of the way heat moves (thermodynamics) is necessary here to explore these processes.

Heat Energy

Heat energy cannot be created or destroyed, but it <u>can</u> be converted into other forms, channeled to and contained in specific places. Whatever renewable energy source is locally available, there is a way to convert it into a form we can use and put it in a place we can use it from. *Heat energy* can be converted into *electrical*, *chemical*, or *mechanical* energy.

Heat Transfer

When free interchange of heat takes place, it is always from the hotter (place or body) to the colder. The hotter will lose energy and the colder will gain energy until a state of equilibrium is attained. Cool mass walls will absorb the sun's heat, but when the sun goes down and the air in the room cools, the heat will slowly be drawn back out of the walls.

conduction

The process of heat energy moving through a material (the sun heats the south side of a mass wall and the heat moves through the wall to the room on the north side of the wall).

radiation

Radiant energy is transmitted as electromagnetic rays, which can travel through space (even a vacuum). They heat any object which intercepts them (the sun heating the earth and you).

convection

Convection is the movement of heat in liquid or gas. The source heats the gas and the currents within that liquid or gas carry the heat to you. (Subtle heat from warm thermal mass travels through the air to warm you).

Comfort Zone

The *comfort zone* is the set of conditions at which humans are comfortable to perform everyday tasks. It is a very different set of conditions for each location and culture, but all are affected by some of the same environmental phenomena:

ambient air temperature

the temperature of the air surrounding the body (without taking humidity into account)

relative humidity

the percentage of water vapor in the air relative to to maximum amount of water vapor it can hold at a given temperature

air movement or speed

how fast the air is moving adjacent to the body, it can be affected by ventilation

temperature of adjacent objects

Sometimes called *mean radiant temperature*, this is the effect of heated mass upon a body (if the air in a room is cool, but the walls and floor are warm, then the <u>perceived</u> temperature is higher)

Matter

All matter is made up of molecules which have weight or *mass* (weight is actually the effect of gravity upon mass).

specific heat

All mass has the ability to store heat, yet some substances have the ability to hold more heat per unit weight than others. The term for this capacity is specific heat.

thermal conductivity

Thermal conductivity is a measure of how fast heat is conducted through a unit thickness of a substance.

thermal mass

Thermal mass is a term for any mass used to hold or contain temperature. For example, our bodies are made up of about 90% water. Our bodies hold a 98° temperature due to the *thermal mass* of this water. **The ideal material for thermal mass would hold a lot of heat and give it off over a long period of time**. Water is one of the best natural materials with regard to these properties. Earth, adobe sand, rock, brick and concrete are also good thermal mass materials. Earth is the least expensive and most readily available, however, and can also be stabilized for structure. This is why it is the ideal material for the Earthship. The more dense the matter, the more heat it will hold. Therefore tightly packed or rammed earth is a very good container or "battery" for storing "comfort zone" temperature in.

LOCATION – MASS

THE INDIVIDUAL SPACES (I.E. INTERIOR AIR VOLUMES) WITHIN THE EARTHSHIP MUST BE INDIVIDUALLY SURROUNDED BY ABUNDANT DENSE MASS TO STORE AND GIVE OFF THE HEAT OBTAINED FROM THE SUN. THE HIGHER THE VOLUME OF MASS, RELATIVE TO THE AIR SPACE YOU ARE TRYING TO HEAT, THE MORE STABLE YOUR COMFORT ZONE COULD BE. THIS CAN BE ACHIEVED BY VERY THICK INTERIOR WALLS AND SUBMERGING THE VESSEL INTO THE MASS OF THE EARTH AS MUCH AS POSSIBLE. IN NORTHERN NEW MEXICO, SOUTH SLOPING HILLSIDES ARE THE BEST, BECAUSE THE EARTHSHIP CAN BE SUNKEN INTO THE MASS OF THE HILL WITHOUT HAVING TO DIG A PIT IN FRONT FOR LETTING SUN IN.

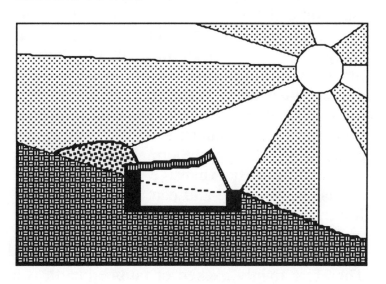

Thermal Movement

When a substance is heated, it will expand; when it is cooled, it will contract. Earth, concrete, wood, and all building materials are affected by weather in this way. This is called *thermal movement*, and can cause a brittle material like concrete or masonry to crack. Masonry buildings may also be pushed by the swelling of frozen earth or water around their foundation walls. An Earthship is more "of the Earth," and it will accept and experience similar thermal movement to that of the Earth. Consequently, it will move with the Earth rather than resisting it. It is very expensive to make foundations that resist the Earth. An Earthship must interface with the Earth, rather than resist it.

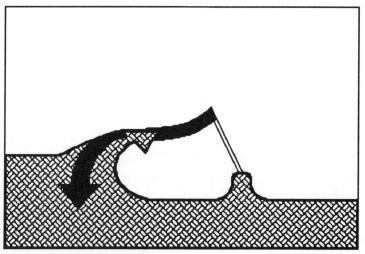

LOCATION-SOIL

EARTHSHIPS MUST BE BUILT OUT OF EARTH ON STABLE, *UNDISTURBED EARTH*. THE

DESIGN IS NOT MEANT TO RESIST THE EARTH, BUT TO JOIN IT.

Energy and Light

Green cells in the leaves of plants and trees harvest the sun's energy. They change the sunlight into chemical energy by the process of photosynthesis. This chemical (food) energy is then transported to the rest of the plant for use or storage.

To make the most of this phenomenon, the Earthship must provide sunlit areas for photosynthesis to happen <u>within</u> its interior space. This allows for year round growing of edible plants. The Earthship must be oriented toward the sun for this to be possible.

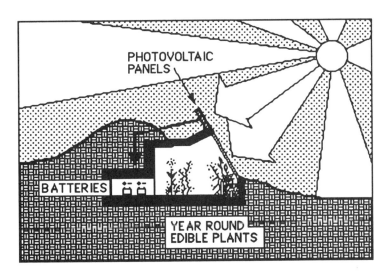

In addition to this, the Earthship must perform a similar "harvest" for electrical energy. Photovoltaic cells, mounted on the roof of the Earthship, change sunlight into electrical energy, which can then be transported to batteries for storage and use.

Natural sunlight can often be used instead of artificial electrical light, if it is appropriately allowed into an interior space. This reinforces the solar orientation of the Earthship once again.

life

The interfacing of the Earth with the sun (and with water) is responsible for what we call life. There are certain functions of life itself that must be interfaced by the Earthship.

The *biosphere* is the region surrounding the Earth that supports life. This includes the *atmosphere*, the *hydrosphere (oceans)*, and the *lithosphere* - the outer layer of the Earth.

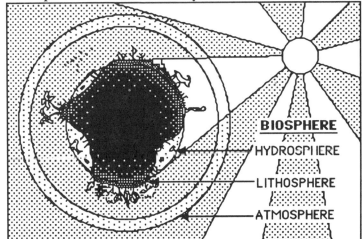

Everything between, including all of life, is powered by the sun. The less we pollute the biosphere the better it will be able to support us. The sun is the most abundant energy source available, it is free and its direct use does not harm our biosphere, where as man made power plants are destroying it.

food chain
Through photosynthesis, the sun's energy is stored in plants, and can then be used by animals, including humans, for their energy.

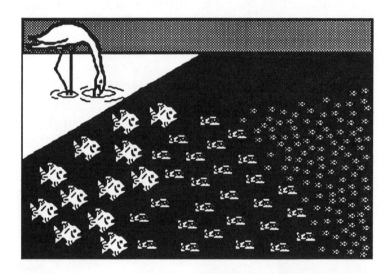

Thousands of plants become the food for hundreds of small creatures who are eaten by scores of larger creatures, who are eaten by single large predators. In a natural *community*, there are just enough of each type of organism to feed the next group and still have enough survivors to propagate the species.

The intertwinings of life, death and decomposition are continuous natural life cycles.

production
The inclusion of greenhouse space in the Earthship design brings some of these processes into everday life, and in doing so, also conserves the energy of commercial food production. Energy does not need to be used for centralized growing of food, (possibly using very much of it to raise livestock), then packaging and transporting the food products to a local market, refrigerating them, and finally bringing them home. By interlacing our homes with natural phenomena, they can produce much of the food we need, thereby greatly reduce general energy consumption.

Geothermal
The earth is not only heated by the sun, but is heated from within. The tremendous pressure of gravity pulls the entire mass of the earth to its center, creating heat and melting rock into magma. The result is called *geothermal* energy.

Ground Temperature
At even the outermost layers of the earth this heat can be felt. Just four feet below the surface, the *ground temperature* remains remarkably constant, especially compared to climatic conditions above the ground. At a four foot depth, the temperature is usually between 55° and 60° degrees F, which is much

more comfortable than weather conditions of both summer and winter. By tapping into this natural *thermal constant*, the Earthship can remain consistently comfortable, because this is only 10 degrees away from the North American comfort zone of 70 degrees. The Earthship tempers this natural constant up to 70° in the winter via heat from the sun. In the summer, this massive constant tends to drag the 100° air temperature down to 70°.

LOCATION-DEPTH

IN NEW MEXICO, THE DEEPER AN EARTHSHIP CAN BE SUBMERGED INTO THE EARTH, THE EASIER IT WILL BE TO MAINTAIN A COMFORTABLE TEMPERATURE.

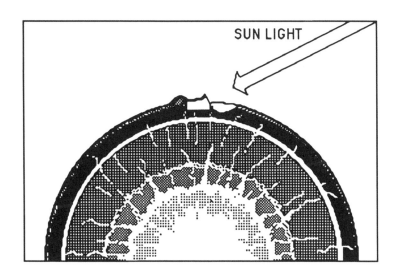

A SUNKEN GARDEN OR "PIT" MAY NEED TO BE DUG IN FRONT OF A SUBMERGED EARTHSHIP SO THAT DESIRED SUNLIGHT IS NOT BLOCKED. MANY UNDERGROUND BUILDINGS HAVE BEEN BUILT THROUGH THE YEARS. IT HAS BEEN CUSTOMARY TO INSULATE THESE BUILDINGS AWAY FROM THE EARTH. AN EARTHSHIP MUST NOT BE INSULATED FROM THE EARTH. IT MUST INTERFACE WITH IT, THUS TAKING ADVANTAGE OF THIS TREMENDOUS THERMAL CONSTANT.

WATER

Water interfaces with the Earth, Sun and Air in many ways to create and sustain life. The Earthship must both avoid and encounter water to provide human habitat.

Runoff

Due to the movement of ancient glaciers, water and wind erosion, earthquakes, volcanos, and other geological phenomena, the surface of the earth has many peaks and valleys. The largest and deepest valleys are full of water-they are the oceans. Water flows from the high points all the way down to these oceans, if it does not flow into an underground reservoir or evaporate first. Water also comes to the Earth by rain. That which is not absorbed into the ground and therefore is free to spill downhill is called *runoff*. On any site there will be some locations which have less runoff passing over them than others. These are the better locations for Earthships. Interfacing with natural runoff patterns can create a dry pocket or island for the Earthship.

LOCATION – HEIGHT ON SLOPE

THE BEST LOCATIONS ARE THOSE WHICH ARE DRIEST - USUALLY CLOSE TO THE PEAK OF THE HILL WHERE THERE WILL BE NO WATER RUNOFF FROM HIGHER PLACES.

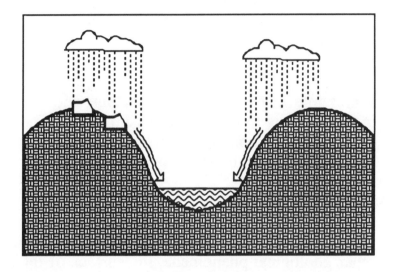

OBVIOUSLY, NOT EVERYONE CAN LOCATE ON THE PEAK OF A HILL, SO RUNOFF LANDSCAPING MUST BE EMPLOYED. THE MOST CRITICAL ISSUE, IS TO NOT LOCATE THE EARTHSHIP WHERE THERE WILL BE A LOT OF WATER RUSHING TOWARD IT. RUNOFF SHOULD BE CHANNELED AROUND THE EARTHSHIP. AVOID PLACES WHERE WATER COLLECTS.

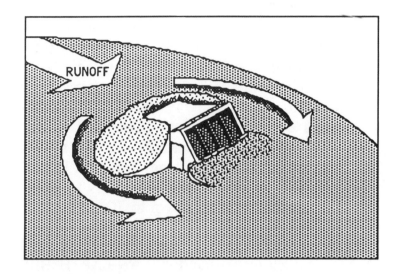

Water Table

Water that is absorbed into the ground may be absorbed by roots of plants or may percolate down into underground voids. Under almost any site there will be some water, although it may be hundreds of feet down. The depth of this moisture is called the *water table*. Often it is within 10 feet and may be only a couple of feet down on a wet site.

LOCATION – MOISTURE

WET SITES MUST BE AVOIDED. AN EARTHSHIP MUST BE AT LEAST FIVE FEET ABOVE THE WATER TABLE! RECORDS ARE OFTEN KEPT FOR THE AVERAGE WATER TABLE OF A SITE, AND FOR THE HIGHEST POSSIBLE WATER TABLE IN THE SPRING. THE BEST THING TO DO IS TO HAVE A HOLE DUG, IN THE HEIGHT OF THE SPRING RUNOFF SEASON, DOWN BELOW THE LOWEST POINT THAT THE EARTHSHIP WILL POTENTIALLY OCCUPY. IF THE EARTH

FIVE FEET BELOW THE EARTHSHIP FLOOR IS TOTALLY DRY, THERE SHOULD BE NO PROBLEM. IF WATER IS DISCOVERED, THE FLOOR SHOULD BE PLANNED TO BE WELL ABOVE IT, OR ANOTHER LOCATION SHOULD BE CHOSEN.

AN EARTHSHIP MAY EVEN SIT ON TOP OF THE GROUND, IF IT IS DRY, AND IF AMPLE DIRT CAN BE OBTAINED TO BERM UP TO THE ROOF ALL AROUND THE HOUSE. OFTEN THE DIRT CAN BE OBTAINED BY DIGGING A SLIGHT RUNOFF MOAT AROUND THE EARTHSHIP.

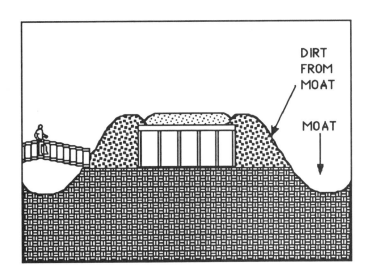

Springs

Springs are small, contained, naturally occurring, streams of water. An underground spring is to a water table as a stream is to a lake on the surface. If an underground spring is discovered on the site, it can be channeled

directly through the Earthship to be used for plants, humidity, etc.

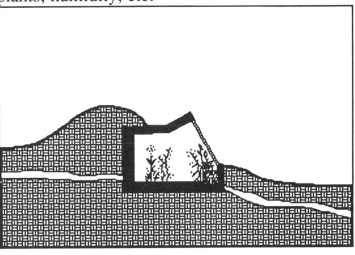

Rain

Since Earthships interface with existing runoff, their roof water can be combined with runoff patterns and caught in cisterns (catch water systems) for domestic use.

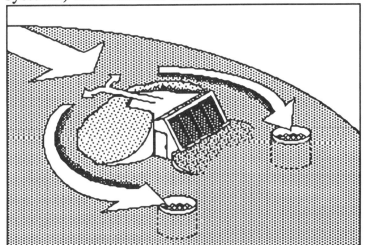

Wells

If enough domestic water is not made available via springs and/or cisterns, then a well is necessary.

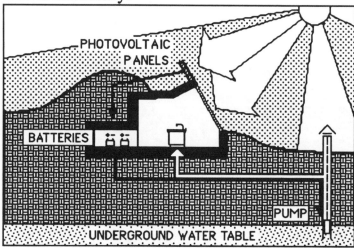

In this case, the well can be pumped with electric energy harvested by the power system of the Earthship, which can be sun or wind generated. Sun power systems are a result of photovoltaic panels on the southern face of the vessel. Wind devices can be incorporated into the structure in the areas where the wind is a reliable source of energy.

AIR

Air plays an important role in the processes that support life. There are also patterns and characteristics of air movement which, when aligned with, enhance the livability of a human habitat.

Respiration

Carbon dioxide must be present for photosynthesis in green plants. By-products of this process are oxygen and water vapor, which can be used in the respiration of animals, who exhale more carbon dioxide. On a huge scale, there is a global breathing exchange going on between all plants and all animals. **By cutting down the rainforests, we are cutting off our own oxygen supply.**

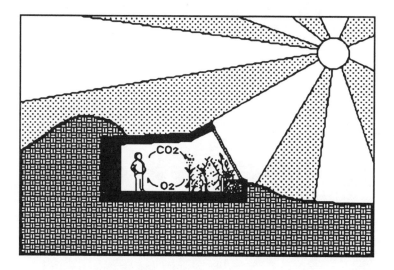

The breath exchange can take place on a small scale inside an Earthship.

Wind

Wind is created by the uneven solar heating of large masses of air. The air rises as it gets heated, pushing and pulling the air masses around it.

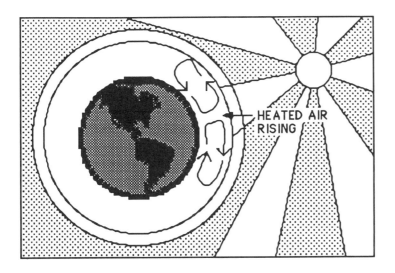

HEATED AIR RISING

to allow warm air to escape and cool air to be drawn in.

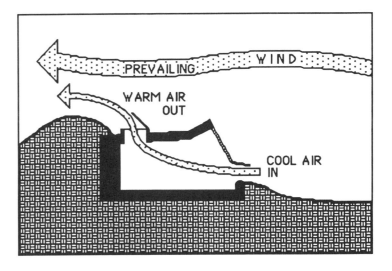

PREVAILING WIND

WARM AIR OUT

COOL AIR IN

Often wind is predictable due to climatic and geographic conditions, and will come from one direction most of the time. If there is such a *prevailing wind*, it can be interfaced with, for ventilation or power. For ventilation, a raised opening facing away from the wind will draw air out of the house as wind blows over the opening. For power, the arms of a windmill can turn a generator, which creates electricity for use or storage.

Stratification

As a fluid (liquid or gas) is heated, it rises; as it is cooled, it settles. This produces what is called *stratification*. If the warmer air at the top of a space is allowed to escape, cooler air will be pulled in, if there is an inlet. Earthships have a high operable skylight and a low window in each room

This also allows individual air movement control in each room. Even when the hot sun is "charging up" the mass, enough natural ventilation can be allowed to keep the space comfortable and full of fresh air.

Through interfacing with the various phenomena discussed in this chapter, the Earthship provides an inviting, comfortable environment for humans and plants without the need of human-made energy. The phenomena around us can provide for all of our needs if we learn to align with them.

LOCATION — REVIEW

We have now seen various ways of interfacing with the four elements: FIRE, EARTH, WATER and AIR. The result is that these natural phenomena have actually determined the design of the Earthship in northern New Mexico. Many methods of interfacing would be the same in any climate. For instance, water run-off is dealt with similarly in Florida and in Ontario. One of the major aspects of the Earthship is that it holds <u>temperature</u> (not just heat). This is why it can be taken anywhere - hot or cold. Some methods of interfacing would be <u>different</u> in differing climates. The most basic modifications for a few climate extremes will now be discussed. If your climate is a combination of these, the Earthship should be designed for the most extreme conditions.

HOT ARID

NO SOLAR GAIN IS WANTED IN A HOT ARID CLIMATE. TO ACHIEVE THIS, THE EARTHSHIP IS TURNED AROUND TO FACE THE NORTH. PLENTY OF REFLECTED LIGHT CAN STILL ENTER THE INTERIOR SPACES, WITHOUT THE DIRECT HEAT OF THE SUN. THE COOLNESS OF THE EARTH CAN STILL BE TAPPED INTO. THE 60 DEGREE EARTH CAN COOL INCOMING 100 DEGREE AIR BEFORE IT REACHES THE LIVING SPACES. HIGH CEILINGS WILL KEEP THE WARMER AIR OVERHEAD. FURTHER COOLING CAN BE ATTAINED BY EVAPORATION, USING

FOUNTAINS OR EVEN CLAY JUGS OF WATER. PLANTS HELP TO LOWER AIR TEMPERATURE. HOWEVER THE FOOD PRODUCING AREA SHOULD BE SEPARATE FROM LIVING AREAS SINCE IT REQUIRES DIRECT SUNLIGHT. EITHER A ROOF GARDEN OR A SOUTH FACING GARDEN WOULD WORK.

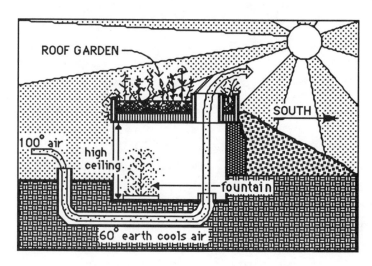

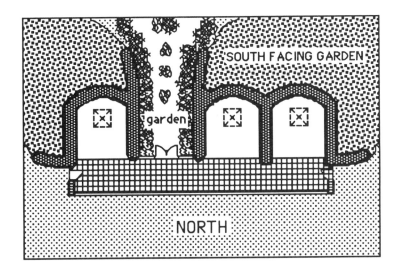

SOUTH FACING GARDEN

garden

NORTH

HOT HUMID

THE EARTHSHIP SHOULD ALSO BE TURNED TO FACE THE NORTH IN THIS CLIMATE. THE CRITICAL FACTOR HERE IS VENTILATION FOR COOLING AND EVAPORATION. AIR PASSING OVER OUR SKIN HELPS PERSPIRATION TO EVAPORATE, THUS COOLING THE BODY. THIS CONCEPT CAN WORK TO COOL AND REDUCE HUMIDITY IN AN EARTHSHIP. TO HELP INDUCE VENTILATION, A DARKLY PAINTED STACK WITH THERMAL MASS BUILT IN TO IT CAN BE USED. IT WILL COLLECT HEAT DURING THE DAY AND SLOWLY RELEASE IT AT NIGHT. THE AIR INSIDE IT WILL THEN BE WARMED UP AND RISE, PULLING MORE AIR BEHIND IT. THIS INDUCED AIR MOVEMENT KEEPS THE EARTHSHIP VENTILATING CONTINUOUSLY. ROOFTOP SPACE CAN BE USED AS AN UMBRELLA TO SHADE THE INTERIOR BELOW. A LOW-MASS ATTIC WILL NOT HOLD HEAT AND WILL ALWAYS COOL OFF AT NIGHT. AGAIN, SUBMERGING INTO THE EARTH WILL HELP

DRAG DOWN THE AIR TEMPERATURE. HOWEVER IN HUMID AREAS MORE ATTENTION MUST BE GIVEN TO GROUND MOISTURE. LOCATING THE EARTHSHIP ON HIGH GROUND IS IMPERATIVE.

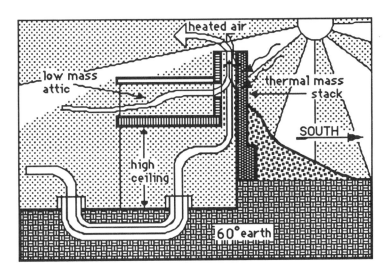

heated air

low mass attic

thermal mass stack

SOUTH

high ceiling

60°earth

TEMPERATE

A TEMPERATE CLIMATE MAY BE A NATURAL CONDITION THAT IS NEARLY COMFORTABLE FOR HUMAN HABITAT. THE MASS OF THE EARTHSHIP WILL BUFFER ANY TEMPERATURE EXTREMES THAT DO OCCUR. THE MASS TO VOLUME RATIO IS NOT VERY CRITICAL SO THE ROOMS MAY BE DEEPENED AND WIDENED TO THE MAXIMUM THE STRUCTURE WOULD ALLOW. THE GLASS DOES NOT NEED TO BE SLOPED, AND THERE CAN EVEN BE AN OVERHANG TO SHADE THE INTERIOR FROM UNNEEDED SUMMER SUN. HERE THE SOMEWHAT REDUCED MASS WILL SIMPLY BE USED FOR A STABILIZING EFFECT ON THE COMFORT ZONE.

45

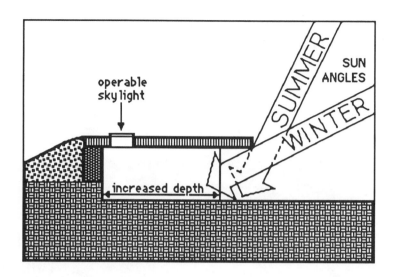

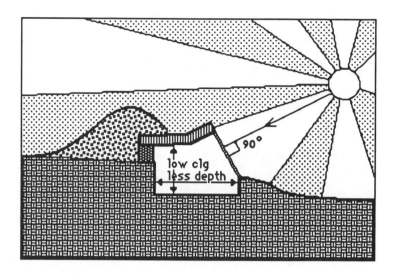

COLD CLIMATE

The Earthship *is* designed for cold climate conditions. For <u>extreme</u> cold, the depths, widths and heights of the spaces should be decreased to increase the mass relative to the air volume. The angle of the glass should be at 90 degrees to the lowest winter sun. The building should be submerged into the earth as much as possible.

Overhangs should be avoided as they effect spring and fall heating potential. Airlocks(see chapter 3) should be considered. Bathrooms should be on the solar face. Earth parapets should be very thick to keep structure below frost line.

The Earthship can be taken anywhere. It is designed for extremes. Solar Survival Architecture is available for consultation on Earthship location for unusual situations.

3. DESIGN

**FOLLOWING THE DIRECTIVES
OF CONCEPT AND
NATURAL PHENOMENA**

- **The basic module**
- **How these modules can be
  combined to design a house**

Fast cars are designed in wind tunnels, i.e. the wind dictates the design of the car. Likewise, natural phenomena dictate the design of an Earthship. The design schematic of existing Earthships is presented in this chapter as it relates to local phenomena. Within these parameters, personal needs and desires are dealt with. The issue of performance versus tradition is discussed from the perspective of "Live simply so that others may simply live."

Chapters One and Two have described the concept and the methods of interfacing that have evolved into the Earthship. They have shown how the elements through their very nature can determine the nature of the architecture. Interfacing with these phenomena delineates the form of the simple module which can provide for the basic human needs of shelter, water, oxygen, food, temperature and energy.

This chapter will review the parameters of this module, and show how these modules can be combined to design a house.

MODULE REVIEW

The module, itself, is an individual U-shaped space or room, with mass on three sides, glass on the fourth, and a skylight in the ceiling above the U of mass. Earth is bermed up on the outside of the mass walls for even more mass. Often the U shape is partially submerged as well. In places where heating is required, the wall of glass is oriented to the south and sloped for maximum solar gain on the coldest day of the year. *Because the modules are U-shaped, they will often be referred to as "U's."*

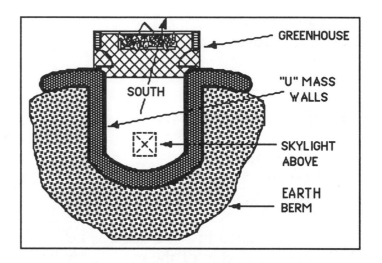

The module is actually constructed in two parts: **the U** (three mass walls), and **the greenhouse** (the glass wall).

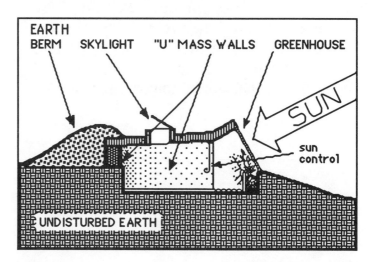

The mass U is the main living space for humans, and the greenhouse is the main living space for plants. The greenhouse is always in sun, whereas the U space has the potential of sun control.

This module can be as small as anyone wants to build it, but it should not be larger than 18 feet wide by 26 feet deep. The 18 foot dimension is the largest recommended span between the mass walls, because longer spanning structural members are uncommon and expensive. The 26 foot dimension is as deep as the module can be and still be comfortably warm. If the total area of the room exceeds these dimensions, the volume of air space becomes so large that the surrounding mass can not keep it within the comfort zone of 65°-75°.

RULES OF COMBINATION

The module is _not_ a house, but is an individual room. This room _cannot_ be expanded to make a house, but must be multiplied. A house is therefore a collection of modules, strategically placed in relation to each other and the site. There are, however, some specific rules of how the modules can be put together.

Straight Row, East to West

U's can be constructed right next to each other with exactly the same solar orientation, and sharing a common mass wall. The greenhouse then becomes a hallway, the means of circulation from one U to any other. It also acts as a heating duct, since it is where the

direct solar heat gain collects. The greenhouse can actually be closed off from some U's while remaining open to others. It is the main circulation vein and the heating duct for servicing the individual U's. This allows the U's to maintain their simplicity and mass without the expense and lack of performance that other circulation patterns would bring. The simple module is preserved.

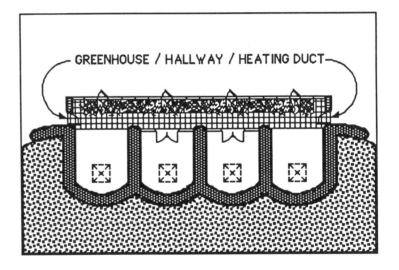

Staggered Row, Relating to Azimuth Angle

As was shown in chapter 2, individual U's can be stepped back from one another without causing shadows on the glass of the adjacent U's. The back U can be located far enough over so the connecting glass is within the effective winter azimuth angle. This angle is derived by the location of the winter sun between 10 A.M. and 2 P.M. It is between these times that the sun is most effective for heating. In northern New Mexico, this is a 60° angle. The space generated between the U's can become a very thick mass wall, or an indirectly heated utility space. All major living U's should get full sun across their south side between 10 AM and 2 PM.

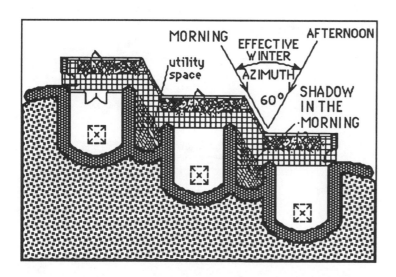

The results of this kind of combination are much like those of the straight row. The greenhouse becomes the circulation hallway and a heating duct, connecting the simple U modules.

Straight Step- On Slope
Two U's can be put one behind and *above* the other, making them like steps on the slope of the site.

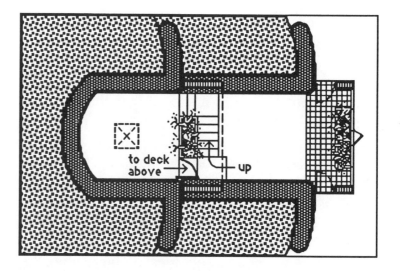

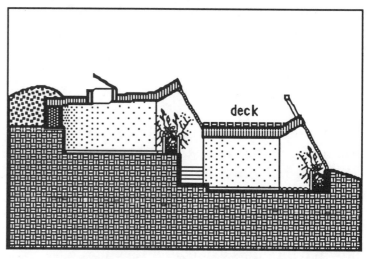

Each level can still be insulated all around by earth, and can still have the full height of glass on the solar side. The roof of the lower U can then become a deck in front of the U above. It is necessary to have a sloping site for this kind of combination.

Many U's can be combined in this way, creating a square grid of U's, in plan, that step up the slope.

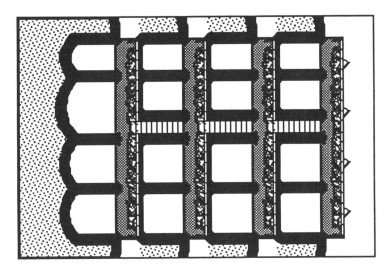

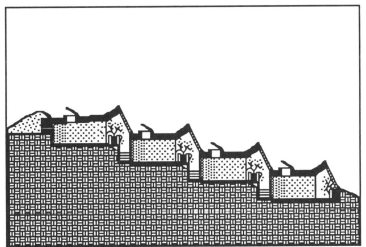

The "greenhouse / hallway / heating duct" still functions as in the previous examples, thus again leaving the simple modules intact.

There can be an overlap between steps, creating a space in the middle that is 2 stories high inside. This is good for fruit and nut trees.

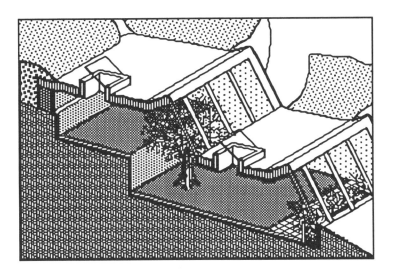

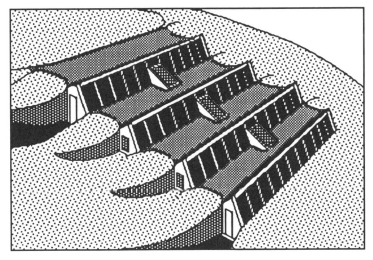

Staggered Step

When U's are combined like steps, the number and size of U's in each row may vary. This allows a series of different U arrangements stepping up a hill. Again, the heating duct / greenhouse / hallway is applied on each level.

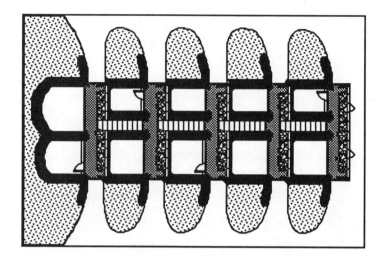

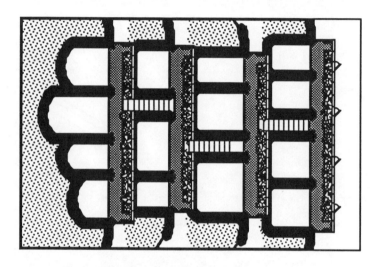

Combined Step and Row

When stepping patterns are multiplied, they are actually combined steps and rows. The resulting set of U's can accommodate almost any spatial plan relationship. Any single-level house plan can be designed and superimposed on a sloping site in steps.

There can be any number of U' or steps in a row. A house can be 2 steps with 5 U's in each row or 5 steps with 2 U's in each row, or anything in between.

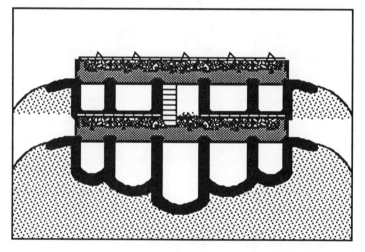

Combinations not Recommended

One U should not be put directly behind another on a flat site, unless heating is not required. This would put a room behind a room behind a greenhouse. The back room would not have any direct sun for light, heat, etc... It would be cooler and darker and difficult to heat without backup systems.

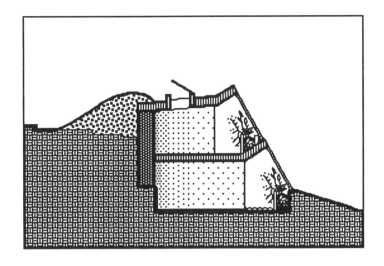

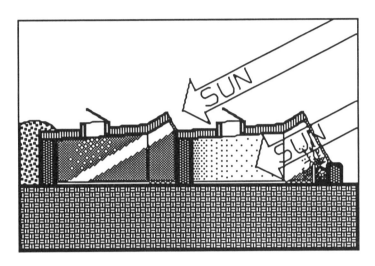

Two U's can be built one directly on top of the other, however in this situation an Architect should be consulted, This makes a more complex design in terms of structure and performance.

SIMPLICITY VS. COMPLEXITY
PERFORMANCE VS. AESTHETICS
ECONOMY VS. EXPENSE

The reason that the Earthship is so economical is that it can be so simple. In fact, a good sized, single family residence can be built with 3 to 5 nearly identical U's in a straight row. Because the U's are so similar in size, detail, construction, etc., it is the most effective use of time and materials possible for an Earthship of its size. In fact, this is the recommended design for most situations. It can fit on a flat or sloping site. It is simply the easiest and the most economical approach.

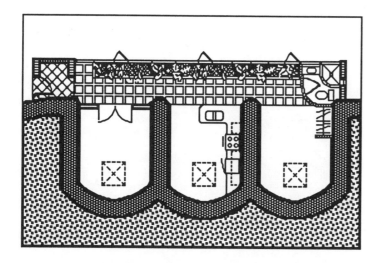

In any situation, the simplest design is usually the best. The rules of combination are the rules of design. Any time that they are broken, there will be extra expense, and usually cause the performance of the Earthship to suffer. When economy and efficiency are the primary goals (as in nature), performance determines the looks of the final design. Some people may find that they have a preconceived idea about what their house should be like, and use this notion as the starting point for their design. An Earthship cannot be designed this way. The layout must initiate from the characteristics of the U module, and then be adapted for the needs of the inhabitants.

POSSIBLE VARIATIONS AND MODIFICATIONS

With this concern for simplicity in mind, we can now review the possible variations that can be made to the basic layout. Every variation will affect the performance of the Earthship, so it is definitely not recommended to stray too far from the basic design. Each variation also takes more time, materials, energy and money, and therefore will affect the performance of the builder / resident as well. This is why one or two changes may be okay if really necessary, but any more will begin to alter the Earthship beyond recognition. It would be possible to change the Earthship, bit by bit, into an English Colonial house with a heating system. This obviously would no longer be an Earthship.

Once an initial basic layout is designed, there are a few necessary variations that will only slightly affect the performance of the Earthship. They will now be discussed.

Bathroom

A bathroom is a small, self-enclosed room, and therefore can fit about anywhere in the design. But bathrooms need to be warm places because people wet from baths or showers tend to be colder than normal. Therefore, if a bathroom is located deep in an Earthship, away from the warm greenhouse, a unit heater should be installed in it. However, the best thing to do is to locate the bathroom right up against the southern glass to maximize the solar heat gain that will go directly into the small room. Bathrooms on the south face need no unit heaters.

Because it is right up against the glass, it will get some of the most intense direct heat in the house. This heat is then intensified because it is such a small room, compared to the rest of the U's.

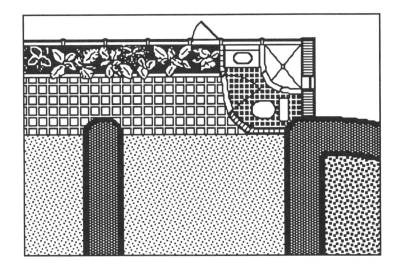

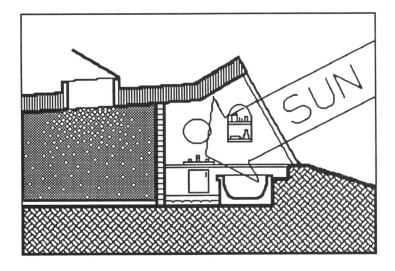

The bathroom can be in this position against the glass anywhere along the front face. Some common positions are at either end, or directly in the middle.

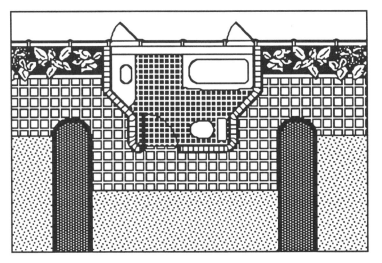

In either position, the bathroom creates a shaded space directly behind it. When on the ends, this shaded space may be slightly cooler than the other rooms. When in the middle of an Earthship, the shaded space is so well surrounded by other warm U's that it is as warm as any other space in the Earthship (except the bathroom itself).

The bathroom can be used to divide the Earthship into segments. In a 3 U design, a central bathroom allows each end room to have a little more privacy. In longer designs, it can separate bedrooms from each other, or from the main living spaces of the house.

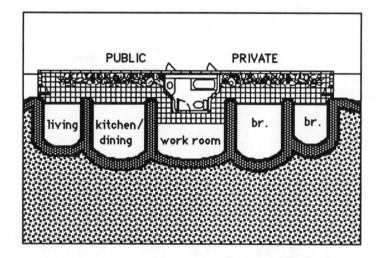

Entry

The entry is best on the East or West end wall, and with an airlock / vestibule / mudroom.

The airlock helps to prevent heated air from escaping whenever the door is opened. It can also be a storage room, utility room, closet, etc... The East and West greenhouse end walls are not structural or solar, and they already

are linked to the circulation. This is the best location for entries.

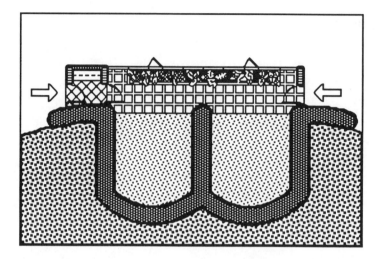

The entry can be made in the south glass wall. This is not recommended when serious heating is required, as it will create shadows and block some of the heat gain. It would also be possible to enter the Earthship from the North side, but this would require the elimination of a substantial part of the berm, which is both mass and insulation. An entry on the north side will affect the performance and the cost of the Earthship significantly but it can and has been done.

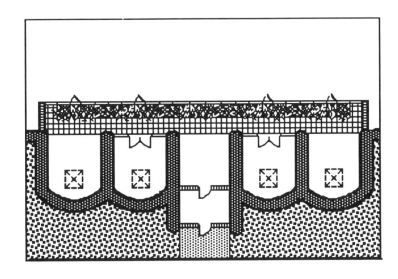

Insulated shades can also be hung directly behind the greenhouse glass to shade the living space and cut down on heat loss at night.

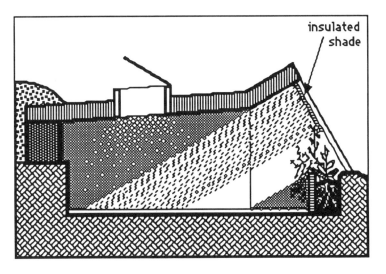

insulated shade

Shading
The living space of each U can be separated from the heating duct / greenhouse / hallway by the following means. Simple cloth or paper rolling shades can be hung, shading the space behind.

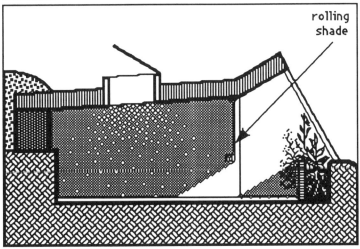

rolling shade

A dividing mass wall can be built between the mass U and the greenhouse. This can give more shade and privacy, but is not always necessary and is an added expense. It does, however, improve the performance by holding heat in the "U" and cutting down on heat loss at night. This mass wall usually has glass above it to allow "borrowed light" to come through the green house to the "U". Privacy and sun control in the "U" can be achieved via drapes or curtains over this glass(diagram next page).

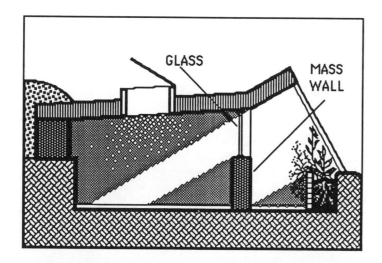

Free-standing closets can give shade and also subdivide space, even within a single U, to have areas of added privacy.

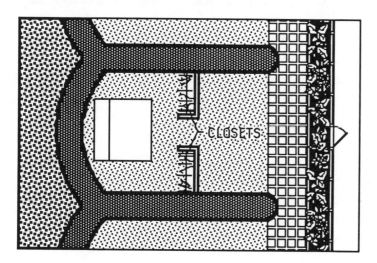

Planters are sometimes used to subdivide space, providing some shade and privacy.

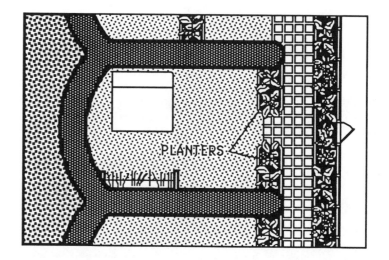

View

It is best if the view from the Earthship is limited to what is shown though the expansive greenhouse windows. If there is an incredible view in another direction, however, it is possible to open up a mass wall, but this eliminates mass and insulation, and obviously reduces the thermal ability of the walls, as well as escalates the cost.

The least disruptive direction for such an opening is to the East. Although mass and insulation are cut down, there is a little amount of early morning solar heat that is gained. It is not enough to make up the loss of mass, but helps a little.

If the opening is to the West, there will be a very small amount of afternoon solar heat that is gained, but not at all as much as that which is lost

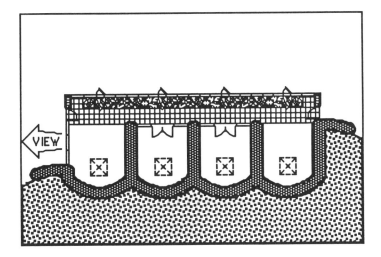

If the opening is to the north, obviously a lot of the berm will be eliminated, greatly reducing the thermal ability of the walls. There is no solar gain from the North (in the Northern Hemisphere), and a lot of heat will be lost through any north windows at night. Northern views are *not* recommended.

Connections Between Rooms

The best way to connect rooms is by means of the common greenhouse hallway. A small opening, such as a window between a kitchen and dining room, can be made through interior mass walls without affecting performance greatly, although this is more expensive. If a larger opening, such as a doorway, is made between interior rooms through a mass wall, it is even more expensive, because a footing and lintel beam are then needed. It also means that the mass wall must be ended, and then started again three feet away, resulting in three "mass wall end details" instead of just one.

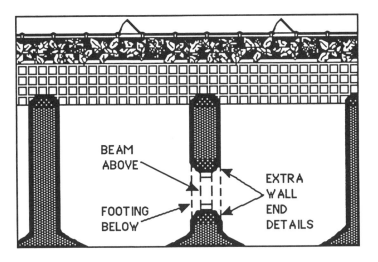

If the width of this doorway increases more, the amount of weight concentrated to either side will be great enough to require columns and beams and footings and reinforced concrete and much more time, energy, materials and overall *expense*. The technology involved in such an adventure is conventional for building contractors, but difficult for the average layperson. The loss of mass also limits performance, so it is really not recommended very often.

Because of the loss of mass and the difficulty of construction, **interior mass walls should never be eliminated!**

EXAMPLE DESIGNS

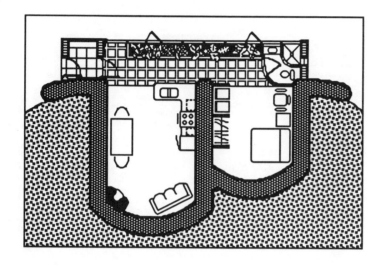

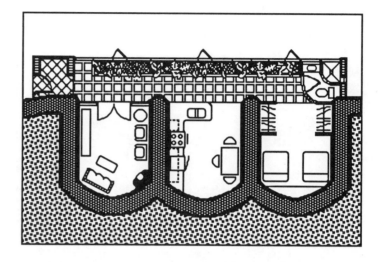

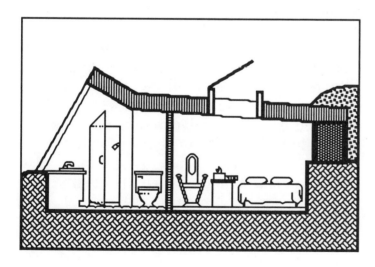

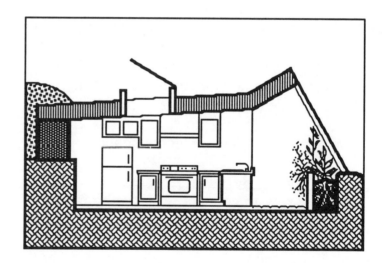

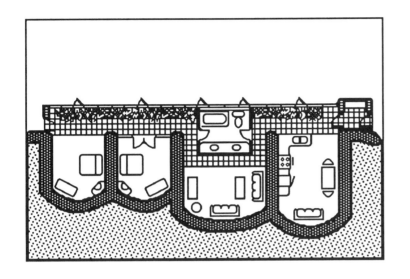 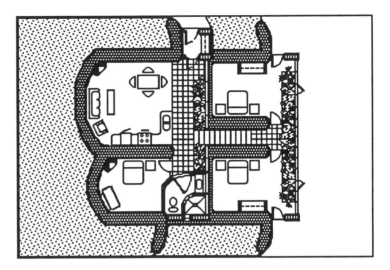

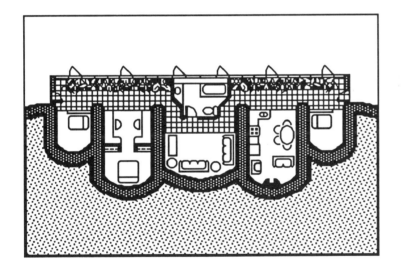 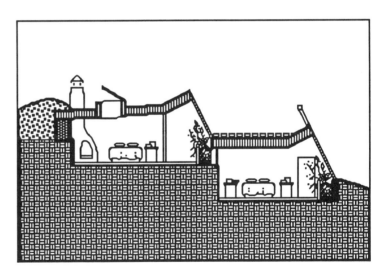

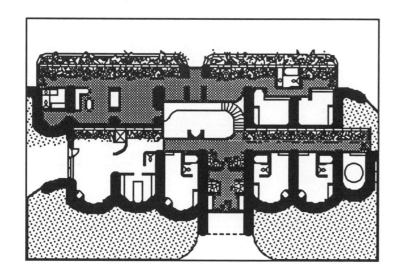 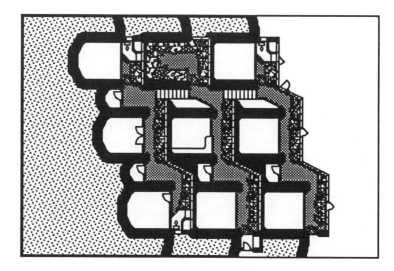

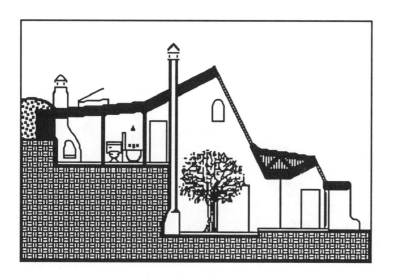 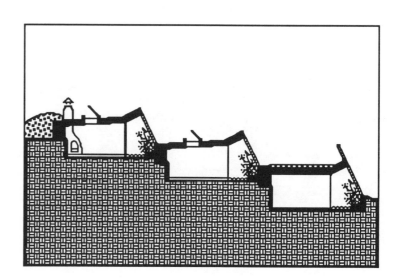

4. STRUCTURE

THE SKELETON OF THE VESSEL

Economy and availability to non-professional builders are important determinants of an Earthship structure. This chapter presents the simple structural integrity of existing prototype Earthships via conceptual diagrams, photographs and three dimensional drawings. This structural system is both designed and explained in terms to which the non-professional builder can relate.

THE STRUCTURE OF BUILDINGS

In order to understand the structure of the Earthship, a general understanding of the concept of structuring buildings is necessary.

Buildings must be able to carry weight, or *loads*. There are two kinds of loads, *dead loads* and *live loads*. The dead load is the weight of the building itself, which is caused by gravity. Just as our skeletons must be able to support the weight of our bodies, the structure of the building must be able to support the weight of its roof. The live load is the weight of more transient and varying things, such as snow, people, and furniture. This is similar to our skeletons also being able to support the clothes we wear and the things we carry.

The combination of these two kinds of loads is the *total load* on the structure, and it is usually expressed in pounds per square foot. The purpose of the structure of the building is to organize, transfer and distribute these loads to the Earth.

Basically, this can be done in two different ways. The loads over an area can be gathered to one point, or a *column*. They will then be transfered down the column, to a *foundation*. The foundation is much wider than the column; it serves to spread the load out to the surrounding earth.

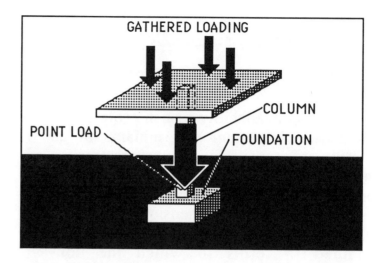

These loads are called point loads, because they bring down intense loads on a few points. There is more chance of movement and settlement where point loads occur. Usually point loads must be analyzed by an architect or engineer. They are avoided in Earthship designs.

The second method is to distribute the loads in a linear fashion, ie. a *bearing wall*. Similar to the column, the loads are then transferred down the wall, to a foundation. The difference is that the load on any part of the wall will be much smaller than the load on the column. Bearing walls are structural walls which act as a continuous unit, distributing loads over an entire wall.

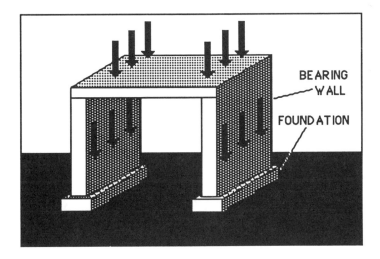

The load on the wall is more evenly distributed to the foundation, thereby spreading the loads over a larger area as they meet the earth. This results in less strain on the structural element and overall reduction of stress on the foundation, since the job of distributing the load has already been partially completed by the wall itself.

THE STRUCTURAL CONCEPT OF THE EARTHSHIP

The structural concept is again based on the "U" module, just as the thermal design concept is. One "U" could be structured independently, and then repeated over and over again.

Most conventional building materials and methods do little to recognize the natural phenomena of the relatively fluid Earth. Structures are designed in and of themselves and then are placed on the earth. In most cases there are a few large loads, and massive foundations are needed to distribute these loads to the earth.

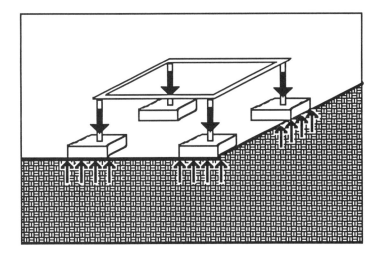

Often the Earth, being rather fluid relative to concrete, has been known to shift, settle, or otherwise move slightly. This can result in major structural cracks in concrete work where intense loads are concentrated and brought to the Earth in great magnitude. To avoid this, much expense is required, plus the employment of an engineer, to build structures with expansion joints and steel reinforcements to resist the tendency of the Earth to move. This is further complicated by the tendency of the materials themselves to expand and contract - see thermal dynamics, Chapter 2.

In contrast, the Earthships are designed to join the Earth, rather than to resist it. The structure (mostly earth itself) is based on a very wide distribution of loads so that by the time all loads reach the earth, they are insignificant in magnitude. An Earthship actually "floats" on the earth. This results in a very forgiving structure that has the potential to move with the Earth.

Conventional buildings set <u>on</u> the earth, Earthships are <u>of</u> the earth.

<u>U-shaped Mass bearing walls are their own foundations</u>

We have already discussed the fact that rooms must be wrapped in mass walls in order for them to store heat. Since we already have these massive walls, we will use them to hold up the roof of the module as well. *They will act as bearing walls as well as mass walls*.

Conventional bearing walls for a room the size of an Earthship module are usually 8" thick, and require a foundation 1'-4" wide to distribute the loads over the earth upon which it sets. The massive walls of the Earthship are 2'-8" thick, and are already wide enough to evenly distribute this load much more than conventional methods require. The Earthship walls themselves are *wider* than the required footing for such a wall.

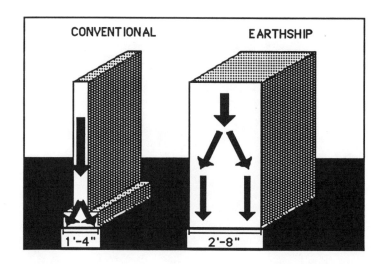

Therefore, the mass bearing walls of the Earthship are also the foundations. So the module is in effect floating with the Earth.

We are achieving thermal mass, structural bearing and foundations all in one shape. The shape is mostly earth itself which is contained in rubber (as later chapters will describe). This results in a massive, durable, resilient structure equipped to handle the seismic loads created by earthquakes. **Brittle, intensely loaded structures are much more vulnerable to earthquakes than resilient, widely distributed structural designs.**

Since most buildings are not surrounded by earth, the foundations need to be well below the rest of the structure to get below the frost line.

66

This is necessary to protect the foundations from the freeze- thaw movements of the earth. This means that the bottom of the foundation must be below the deepest point where the ground will freeze. These depths vary from region to region. Because Earthships are buried at the perimeter. The bottom of the mass wall will be well below the frost line, and there is no danger of thermal movement.

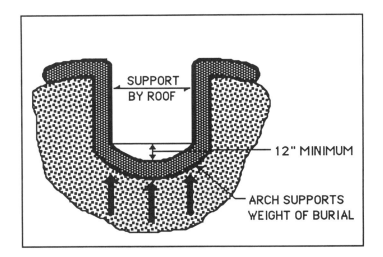

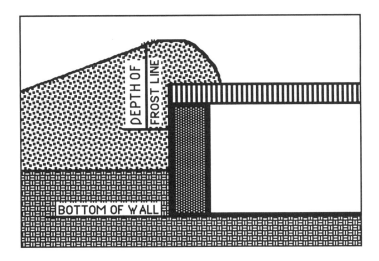

Although the north wall, or rear of the "U" is not necessary to support the roof, it is needed to retain the weight of the burying up against the building. The ability of this wall to retain the earth is strengthened if the wall is arched. This arch should be a minimum of 12" deep and can be as rounded as a semi-circle.

Framing the Roof
The roof structure is framed with beams running in the east-west direction, so that the loads are transferred directly to the mass bearing walls. This distributes the loads in many small increments along the wide, massive walls.

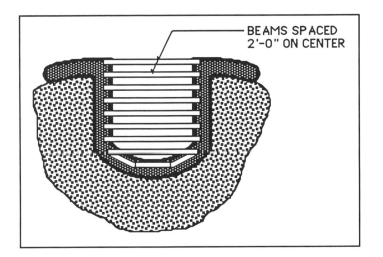

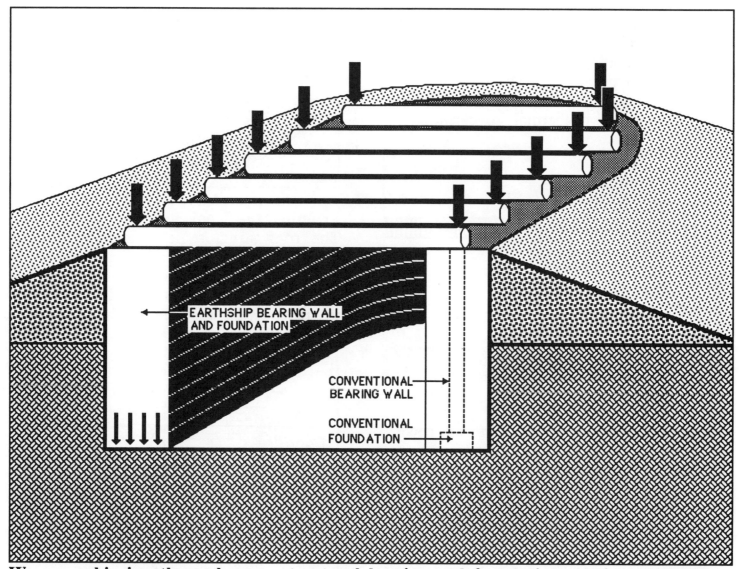

Within the figure:

EARTHSHIP BEARING WALL AND FOUNDATION

CONVENTIONAL BEARING WALL

CONVENTIONAL FOUNDATION

We are achieving thermal mass, structural bearing and foundations all in one shape.

Point loads are avoided. An even distribution of loads throughout allows the structure to "float" with the earth.

Greenhouse Lean-to

The other major structural component is the greenhouse. The greenhouse is a relatively light piece of carpentry work, compared to the massiveness of the U structure. It is a lean-to element which rests on the southernmost beam.

As the loads come down on the roof of the greenhouse, they are distributed in part to this beam, however, most of this relatively light stress will be transferred down to the mass wall which supports the greenhouse. All of these loads are minimal. This mass wall is also 2'-6" thick, thus continuing the "floating" concept of the Earthship.

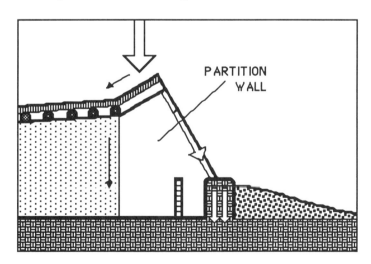

Partition walls

Partition walls are non-structural walls. They will be used to fill in the space between the greenhouse face and the mass walls as well as to enclose bathrooms, etc. Since they do not need to carry any loads additional to their own weight, they simply set on foundations which are about the same width as the walls themselves.

There are two types of partition walls in the Earthship - interior walls and exterior walls. (The method of building these walls out of aluminum cans will be discussed in Chapter 6 & 7). Interior partition walls are 6" thick and require an 8" wide by 8" deep footing with one piece of 1/2" steel reinforcement bars (rebar) to hold it together. Exterior partition walls are insulated which makes them 14" thick and they require a 16" wide footing with two pieces of rebar.

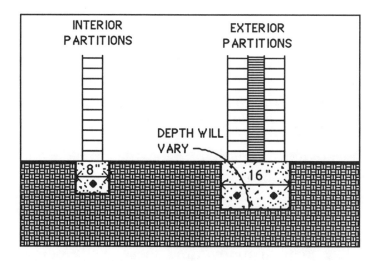

The depth of the footing will vary, relative to different conditions. If the bottom of the wall will be *below* the frost line after berming, a concrete pad 12" deep will be needed.

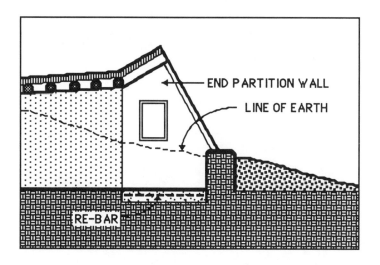

If the bottom of the wall is *above* the frost line, the foundation will need to go as deep as the frost line.

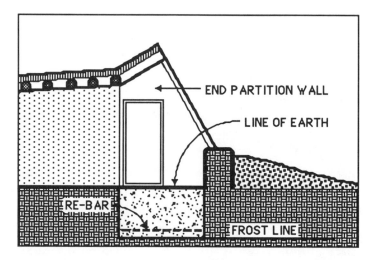

This will insure there will be no thermal movement. These foundations will have (2) 1/2" pieces of steel rebar.

STRUCTURAL ECONOMY

As was discussed in Chapter 3, Earthships are designed with performance and economy in mind. Building a house made up of several simple "U" modules is the easiest, cheapest way to go. The structure is simple and has very few variations. This is critical when cost is an issue.

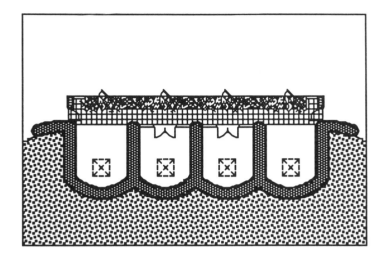

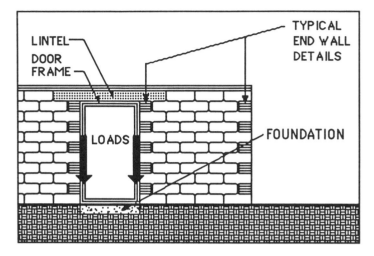

Deviations from the simple structure of the "U" module are possible, but _they will add to the cost and subtract from the performance_ of the building. For example, a doorway could be cut through a tire wall, providing a passageway from one room to the next.

However, as you will learn more about in Chapter 6, this would entail cutting many extra blocks which are used for half tires, making a lintel and a frame, pouring a concrete foundation in which to set the frame, securing the frame to the tire wall, etc...

This requires time, conventional materials, and additional skills and _all of these cost more money_. Also, this will reduce the mass of the room, and reduce the possibility of individually controlling the temperature of each room.

If you do want to deviate from the structural simplicity of the "U" module, consider the consequences, and make as few of these changes as you can. The extreme, replacing all interior tire walls with columns, will leave you with a house which costs as much, and performs almost as badly, as a conventional compartment.

72

5. MATERIALS

THE PRIMARY BUILDING BLOCKS
OF THE VESSEL

– What they are
– Why we use them

The nature of the materials used to execute an Earthship design is explored. The earth-rammed automobile tire is presented as the most appropriate method for its strength, economy, lack of skill needed, and the fact that it makes use of an otherwise discarded "natural resource." The aluminum beverage can used as masonry unit for filler walls is also presented for similar reasons.

What if we found a way to make building blocks out of compressed oxygen. We simply extracted the oxygen out of the air and compressed it into bricks. This would be great because oxygen is everywhere. However, we are intelligent enough to understand that we breathe oxygen. It is what enables us to stay alive. We would not want to deplete our life giving breath would we? Trees are a source of oxygen on this planet. We currently build with trees as well as simply clear them out of the way for more important things - like cattle.

THE NATURE OF THE MATERIALS

In keeping with the design and conceptual information presented in the previous chapters, the nature of the building materials for an Earthship must have certain characteristics of definition established before we can go looking for them. The following outline will establish the nature of the materials necessary to build a vessel that aligns with rather than deteriorates the environment of the planet. We will think in terms of ideals here in an effort to lift us from the conventional alleys that have lead us to our present dilemma.

Indigenous
Ideally the materials for an Earthship would want to be indigenous to many parts of the planet. Shipping materials for long distances presents an energy impact not in keeping with the Earthship concept. In order for the Earthship to be easily accessible to the common person and to maintain a low impact on the planetary energy situation, a "building block" found all over the globe would be required.

Able to be fashioned with little or no energy
If a building material was found that was indigenous to many parts of the planet but it required massive amounts of energy to fashion into a usable form, we still would not be meeting the conceptual requirement of an Earthship. The major building materials for an Earthship must require little or no manufactured energy to fashion into use. This keeps them easily available to common people and at the same time would allow the large scale production of Earthships to maintain a relatively low impact on the planet. Since there are so many of us, if we are to survive without literally consuming the planet, everything we use must be chosen with consideration to the impact of large scale application. We must explore building materials and methods that are not dependant on manufactured energy and that have the potential to contribute to the general well-being of the planet rather than exploit it.

Mass
The materials that surround the spaces of an Earthship must be dense and massive in order to store the temperatures required to provide a

habitable environment for humans and plants. The Earthship itself must be a "battery" for storing temperature. This massive battery must be achieved without large amounts of energy. This suggests built-up dense mass in "bite-size" human manageable pieces. This built-up mass must also have the capacity for structural bearing and a cohesive homogeneous quality. Any light porous material, no matter how strong, is ridiculous for a building material if it has no mass. In anything but a temperate climate where no heating or cooling is necessary, mass is a primary factor in selecting a building material. Making houses out of heavy dense mass is as important as making airplanes light. Obviously a heavy airplane takes more fuel to fly. Obviously a light house takes more fuel to heat or cool. Why do we see the forest but not the trees?

Durability

We have built out of wood for centuries. Wood is organic and biodegradable. It goes away. So we have developed various poisonous chemical products to paint on it and make it last. This, plus the fact that wood is light and porous, makes it a very unsatisfactory building material. This is not to mention the fact that trees are our source of oxygen. For building housing that lasts without chemicals we should look around for materials that have durability as an inherent quality rather than trying to paint on durability. Wood is definitely a good material

for cabinet doors and ceilings where mass is not a factor and where it is protected so it will not rot, but the basic massive structure of buildings of the future should be a natural resource that is inherently massive and durable by its own nature.

Resilient

Earthquakes are an issue in many parts of the world. They are actually a potential anywhere. Any method of building must relate to this potential threat. Since earthquakes involve a horizontal movement or shaking of the structure, this suggests a material with resilience or capacity to move with this shaking. Brittle materials like concrete break, crack, and fracture. The ideal structural material for dealing with this kind of situation would have a "rubbery" or resilient quality to it - something like jello. This kind of material would allow movement without failure.

Low specific skill requirements

If the materials for easily obtainable housing for the future are to be truly accessible to the common person they must, by their very nature, be easy to learn how to assemble. If it takes years of apprenticeship to learn a skill then that method is not the answer for housing. The nature of the materials for building an Earthship must allow for assembling skills to be learned and mastered in a matter of hours, not years. These skills must be basic enough that specific talent is not required to learn them. **General application of common human capabilities must guide in the evolution of materials and methods for housing of the future.**

Low tech use/application

Some systems of building today are simple if one has the appropriate high-tech expensive energy dependant device or equipment. This, of course, limits the application of these methods to the professionals who have invested in the technology to enable them to use such methods. Because of the expense and energy required to get set up for these systems the common person is left totally dependent on those professionals for accessibility to these particular housing systems. Therefore the common person must go through the medium of money (bank loans, interest approvals, etc.) to gain access to a housing system that usually dictates performance and appearance. The point here is that if high-tech systems and skills are between the common person and their ability to obtain a home, we are setting ourselves up to place the very nature of our housing in the hands of economics rather than in the hands of the people themselves. This situation has resulted in inhuman, energy-hog housing blocks and developments that make investors some quick money and leave the planet and the people with something that requires constant input of money and energy to operate. The technology required to build an Earthship must be beyond the type of technology that we are so impressed with today. Earthship technology is the technology of natural phenomenon like the physics of the sun, the earth and people themselves. The methods and materials for obtaining housing of the future must be within the immediate grasp of the common person with a minimum of easily accessible devices. We must employ a much more thorough understanding of the nature of ourselves and the physics of our environment.

The requirements above describe the nature of the ideal "building block" for constructing Earthships - Housing of the future. Many conventional materials satisfy one or two of these requirements but no conventional material satisfies all of them. We will be evolving a new material or building block for the primary structure of the Earthship.

THE PRIMARY BUILDING BLOCK

Obviously all of the materials used in an Earthship would want to meet the requirements outlined above. However, as a first step toward a vision we must begin with the primary building block - that which provides the major structure and performance of the Earthship. The major structure and performance of the Earthship is encompassed in the design element termed a "U" in the previous chapters. Modules are constructed in this "U" shape for reasons already described. This "U" shape must therefore be constructed of a primary building block that meets all of the above requirements. Throughout twenty years of exploring the ideals that have resulted in the concept of the Earthship, we (Solar Survival Architecture) have developed/found a natural resource that meets these requirements. This building block is a rubber automobile tire rammed with packed earth. Let's take it through the outline of requirements and see how it "stacks up".

Indigenous

The rubber (sometimes steel belted) automobile tire is indigenous all over the world as a "natural resource". Every city is a natural supplier of this item. It can be "harvested" with absolutely no technical devices or energy other than two human hands to pick it up and throw it into a pickup truck. The automobile tire is definitely an indigenous material to every heavily populated area of the planet. It is readily available without the energy and economic impact of shipping to every potential building site.

Able to be fashioned with little or no energy

The rubber automobile tire can be used as found without any modification. The process of ramming them full of densely packed earth is achieved with simple human labor and can be done with whatever type of earth is available on the building site. Common people of all shapes and sizes can easily learn to gather tires and pack them full of earth with simple hand tools and with the same type of human energy that they use while trying to tone up their bodies in the local spa. The impact of large scale use of this idea would result in depletion of the giant tire mountains that have become a serious problem in many cities, and in many people getting in a lot better shape without having to spend money for a spa membership. This building block is therefore achieved with little or no manufactured additional energy.

Mass

There are few materials of any kind that would provide better, more dense mass for storing temperature than rammed earth. The rubber tire casings provide a natural form for humanly manageable production of thermal mass building blocks with little more than human energy. There are also very few materials that would provide the structural bearing capacities and homogeneous qualities of an earth rammed tire wall. The diameter of the tires (2'-4") sets the thickness for the walls surrounding the "U" modules - 2'-8" with plaster. This amount of dense mass surrounding every room of an Earthship would provide a thermal battery like no other in construction history.

Durability

The durability of tires filled with earth can not be surpassed. A buried tire (which is in effect what we have in a tire wall) will virtually last forever. The only thing that deteriorates rubber tires is sunlight or fire. Since they are filled with earth and ultimately covered with earth they never see sunlight when built into an Earthship. Tires only burn when surrounded by air. When they are filled and coated with earth, trying to get them to burn would be like trying to light a phonebook on fire as compared to a wad of paper. The very qualities of tires that makes them a problem to society (the fact that they won't go away) makes them an ideal durable building material for Earthships. Earth and tires by virtue of their very nature will last forever.

Resilient

Whereas a rubber tire/rammed earth wall is amazingly strong, it is obviously not brittle. It can vibrate or move without fracture or failure. Since these walls are so wide and the loading on them is widely distributed, the entire structure would have the potential of absorbing and moving with a considerable horizontal shock from an earthquake. There is probably no other material available at any price that has the reliance that earth rammed tires would have. They do provide a dense, rubbery, flexible wall much more akin to the nature of "jello" than any other material.

Low specific skill requirements

Over the past fifteen years many people of all shapes and sizes have been taught to "pound tires" (the term used for the process of densely packing the tires with earth). Within one or two hours the average human can be an expert. It requires physical energy more than brute strength. A team of two people, one shoveling and one pounding, can pound about four tires an hour. The shoveling job is easiest while the pounding requires a little more strength and energy. The general application of common human capabilities is definitely all that is required here. This is a skill that the very lowest people on the labor force can become good at.

Low tech use/application

The only real major piece of equipment needed to build a tire building is a backhoe. This is a common piece of equipment needed for all building of any type. Backhoes and operators rent almost anywhere for 30 to 50 dollars per hour. Other typical tools needed are a chain saw, skill saw, and a cement mixer. Common people use these tools all the time and they are very easily accessible to all. This places the building of an Earthship easily within reach of typical contractors and owner builders.

SECONDARY MATERIALS

The same requirements should be related to for the secondary materials. Some secondary materials such as glass are the same everywhere while others will vary with different locales. The secondary materials are those which make up the fill in walls, ceilings, floors, glazing, and miscellaneous carpentry.

Fill in walls

The most significant secondary material is that used for bathroom walls, closet walls, non-structural end walls of the greenhouse hallway, and all other miscellaneous infill areas. The material we have found for these areas is one that meets all the requirements outlined in the nature of materials except for mass which in the case of fill in walls is not necessary. This material is a little durable aluminum brick that appears "naturally" on this planet. It is indigenous to most parts of the planet that are heavily populated. It is also known as the aluminum beverage can. Its evolution as a low tech, easy to use brick has been taking place for almost twenty years in New Mexico. It has been used for structural walls, non-bearing interior walls, filler walls, domes, vaults etc. Whole buildings have been built with aluminum cans. Due to its light weight, the fact that it requires very little skill to learn to use, that it can be plastered over without conventional metal lath, that it will never wear out or burn and that it is very easy to obtain; it has become the ideal material for fil in walls in Earthships. It is another natural resource of the twentieth century.

Ceilings

The ceiling decks and beams of the Earthship can be made of whatever local beams and decking are available. In New Mexico standing dead trees are cut for round log beams called vigas. Decking is usually made from wood planks. The ceiling decks and beams are usually made from some kind of wood, however this is not mandatory. Concrete or steel beams and decking could be used as well as any other method of spanning distances of ten to twenty feet. We are currently experimenting with a product made by A.I.R. Research of Wisconsin that is made by grinding up garbage and mixing it with a slurry of adhesives to produce a poured beam almost as strong as and having similar qualities of concrete. Conventional vapor barriers and rigid insulation (R60) are used above the ceiling. See chapter six for specifics on these materials and their detailing.

Floors

Floors can also be made from any local indigenous material from concrete to flagstone to tile or wood. Some Earthships in New Mexico have used adobe mud floors which are traditional in the area. They are very beautiful and will work anywhere. Floors should take advantage of local materials that are of a low energy impact nature, however they are quite conventional in the application to the Earthship structure.

Glazing

The southern glazing on Earthships that wants to collect heat should be double-paned, insulated glass as manufactured by most glass companies in standard sizes. The size most often designed for in typical Earthships is 46" x 90". All other glazing should be either triple pane or one of the new heat retaining glazings (consult your local glass dealer).

If Earthships were to become the way of the future, on a large scale, the resulting impact would be significant. There would be a radical reduction in the use of global energy to both manufacture and transport the various materials that dominate the housing industry. There would also be a radical reduction in the amount of automobile tires discarded on the planet and the need to find some way to dispose of them. There would also be a significant reduction in deforestation which is and will be a continuous threat as long as wood is a major building product for housing. Anything that we do on as large a scale as housing must (like the trees) be born of something that we ourselves produce. Our numbers are too great for the planet to continue being the sole supplier of our needs. The by-products of the tree itself, through decay and biodegrading, provide soil for the nourishment of its offspring. Likewise **the by-products of our society must provide the materials for housing our future generations.**

6. THE "U" MODULE

THE DETAILS AND SKILLS USED TO BUILD THE "U" MODULE

The fundamentals of how to build your own Earthship are presented here. A well illustrated and explained collection of easy to learn skills, available to all types of people of various strengths, shapes and sizes is presented. This includes how to lay the rammed earth tires, how to lay the aluminum cans in mortar, connections, mistakes commonly made, etc...

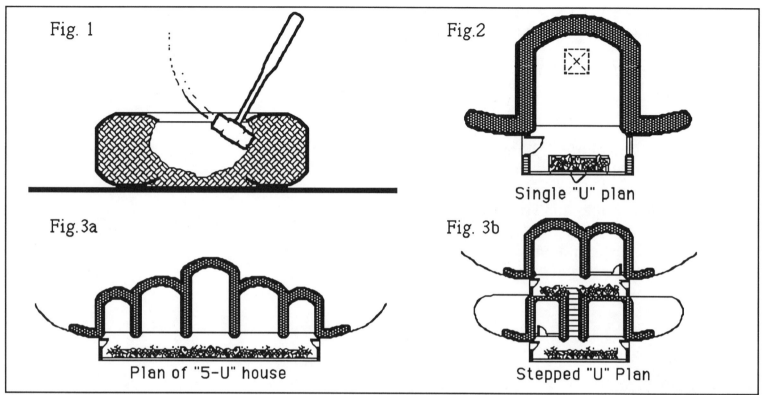

Fig. 1

Fig.2

Single "U" plan

Fig.3a

Plan of "5-U" house

Fig. 3b

Stepped "U" Plan

This chapter begins with an explanation and illustrations of how to pound a rammed earth tire. This is the building block of the "U" module. (Fig. 1)

Next, the construction materials and methods used to build the entire "U" module out of these rammed earth building blocks will be explained and illustrated. (Fig. 2)

Our objective is to provide a thorough understanding of how to build one single "U" module. Since the Earthship is made up of several of these "U" modules, an understanding of how to build the module is a basic understanding of how to build the Earthship. Chapter 8 will deal with how to assemble the modules into an Earthship. (Fig. 3a - 3b)

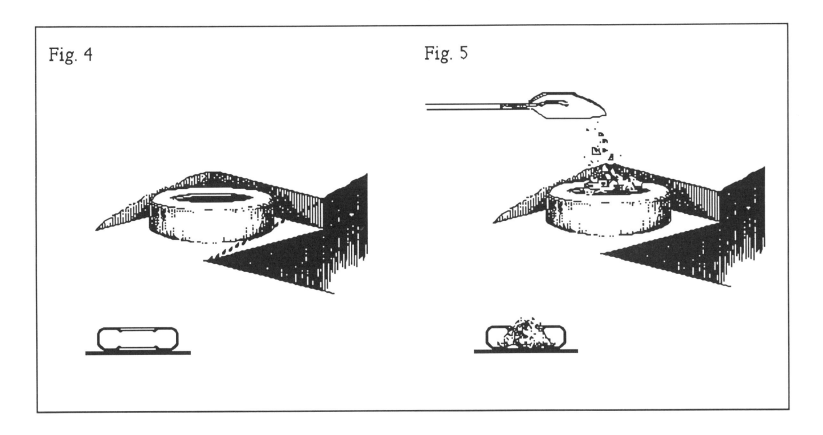

Fig. 4

Fig. 5

HOW TO POUND A TIRE

Tire walls are made by laying tires in staggered courses like brick or concrete block. Each tire is filled with compacted earth, so that it becomes a rammed earth brick encased in steel belted rubber. As you will find, a pounded tire weighs over 300 pounds, so all tires are pounded in place and only minor movements can be made.

First, level a section of undisturbed earth large enough to receive a 2'-4" tire. This is approximately 3'-0" square. Remove all loose topsoil which would otherwise settle under the weight of the wall. Set the tire on the leveled undisturbed ground. (Fig. 4)

Tire pounding should be done in teams of two people, a shoveler and a pounder. Depending on your strength and endurance, a team should be able to pound a tire in 5-15 minutes. First,

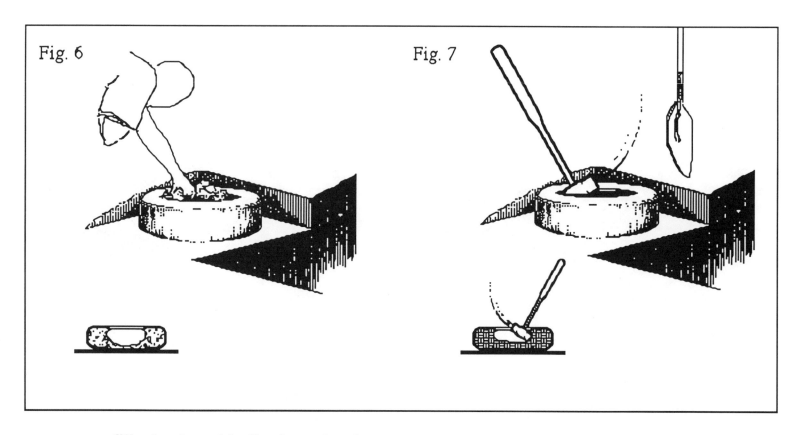

Fig. 6

Fig. 7

one person fills the tire with dirt from the site. (Fig. 5)

Slightly damp soil is easiest to compact, however any type of soil with or without gravel will work.

The dirt is pushed by hand into the casing by the pounder. Gloves are advised for both workers. (Fig. 6)

Keep pushing the dirt into the casing until it is as full as you can pack it by hand. Now begin pounding the dirt into the casing with a 9 pound sledgehammer.

The shoveler continues to add more dirt, while the pounder packs it in. (Fig. 7)

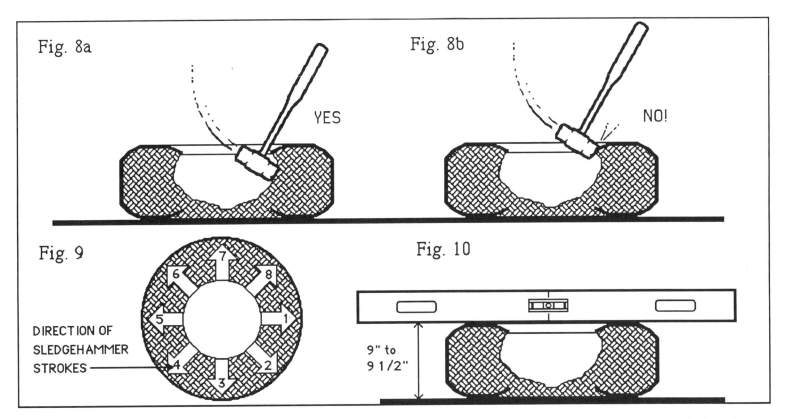

Fig. 8a YES

Fig. 8b NO!

Fig. 9

DIRECTION OF
SLEDGEHAMMER
STROKES

Fig. 10

9" to
9 1/2"

Each tire takes about three or four wheelbarrows of dirt. When serious pounding begins, large amounts of dirt will be generated from the initial excavation (which is explained later).

The tire will become full of dirt and begin to swell up.

The sledgehammer strokes shown go <u>into</u> the casing. Do not hit the casing itself. (Figs. 8a-b)

As you pound the dirt, move around the tire to keep the tire pounded evenly. (Fig. 9)

This is done until the tire has swelled to about 9 or 9 1/2 inches. After the outer casing is sufficiently packed and swollen, it will need to be leveled. Lay a 4'-0" level across the tire, letting it rest on the swollen rubber casing. (Fig. 10)

Make sure that the tire is level in all directions. Add more dirt to build up the tire if necessary.

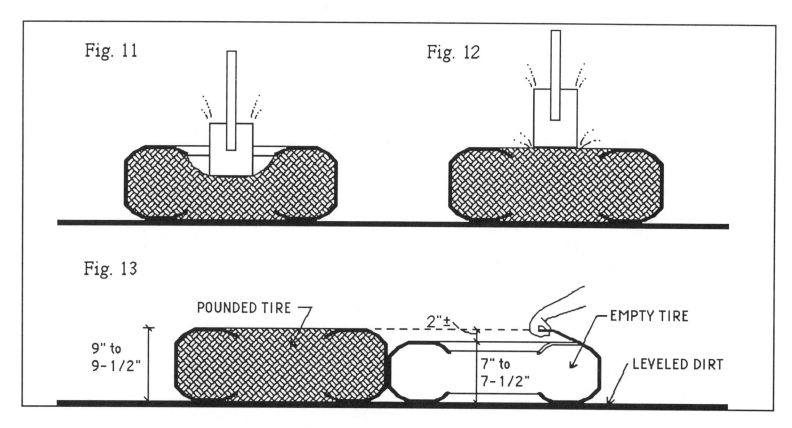

Fig. 11

Fig. 12

Fig. 13

POUNDED TIRE

9" to 9-1/2"

2"±

7" to 7-1/2"

EMPTY TIRE

LEVELED DIRT

Next, the interior of the tire is filled with more dirt and tamped until it is packed as tightly as the inner casing. Do not fill completely and then tamp. Tamp as you fill; i.e. fill a little then tamp a little. This allows a tighter tamping job. (Fig. 11-12)

This ensures that the whole tire brick has consistently packed earth throughout.

The ground next to the pounded tire must be leveled now in preparation for pounding another tire. Level the ground so that it is 9" to 9-1/2" below the top of the pounded tire. An unpounded tire is 7" to 7-1/2" high. This allows for about 2" of swell when pounded. (Fig. 13)

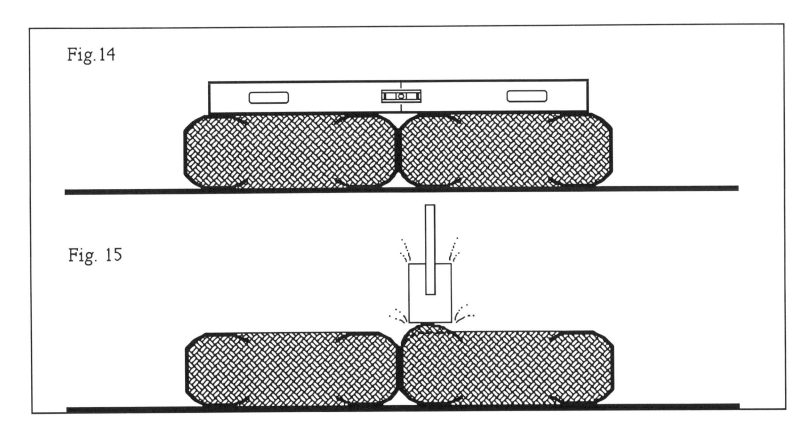

Fig. 14

Fig. 15

Continue the above procedure, laying the second tire so it is touching the first. After the next tire is pounded, level it with the first tire. (Fig. 14) Also level it with itself in the other direction.

If you arc too high with any part of the second tire, it can be beat back down with the tamper. (Fig. 15)

It is important that each tire be level in itself and with the adjacent tires, so eventually the entire course will be level. This is the procedure for the ground course of tires.

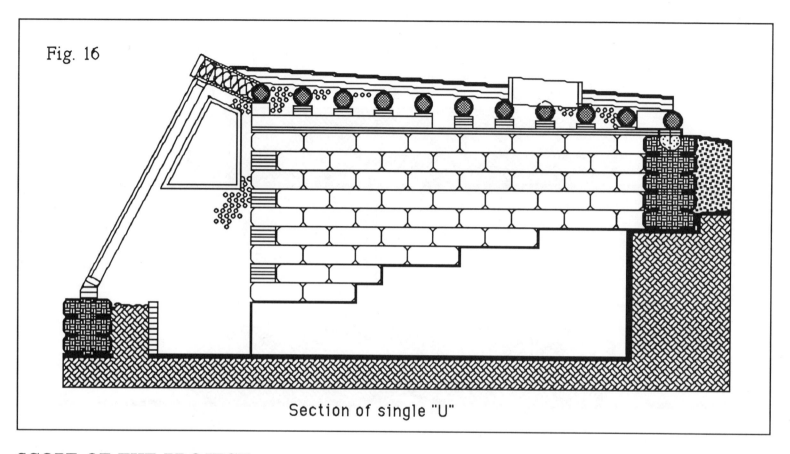

Fig. 16

Section of single "U"

SCOPE OF THE PROJECT

Now that you know how to pound a tire, you are ready to begin a "U" module. Here is a set of diagrams for this module, including a cross section and floor plan. (Figs. 16-17) It is a good idea to get a feel for the general scope of the project before you begin. The example shown is a building on a sloping site. For your own project, use the information you learned in Chapter 2 - Location, to locate your Earthship.

These "U" modules can vary in width and depth, however the basic details remain the same. Maximum recommended width is 18'-0" and maximum recommended depth is 26'-0".

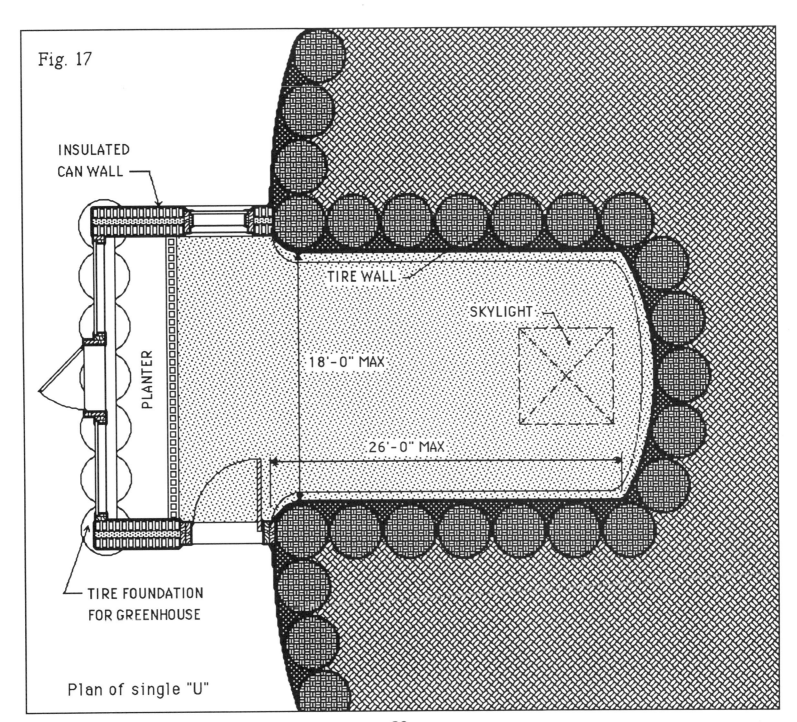

Fig. 17

INSULATED
CAN WALL

TIRE WALL

SKYLIGHT

PLANTER

18'-0" MAX

26'-0" MAX

TIRE FOUNDATION
FOR GREENHOUSE

Plan of single "U"

89

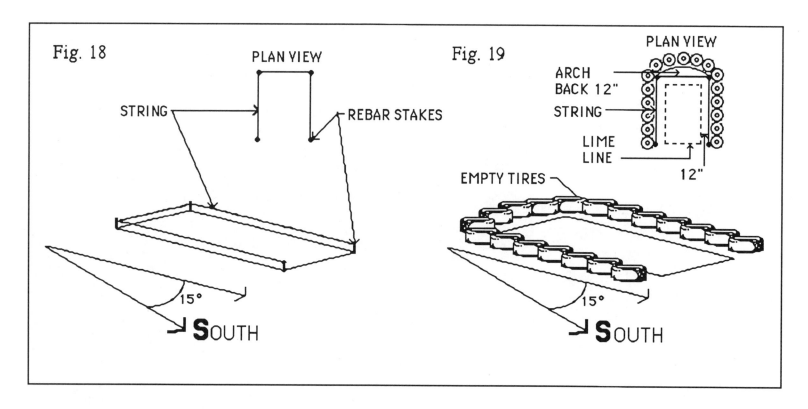

Fig. 18

PLAN VIEW

STRING

REBAR STAKES

15°

SOUTH

Fig. 19

PLAN VIEW

ARCH
BACK 12"

STRING

LIME
LINE

12"

EMPTY TIRES

15°

SOUTH

LAYOUT

First, you will need to stake out a rectangle which will be the size of the interior of your room. Stretch a string line around rebar stakes to mark this line. (Fig. 18) Orient this room 15 degrees east of south to catch the morning sun (see chapter two).

INITIAL EXCAVATION

Lay out your first course of empty tires along your string line, allowing for your arch in the back. (Fig. 19)

The arch should be a <u>minimum</u> of 12" from the string line. As discussed in Chapter 4 - Structure, the arch is for additional support against the burial.

Always use larger tires, #15 and #16, on the first course. #15's will be used throughout the body of the wall, and #14's will be used for the top course.

After you have laid out the tires, (touching the string on the sides) measure 12" from the string to the interior. Mark this line with lime

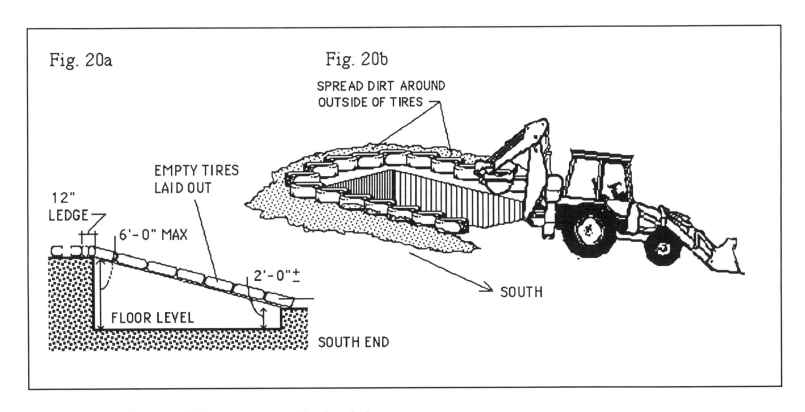

Fig. 20a

Fig. 20b

SPREAD DIRT AROUND OUTSIDE OF TIRES

EMPTY TIRES LAID OUT

12" LEDGE

6'-0" MAX

2'-0"±

FLOOR LEVEL

SOUTH END

SOUTH

on the ground - it will be the outer limit of the initial dig. **Do not let the initial dig get any closer than 12" from the tires.** This is an earth cliff and must be protected from erosion by being further from the tires now than the final design requires. It will be carved back by hand later.

Have the backhoe driver dig out the room as marked within the lime lines, (Fig. 20a - 20b).The maximum depth on the north end is 6'-0". The depth on the south end will vary

from zero to 3'-0" according to your specific site slope, the depth of the rooms, and other site conditions.

As the dirt is dug out of the ground, have the backhoe driver spread it around the outside of the U. This dirt will be used to fill the tires later.

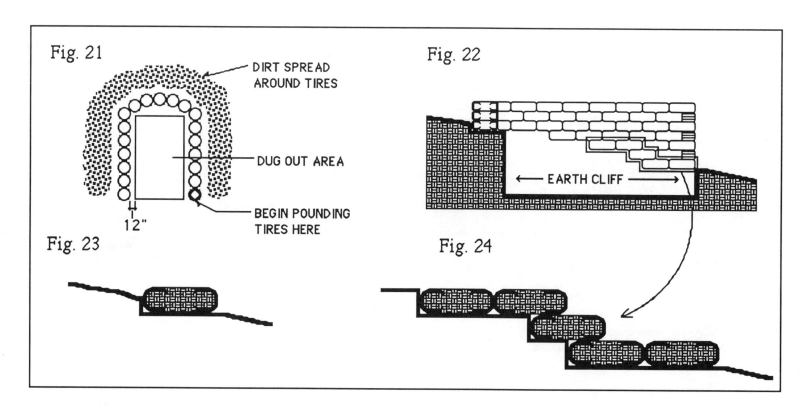

Fig. 21

DIRT SPREAD AROUND TIRES

DUG OUT AREA

12"

BEGIN POUNDING TIRES HERE

Fig. 22

EARTH CLIFF

Fig. 23

Fig. 24

THE FIRST COURSE OF TIRES

Beginning with the front right tire, level a section of earth, then pound and level the first tire. (Fig. 21 & 23)

How you proceed will depend on the slope of your specific site. On a steeper site, you can step the tirework up the hill. (Figs. 22-24)

This results in less tires to pound on the up hill side of the "U".

On a flatter site, the entire first course will set on the same level.

Fig. 25 shows the first course of tires on a typical sloped site. Notice the wing walls going to the east and west. These only occur when another "U" is not being placed next to the one you have started i.e. they occur at the east and west ends of the building. If you are just building one "U" both wing walls occur as shown.

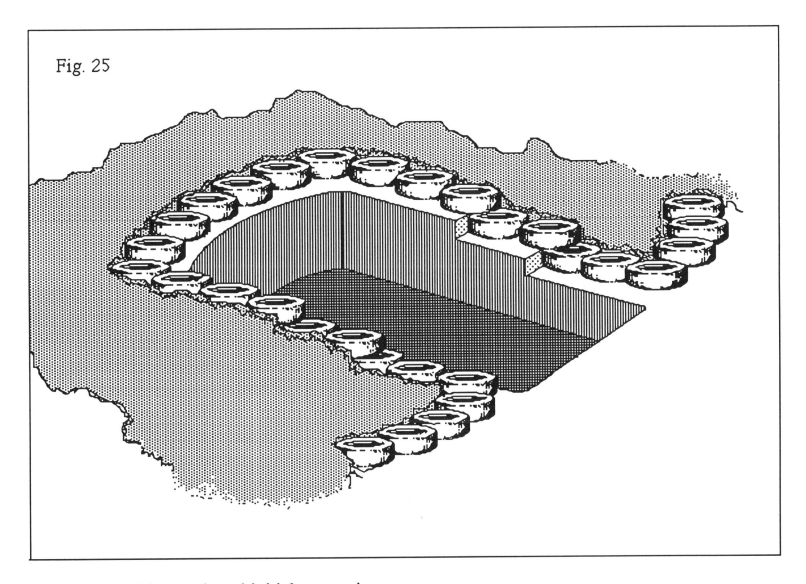

Fig. 25

First course of tire work and initial excavation.

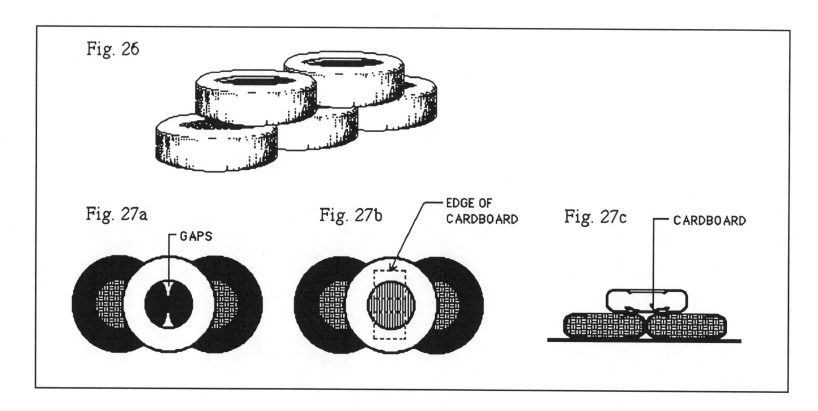

Fig. 26

Fig. 27a

GAPS

Fig. 27b

EDGE OF
CARDBOARD

Fig. 27c

CARDBOARD

THE SECOND COURSE

Courses of tires are staggered, in the same way as brick or concrete block. (Fig.26)

You will find that when you lay a tire for the second course, the dirt will fall through the gaps created where the tires round inward. To remedy this, lay a piece of cardboard inside the tire to temporarily hold the dirt.
(Figs. 27a-c)

This is usually done with two pieces as it is easier to fit two small pieces in than one big one. Use discarded boxes from the grocery store. After the tire is pounded, the compacted dirt will no longer need a form; and, since both sides of the tire wall will eventually be sealed and covered by dirt or mud plaster, the cardboard can decompose without affecting the structure. The cardboard is only a temporary device.

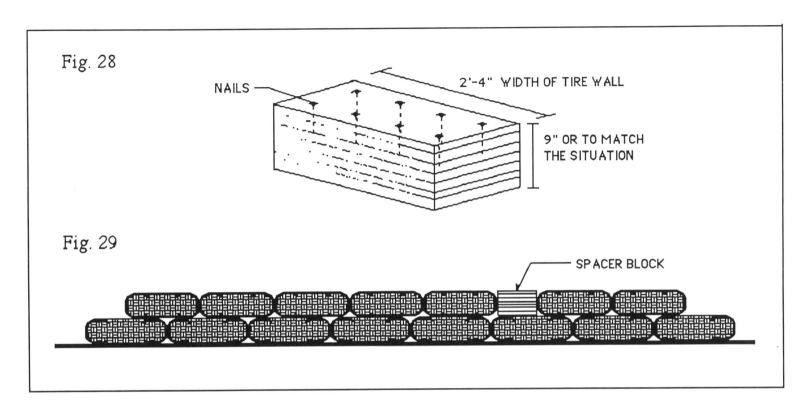

Fig. 28

NAILS

2'-4" WIDTH OF TIRE WALL

9" OR TO MATCH
THE SITUATION

Fig. 29

SPACER BLOCK

BLOCKING

There will be times when a half tire is necessary. In these situations, solid wood blocking is used. It is constructed by laminating 1x12 and 2x12 pieces of lumber and plywood scraps together. (Fig. 28) There are four different types of blocking -

1. spacer blocks   3. L connection blocks
2. end blocks   4. Y connection blocks.

In a single "U", you will use only spacer blocks and L connection blocks. The other types are used when two or more U's are joined together. This will be discussed in Chapter 8. **All blocking should be coated with two coats of wood preservative and wrapped in two layers of 6 mil plastic.** Slash the plastic on the side of the blocking that faces the inside of the room so that it will not trap moisture.

Spacer blocks

Because of the irregularities in the size of tires, you will encounter situations where the tires will begin to line up vertically, rather than be staggered. When this occurs, a solid

95

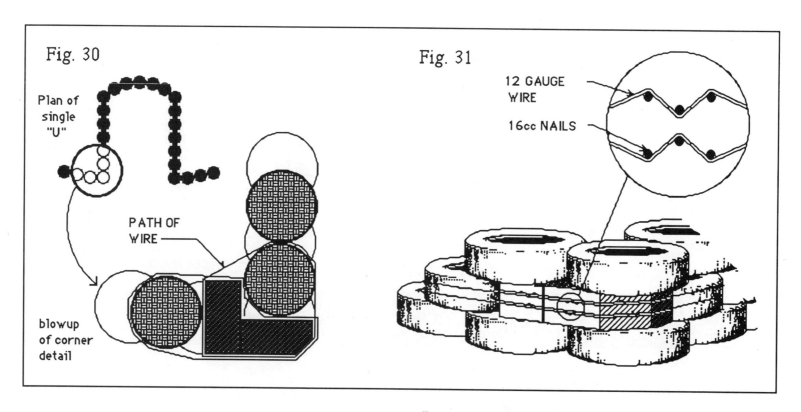

Fig. 30

Plan of
single
"U"

PATH OF
WIRE

blowup
of corner
detail

Fig. 31

12 GAUGE
WIRE

16cc NAILS

wood block, the size of a half tire, should
be inserted. (Fig. 29)

This will put you back on staggered coursing.
Staggered coursing is important, as it knits the
wall together.

If a spacer block is necessary on the ground
course, put a board on either side of the tires
and fill the space with concrete as it is not a
good idea to put wood on the ground.

L connection blocks
These will vary with each situation and must
be custom fit. This can be done with two
blocks. One example is shown. (Fig. 30)

Tie these blocks into the tire walls, using 12
gauge wire. Nail the wire to blocks and tires
with 16 cc nails. Use the placement of the
nails to stretch and tighten the wire. (Fig. 31)

Tires do vary in diameter. It is a good idea to
lay out empty tires around the U for each
entire course, selecting tires larger or smaller

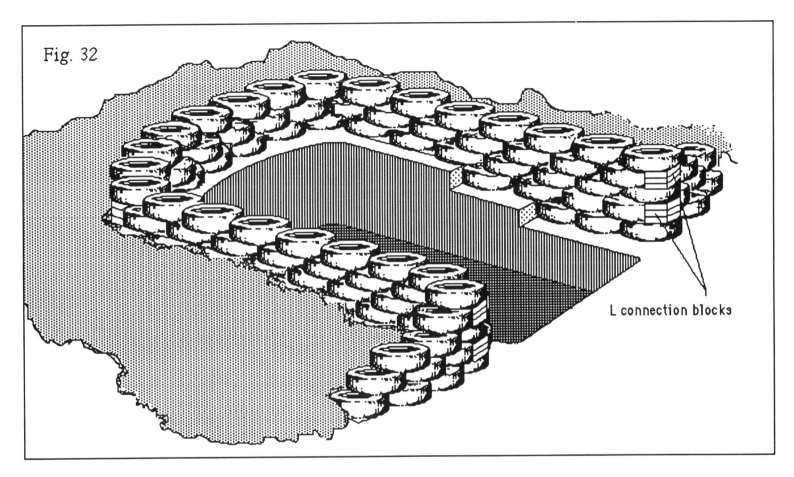

Fig. 32

L connection blocks

Typical "U" all pounded out and ready for backfilling and bond beam plates.

to try and achieve a layout that requires little
or no blocking. Blocking is time consuming,
more expensive, and not as thermal as
earthrammed tires.

In many simple buildings, spacer blocking can
be totally avoided.

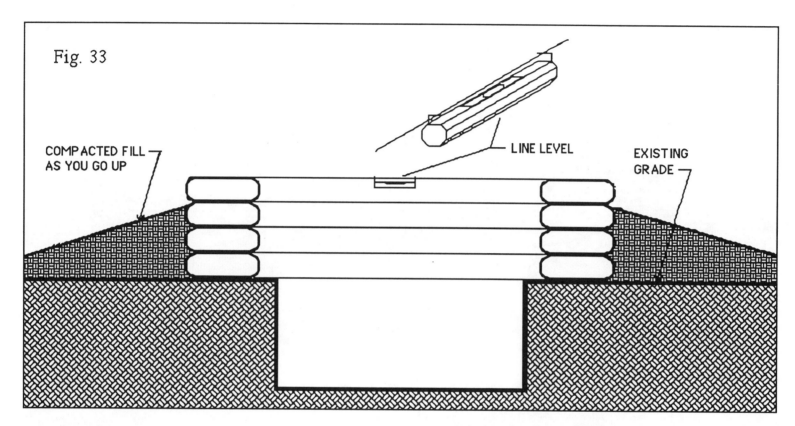

Fig. 33

COMPACTED FILL
AS YOU GO UP

LINE LEVEL

EXISTING
GRADE

BACKFILLING

Backfill behind the tires as you get higher. This will allow you a place to stand while pounding. This dirt needs to be compacted. Some compacting will be achieved through normal work traffic, but compacting by back dragging with the scoop of the backhoe is also necessary. **Drop** the fill against the tire wall. **Do not push it up against the tire wall or you will push the wall out of plumb.**

LEVELING COURSES

As you finish each course of tirework, check to make sure each course is level by stretching a line level (Fig. 33) from east to west, or shooting elevations with a transit, across the U. When you are completely finished pounding tires, level across the U, from east to west, in several places. It is important that this is level, so that the roof structure can rest on a flat surface, distributing its weight evenly throughout the wall.

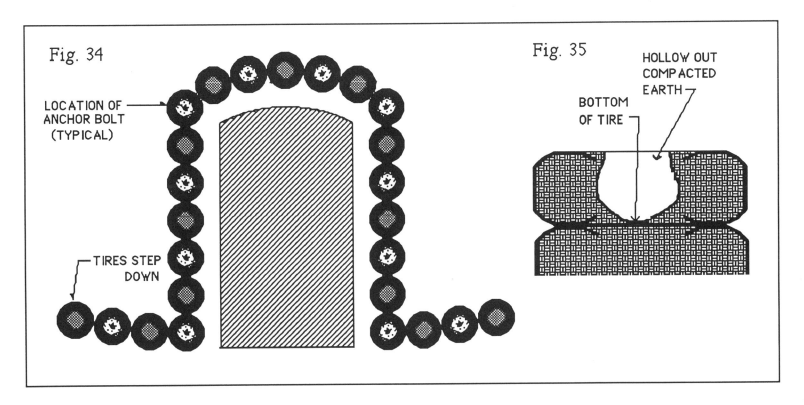

Fig. 34

LOCATION OF ANCHOR BOLT (TYPICAL)

TIRES STEP DOWN

Fig. 35

HOLLOW OUT COMPACTED EARTH

BOTTOM OF TIRE

SETTING THE ANCHOR BOLTS

The roof structure will be fastened to the tire wall using anchor bolts set in concrete. Bolts will be located in every other tire on the top course. (Fig. 34)

If it doesn't work out even, then double two bolts in adjacent tires.

To set the bolts, first hollow out about one gallon of compacted earth from the tires indicated. (Fig. 35) Hollow out all the way down to the bottom of the tire.

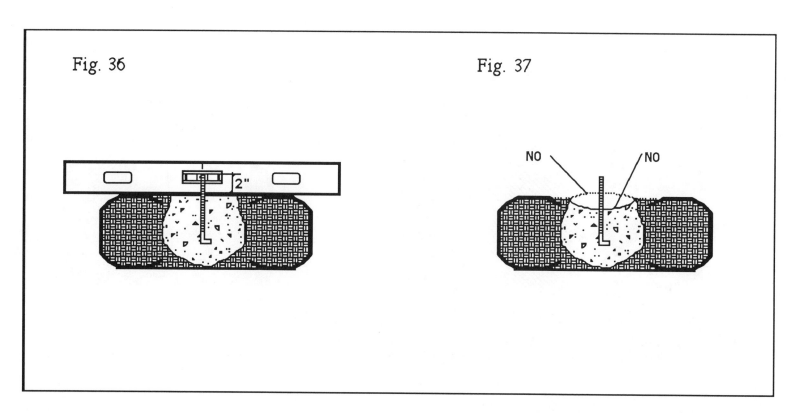

Fig. 36   Fig. 37

Next mix the concrete, using a concrete mixer or a wheelbarrow. The mixture is 3 parts sand to 1 part cement.

The mixture should be what is called a 'stiff mix' (ie. not soupy), so that the bolts can set up straight in the concrete.

Now, fill the void with concrete, flush with the bottom of the level. Set one 1/2" diameter, 8" long anchor bolt in the center of each concrete filled tire. Allow the bolt to stick out 2" above the top of the tire. (Fig. 36)

It is important that the cement be flush with the top of the tire as in Fig. 36. Do not let the cement get above or below (Fig. 37) as this will cause problems with the wood plate that will be anchored on next.

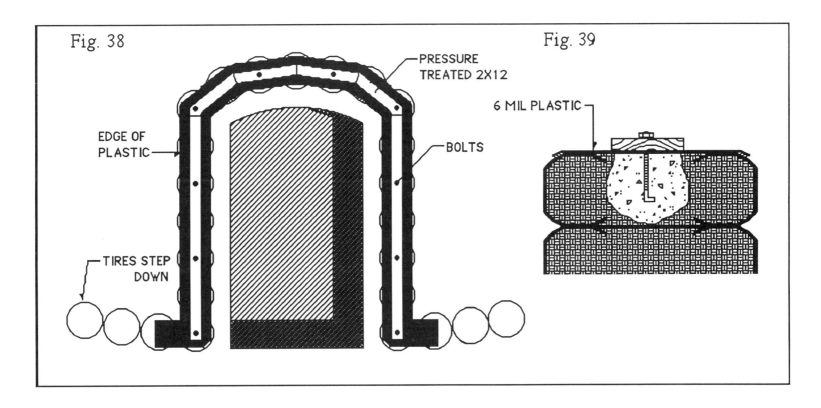

Fig. 38

PRESSURE TREATED 2X12

6 MIL PLASTIC

EDGE OF PLASTIC

BOLTS

TIRES STEP DOWN

Fig. 39

THE TOP PLATE

After the concrete has dried, apply 2 layers of 6 mil. plastic over the entire top of the wall. Staple it down with a staple hammer.

The top plate will be made of 2 layers of 2x12 pressure treated dimension lumber (or two layers of rough sawn 2x12's coated with wood preservative), centered over the bolts. (Fig. 38)

Drill 1/2" holes in the first layer to match the location of the bolts. This can be done by placing the board over the bolts and tapping with a hammer so the bolts leave an indention in the wood. Drill at the indentions. Bolt this wood down with washers over the plastic. (Fig. 39)

Tighten the bolts with washers <u>just snug:</u> if they are too tight, they will pull the concrete loose from the tire.

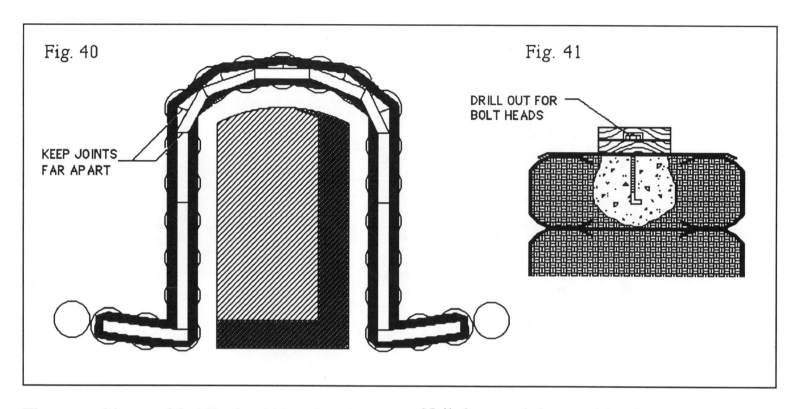

Fig. 40

KEEP JOINTS
FAR APART

Fig. 41

DRILL OUT FOR
BOLT HEADS

The second layer of 2x12's should be placed so that the joints are well away from the joints of the first layer. This provides a continuous 4x12 treated wood bond beam. (Fig. 40)

With a spade bit, drill holes in the second layer to match the bolt locations. Drill holes big enough to cover the nut and washer, usually 1¹/₄" diameter. This will allow the wood to set flat on the first layer. (Fig. 41)

Nail the wood down with 16cc nails in several places, with at least 4 nails per foot. Nail more heavily around all joints.

Now you can backfill up to the top of the tirework. Compact this fill by back dragging with a backhoe.

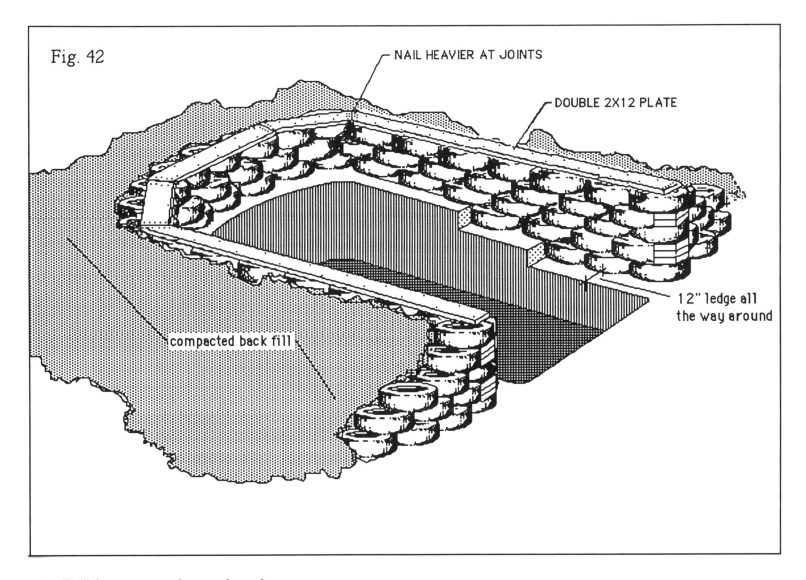

Fig. 42

NAIL HEAVIER AT JOINTS

DOUBLE 2X12 PLATE

12" ledge all the way around

compacted back fill

The "U" is now ready to place beams.

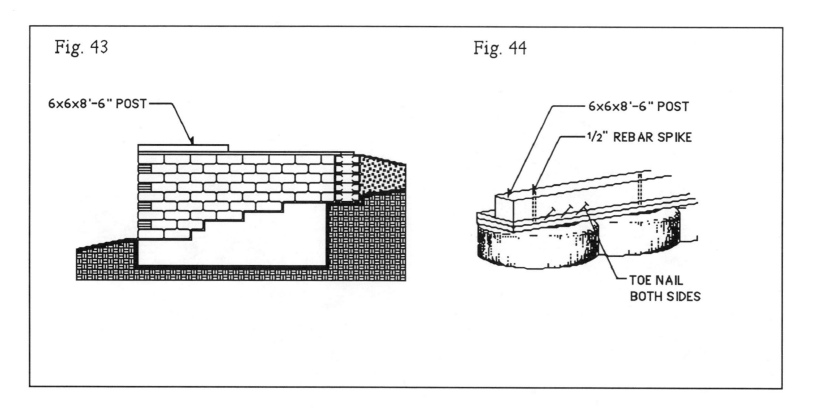

Fig. 43

6x6x8'-6" POST

Fig. 44

6x6x8'-6" POST

1/2" REBAR SPIKE

TOE NAIL
BOTH SIDES

SHIMMING BLOCKS FOR BEAM PLACEMENT

It is necessary to slope the roof structure, so that it may properly shed water. To achieve this slope, you will need to 'shim up' the beams. This process should be done on the east and west walls at the same time.

Locate a 6x6x8'-0" long post on the top plate, flush with the inside of the plate. (Fig. 43 and 44) Toe nail it in on the sides.

Drill a 1/2" hole through the 6x6 and the top plate with a 16" auger bit.

Be careful not to drill through the plate into the concrete. This would destroy the structural integrity of the concrete and dull the bit.

Pin the 6x6 to the plate with a spike made from 1/2" rebar. This spike is then driven like a nail into the pre-drilled hole (Fig. 44) **Do not drive the spike into any of the concrete. This will crack it and destroy its ability to hold the anchor bolt.**

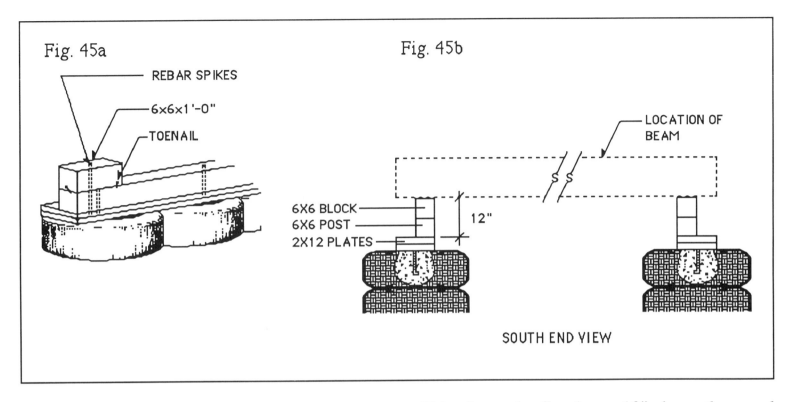

Fig. 45a

REBAR SPIKES

6x6x1'-0"

TOENAIL

Fig. 45b

LOCATION OF
BEAM

6X6 BLOCK

6X6 POST

2X12 PLATES

12"

SOUTH END VIEW

Rebar comes in 20'-0" lengths; it can be cut to the various lengths needed for spikes, using a hacksaw, welder's torch, or a rebar cutter at a lumber yard. Drive the spikes in with a hand sledge.

Cut another 6x6, 1'-0" long. Using the same method, fasten this block to the one below it, staggering the spikes. (Fig. 45a-b)

This places the first beam 12" above the wood plates. The last beam will be directly on the wood plates thus providing a 12" drop from front to back of the "U". This same process may be done with 8x8 stock for deep "U's" thus creating a steeper slope.

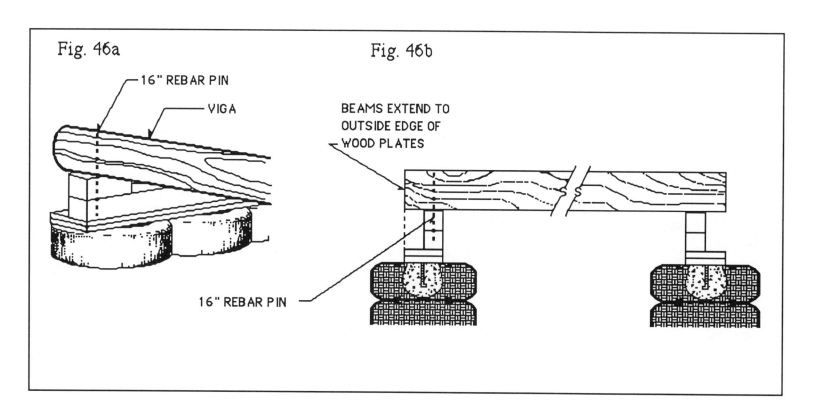

Fig. 46a

Fig. 46b

16" REBAR PIN

VIGA

BEAMS EXTEND TO
OUTSIDE EDGE OF
WOOD PLATES

16" REBAR PIN

BEAMS

In New Mexico, where most of the prototypes for this construction exist, vigas (round logs) are used for beams. Vigas are preferred because they require less energy to "manufacture" than dimension lumber. In many regions these are not available, so you will have to substitute standard wood beams. The size of these will depend on variables, such as snow load, distance of spans, etc.

An engineer or builder should be consulted to size beams for specific situations. These beams can be rough sawn timbers or laminated from 2" thick lumber. They are usually 6" wide and 10" deep. All types of beams are placed 2'-0" on center.

After the first blocking has been secured, lay the first beam across the structure flush with the front of the tire wall. Pin this beam with rebar spikes, similar to the way the blocking shims were installed. (Figs. 46a-b)

106

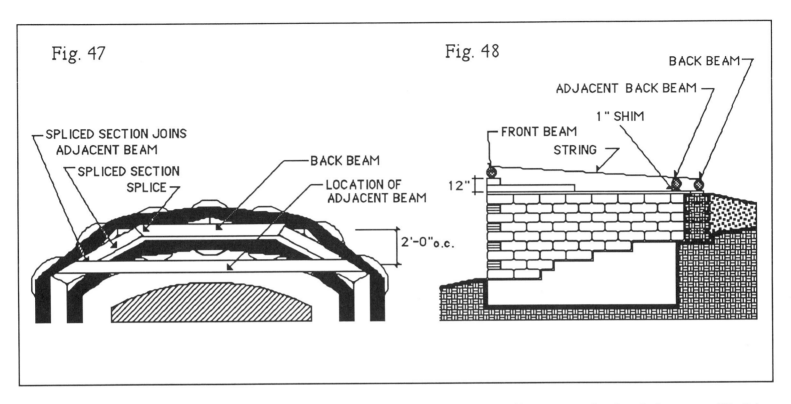

Fig. 47

Fig. 48

SPLICED SECTION JOINS ADJACENT BEAM

SPLICED SECTION

SPLICE

BACK BEAM

LOCATION OF ADJACENT BEAM

2'-0"o.c.

BACK BEAM

ADJACENT BACK BEAM

1" SHIM

FRONT BEAM

STRING

12"

Next locate a beam directly on the plate at the back of the "U", flush with the outside of the plate. This beam will have to be spliced to two other short sections of beam in order to follow the curve of the back plate. It will not span it will simply be sitting on the plate. Extend the spliced section until it joins the location for the adjacent beam which is 2'-0" away. (Fig. 47 and 50)

The beam adjacent to the back beam will shim up about 1" higher than the back beam to maintain a slope. (Fig. 48)

Now, stretch a string from the front beam to the beam adjacent to the back beam. Do this on each side centered over the wood top plate. This will be the guide for the height of the beams in between these two, thus illustrating the roof slope. (Fig. 48)

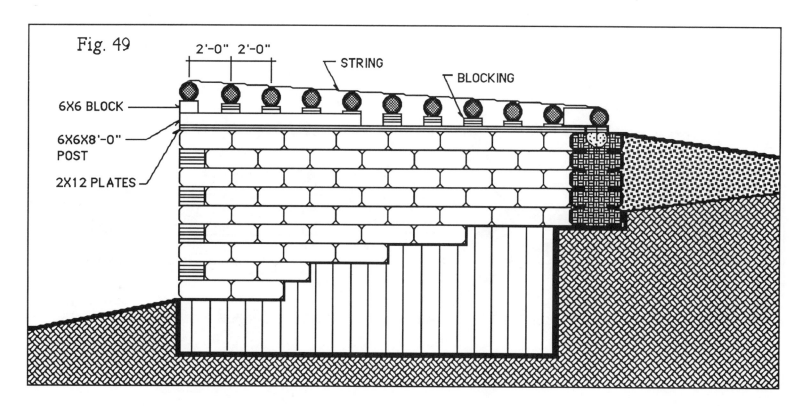

Fig. 49

2'-0" 2'-0"

STRING

BLOCKING

6X6 BLOCK

6X6X8'-0" POST

2X12 PLATES

The beams will be 2'-0" on center. Cut and nail 2x6's to make blocking which will raise the beams to the correct height. Small blocks can be nailed into the plate and to each other. Continue pinning the beams with rebar **through the blocking into the plate.** (Fig. 49) Be careful not to drive pins into concrete around anchor bolts. The concrete will shatter and the anchor bolts will be worthless.

When vigas are used, alternate large and small ends for a neater over all appearance.

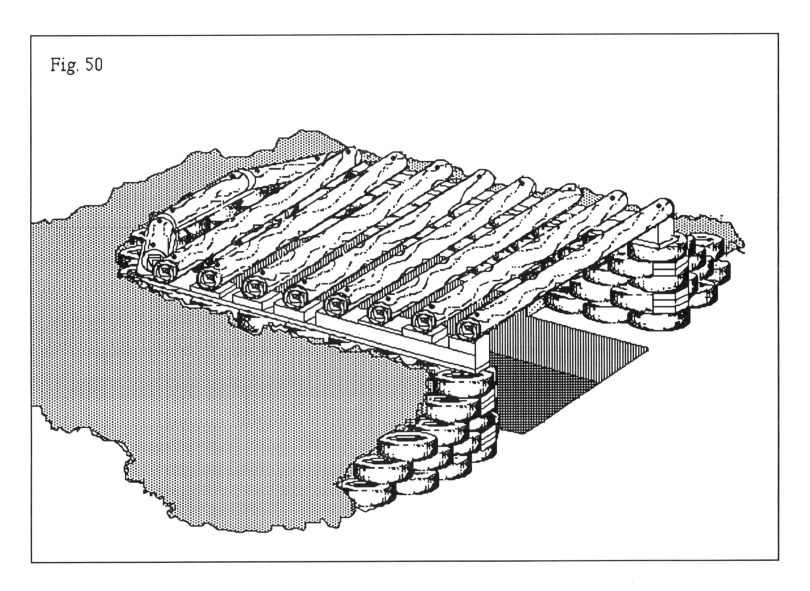

Fig. 50

The "U" module is now ready for can infill, roof decking, and perimeter insulation.

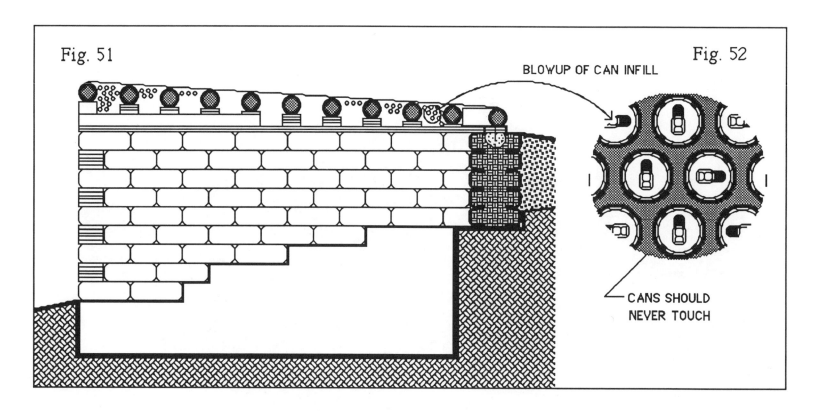

Fig. 51

Fig. 52

BLOWUP OF CAN INFILL

CANS SHOULD NEVER TOUCH

CAN INFILL

The spaces between the beams and blocking will be filled, from the plate up to the string, with aluminum cans set in a cement mortar. (Fig. 51)

Cans are laid in a cement mortar mixture which is 3 parts course sand to 1 part portland cement. This can be mixed in a wheelbarrow or a concrete mixer, depending on how much you will be mixing at once. Regular portland cement should be used.

The cans themselves are not structural; they act as spacers within a perforated concrete network. **It is the matrix of concrete which gives the can wall its strength**.

In this situation, all cans should be laid with the mouth facing toward the inside of the room. The mouths will act as a metal lath to hold the plaster later. (Fig. 52)

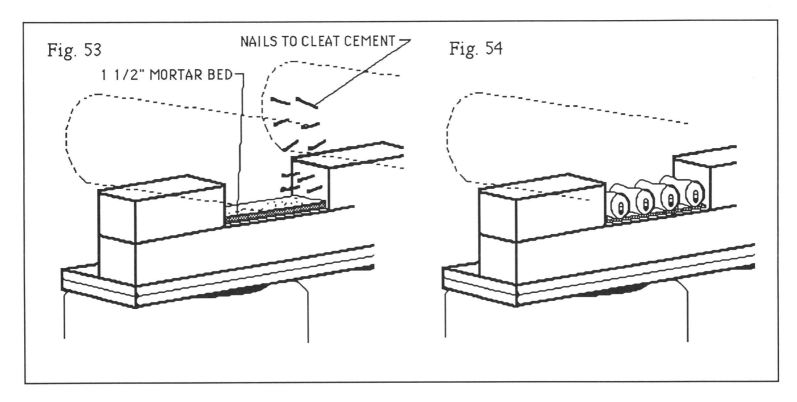

Fig. 53

1 1/2" MORTAR BED

NAILS TO CLEAT CEMENT

Fig. 54

Always wear rubber gloves whenever you are working with portland cement. It will irritate your skin.

The mortar should be a stiff mix, so that it does not ooze out from around the cans. A loose wet mix would make this operation very difficult.

Drive a few nails in the wood where the cans and cement will make contact with the wood. This anchors the cement work to the woodwork.

Now, lay a 1 1/2" bed of mortar on the blocking. It should be about 3 1/2" wide. (Fig. 53)

Slightly crimp each can, so that once the mortar is dry, it cannot be pushed out of the wall. Lay the cans about 3/4" apart, flush with the inside of the blocking. (Fig. 54)

Never let the cans touch each other. This would interrupt the structural concrete matrix.

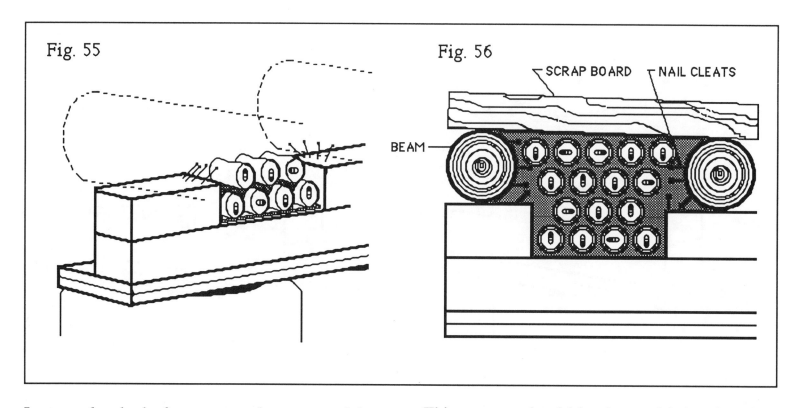

Fig. 55

Fig. 56

SCRAP BOARD   NAIL CLEATS

BEAM

Lay another bed of mortar on the center of the first course of cans, and add another row of cans. If the mortar is oozing out and running, it is too wet. (Fig 55)

Continue the process until you reach the string. (Fig. 56) Use a scrap board for a straight edge to assure that you have cement coming up to the line of the decking which will be applied later.

This process should be done with hands only - (wearing household rubber gloves). Trowels and regular masonry tools will simply slow you down. Your mortar should be stiff enough to allow the whole area to be filled at once.

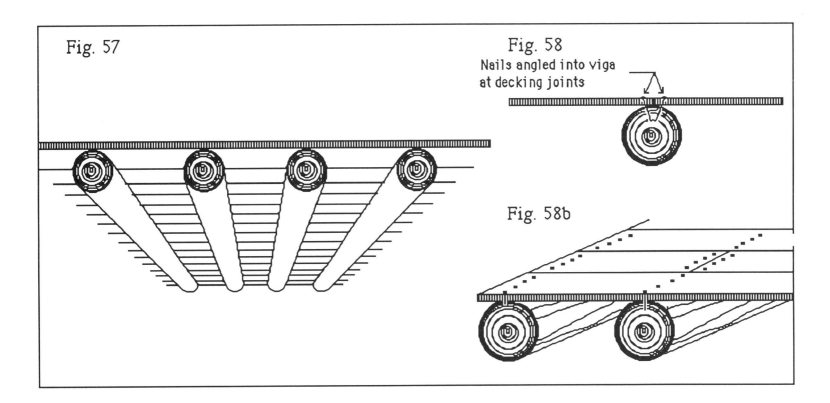

Fig. 57

Fig. 58
Nails angled into viga
at decking joints

Fig. 58b

ROOF DECKING

The roof decking can be made of any wood material, but keep in mind that this will be visible as your ceiling. (Fig. 57)

This wood should be a minimum 5/8" thick. Rough sawn 1x12 lumber is recommended, because it is cheap and looks nice, however it is not always available. Other usable materials include 1x8 dimension lumber, 1x6 tongue and groove, or any planking 6" or wider.

Lay the roof decking side by side, perpendicular to the beams. Nail it down into the beams with 16cc nails. (Fig. 58b). Keep the nailing over the center of the beam or it will show from below. Slope the nailing at the joints (figure 58a). This will keep nails from showing below. Start from one side and work towards the other side.

Stop at the point where the skylight is to be placed. Install the skylight and then continue laying the roof deck around the skylight box. (Fig. 59)

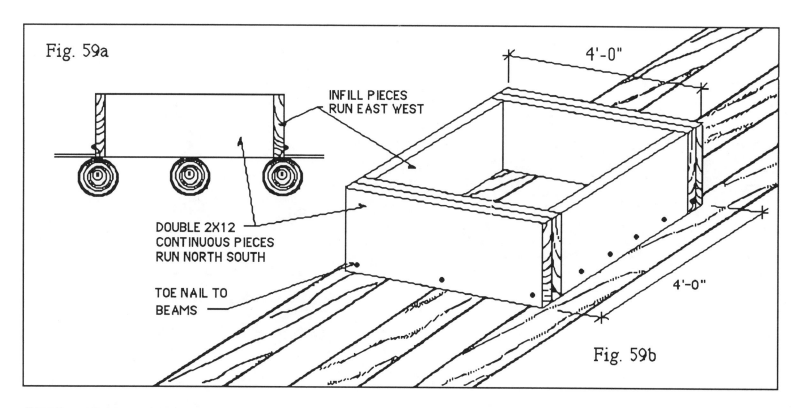

Fig. 59a

INFILL PIECES
RUN EAST WEST

DOUBLE 2X12
CONTINUOUS PIECES
RUN NORTH SOUTH

TOE NAIL TO
BEAMS

4'-0"

4'-0"

Fig. 59b

SKYLIGHT BOX

The skylight box is simply a 4'-0" square box
made from 2x12 stock. In piecing together
the box <u>make sure the pieces that run north-
south are continuous for the full 4'-0"</u>. They
should also be doubled. They must get a good
"seat" on the beams. Sometimes the middle
beam is later cut out and the cut ends are hung
from this double member. Toe nail the
skylight box to beams. Make sure the skylight
box is built and installed square.

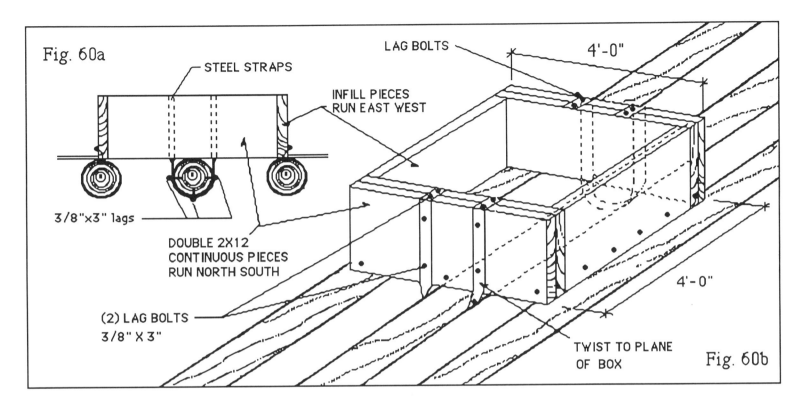

Fig. 60a

STEEL STRAPS

INFILL PIECES
RUN EAST WEST

3/8"x3" lags

DOUBLE 2X12
CONTINUOUS PIECES
RUN NORTH SOUTH

(2) LAG BOLTS
3/8" X 3"

LAG BOLTS

4'-0"

4'-0"

TWIST TO PLANE
OF BOX

Fig. 60b

CUTTING OUT THE MIDDLE BEAM

After the skylight box is installed you may want to cut out the middle beam. Before you cut it out, the ends of the beam are hung with 1/8" x 2" steel straps as shown in Fig. 60. The straps are wrapped around the beam then twisted to the plane of the box and folded over the top of the box. Use 3/8" x 3" lag bolts to screw the straps to the skylight box as shown. The straps must also be screwed to the beam with (3) 3/8" x 3" lag bolts. This is to insure that the strap will not slip off the beam. The

beams tend to shrink and the strap gets loose without these bolts.

Now the beam can simply be cut out with a chainsaw.

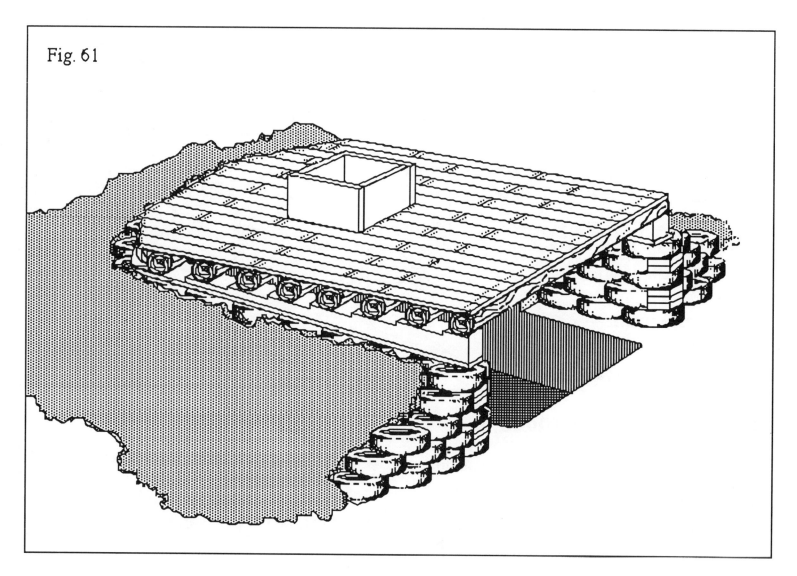

Fig. 61

Your "U" module should now look like this.

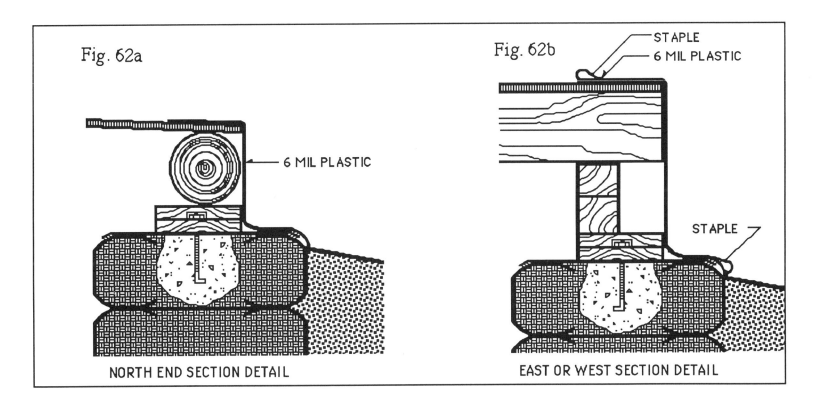

Fig. 62a

6 MIL PLASTIC

NORTH END SECTION DETAIL

Fig. 62b

STAPLE

6 MIL PLASTIC

STAPLE

EAST OR WEST SECTION DETAIL

VAPOR BARRIER

Now, paint all the wood on the perimeter with 2 coats of wood preservative. This will guard it against moisture and bugs.

Then, a vapor barrier must be applied. A vapor barrier usually goes on the warm side of the insulation.

Staple 6 mil. plastic to the perimeter of the roof decking and drape it over the wood, down over the top tire. (Figs. 62a-b)

Fold over the end of the plastic to make it double ply, so that the staples do not tear the plastic.

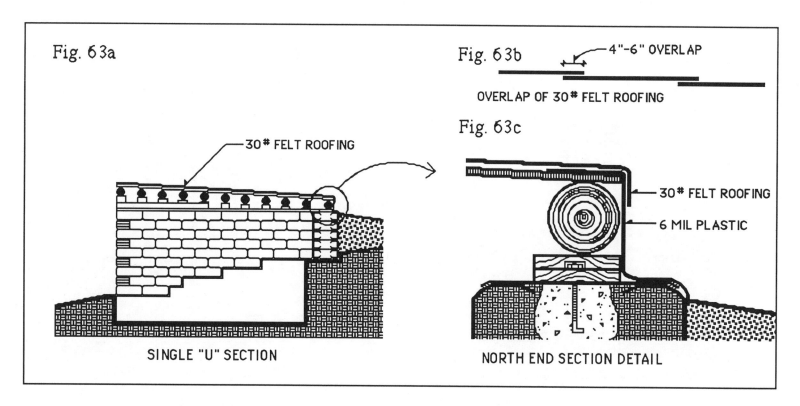

Fig. 63a

Fig. 63b

4"-6" OVERLAP

OVERLAP OF 30# FELT ROOFING

Fig. 63c

30# FELT ROOFING

SINGLE "U" SECTION

30# FELT ROOFING

6 MIL PLASTIC

NORTH END SECTION DETAIL

Next, you will apply 30# felt roofing to the roof deck. (Fig. 63a)

This material comes in a roll. Begin at the north end, rolling out the roofing and stapling it to the roof deck. Overlap the seams about 4"-6" and staple. (Fig. 63b)

This should also overlap the 6 mil. plastic at the perimeter. (Fig. 63c)

This 30# felt provides a vapor barrier on the warm side of the roof insulation.

The wind will rip this material off no matter how much you staple it. For this reason you should do it just before you insulate the roof.

118

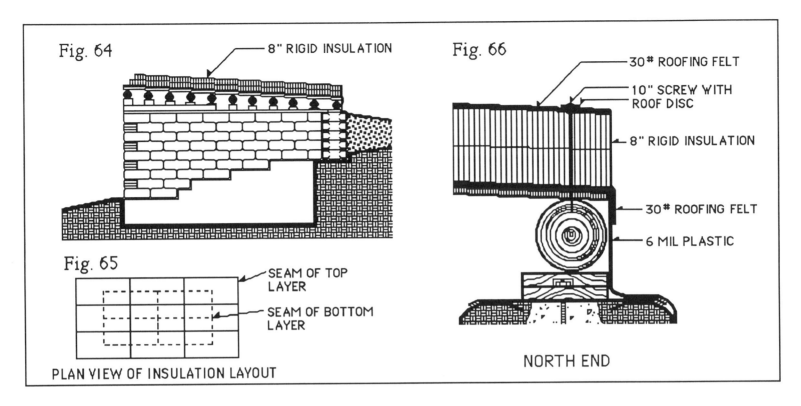

Fig. 64 — 8" RIGID INSULATION

Fig. 65
SEAM OF TOP LAYER
SEAM OF BOTTOM LAYER
PLAN VIEW OF INSULATION LAYOUT

Fig. 66
30# ROOFING FELT
10" SCREW WITH ROOF DISC
8" RIGID INSULATION
30# ROOFING FELT
6 MIL PLASTIC
NORTH END

INSULATING THE ROOF AND PERIMETER

Insulative qualities are measured in "R-values." Since most heat would be lost through the roof of the structure, it should have a <u>minimum</u> R-60. 8" of foam insulation board, plus the added insulative qualities of the deck and roofing materials, will be sufficient. (Fig. 64)

There are many brand names of rigid insulation. Choose one that provides R60 (or close to it) for 8".

Foam insulation board comes in 4'x8' sheets, 4" thick. You will use two layers. The seams of the two layers should be staggered to prevent any seams from lining up for the full 8" (Fig. 65).

Screw the insulation through the decking into the beams using 10" deck screws with roof discs. (Fig. 66). 9" gutter spikes with roof discs can also be used for this.

It is important that you bolt or spike <u>into the beams</u>; otherwise the bolts will show on the interior ceiling.

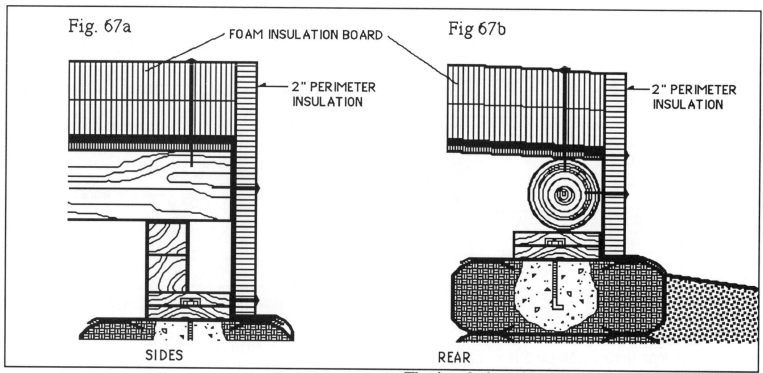

Fig. 67a

FOAM INSULATION BOARD

2" PERIMETER INSULATION

Fig 67b

2" PERIMETER INSULATION

SIDES

REAR

It is best to tack the first 4" layer of insulation down with a few 6" barn spikes (over the beams only). Then apply the next layer staggering the joints and using the 10" screws or spikes with roof discs. Again just tack it down with a few screws or spikes as it will be permanently fastened with the application of the roof underlayment.

The deck screws are difficult to find. They can be ordered through a commercial roofing contractor.

The insulation should be stopped 12" short on the south end, where the greenhouse will attach. (Fig. 69a) This gap will be filled in later. Stop insulation flush with the beams at the sides and rear.

The perimeter space behind the can infill and beams down to the tire wall will also need to be insulated. Using 16cc nails driven through roof discs, nail 2" of rigid <u>waterproof perimeter insulation</u> into the beams, all the way around the structure. This should be level with the top of the foam insulation board. (Figs. 67a-b)

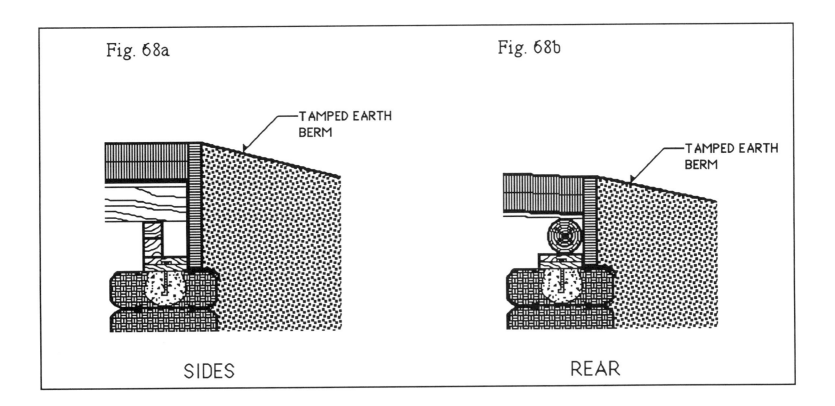

Fig. 68a

Fig. 68b

TAMPED EARTH BERM

TAMPED EARTH BERM

SIDES

REAR

THE FIRST BURIAL

Next, finish berming up to the top of the roof insulation. Now, have the backhoe driver tamp this earth by back-dragging with the scoop. (Figs. 68a-b)

The underlayment for the roofing can be installed now. It is 30# or 40# roofing paper. It is spiked or screwed on through the insulation to the beams with spikes or screws and roof discs.

This process permanently installs both the insulation and the roof underlayment. This should happen very soon after tacking down the rigid insulation as the rigid urethane type insulation should not get wet. Use about 8 screws or spikes per 4x8 sheet. Place screws or spikes over beams. Locate the beams on top of roofing paper and snap a chalk line to guide your nailing.

121

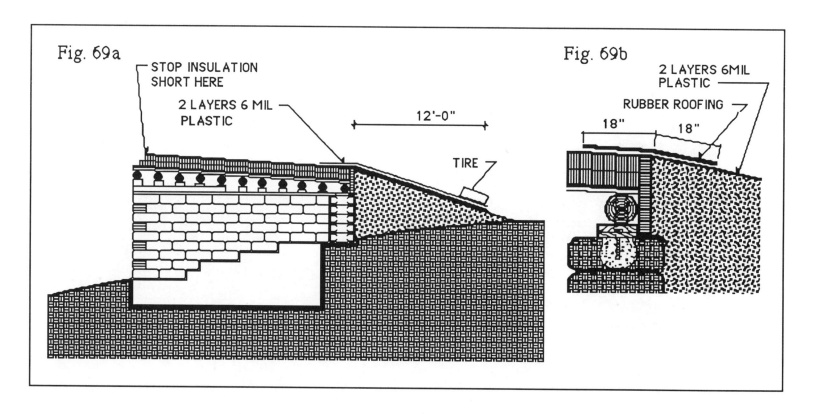

Fig. 69a

STOP INSULATION SHORT HERE

2 LAYERS 6 MIL PLASTIC

12'-0"

TIRE

Fig. 69b

2 LAYERS 6MIL PLASTIC

RUBBER ROOFING

18"   18"

ROOFING OVER THE BERM

Staple 2 layers of 6 mil plastic (or one layer of 10 mil) to the foam insulation. Drape it over the sloping berm all the way around the "U" until it is about 12'-0" away from the structure. Weight it down temporarily with empty tires. (Fig. 69a)

The joint between the structure and the dirt must now be covered and reinforced with heavy rubber roofing. (Fig. 69b) It comes in a roll and there are many manufacturers. Consult a roofer or building supply store.

This roofing comes 3'-0" wide and should be installed half on and half off the structure for a good overlap at the joint. It can be melted on or glued with tar. A roofing contractor should be consulted for roofing materials in your area. Listen to the roofing contractor as far as how to handle the materials but follow these instructions for roofing this type of building.

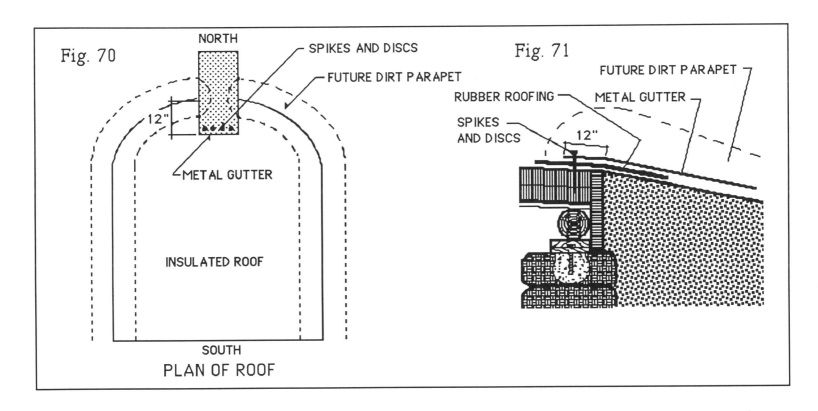

Fig. 70

NORTH

SPIKES AND DISCS

FUTURE DIRT PARAPET

12"

METAL GUTTER

INSULATED ROOF

SOUTH

PLAN OF ROOF

Fig. 71

FUTURE DIRT PARAPET

RUBBER ROOFING

METAL GUTTER

SPIKES AND DISCS

12"

DRAINAGE

Water will be channeled from the roof down a canal until it is well away from the structure. This will be achieved by forming a dirt parapet which will channel water into a metal gutter. The metal gutter is laid before the final roofing, and before the dirt parapet is formed .

The canal is centered in the back of the U, at the lowest point of the roof. (Fig. 70)

Lay a 3'x8' piece of 26 or 28 gauge sheet metal overlapping on to the roof by about 1'-0" and sloping down over the berm. (Fig. 71) Spike or screw it in with the same spikes and discs you used for attaching the insulation.

The sheet metal used should be painted with tar on the underside and with an earth color paint on the top, to prevent it from rusting.

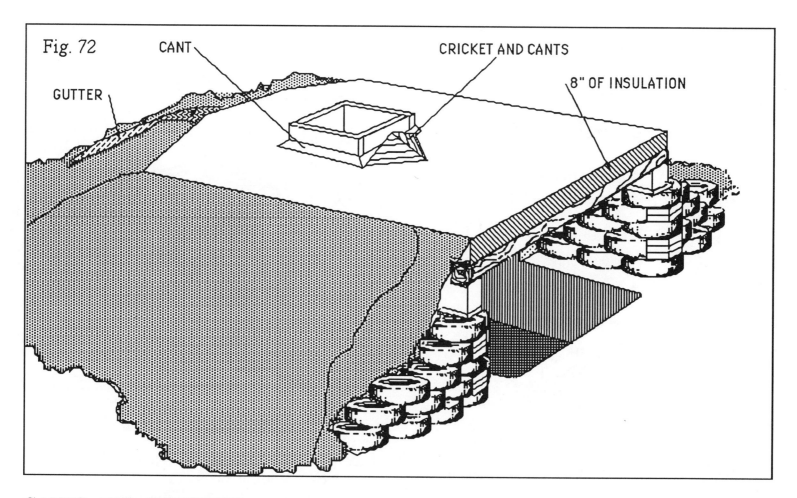

Fig. 72

GUTTER

CANT

CRICKET AND CANTS

8" OF INSULATION

CANTS AND CRICKETS

Cants are angular (45°) prisms of foam insulation board placed against the skylight box on four sides. The cants guide the roofing up against and on to the skylight box (figure 72). These are installed now and roof underlayment (30# felt) is installed over them.

Crickets are built up layers of plywood or celotex on the uphill side of roof openings to direct water around them. These are glued down with tar, spiked and roofed over (figure 72).

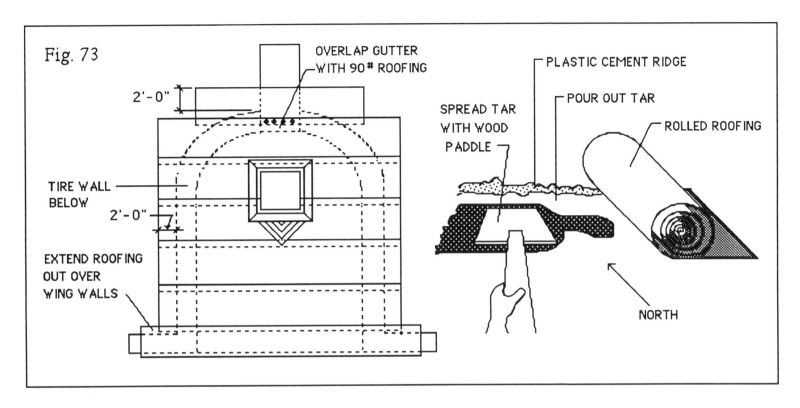

Fig. 73

OVERLAP GUTTER
WITH 90# ROOFING

2'-0"

TIRE WALL
BELOW

2'-0"

EXTEND ROOFING
OUT OVER
WING WALLS

PLASTIC CEMENT RIDGE

POUR OUT TAR

ROLLED ROOFING

SPREAD TAR
WITH WOOD
PADDLE

NORTH

COLD PROCESS ROOFING

Now 90# rolled roofing is applied over the underlayment with cold process tar. This tar is available at builders supply store along with the 90# roofing. The tar is poured out in the path of the roll, spreading it out with a scrap wood paddle. This is very similar to applying paste for wallpaper. Due to the roof slope, the tar will run north. This can be prevented by

first running a little ridge of plastic cement (another tar product) along the north edge of the roll. This will act as a seal for the lap joints as well as a dam for the cold process tar.

Take roofing out 2'-0" over the edge of the building, and extend roofing out over tamped earth at wing walls (Fig. 72).

125

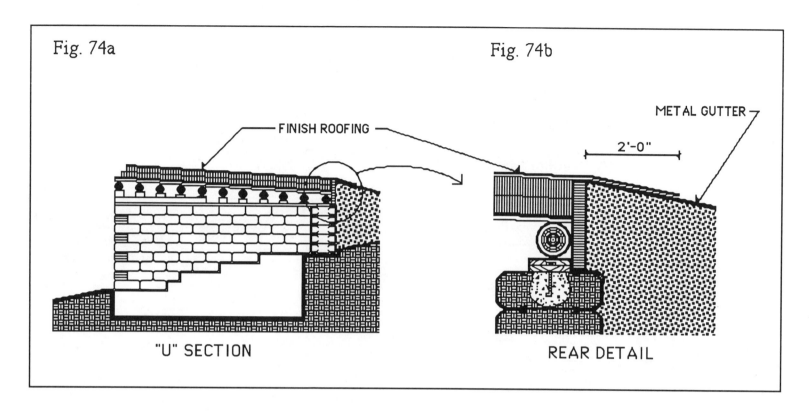

Fig. 74a

Fig. 74b

FINISH ROOFING

METAL GUTTER

2'-0"

"U" SECTION

REAR DETAIL

ROOFING ALTERNATIVES

Several different types of roofing can be used for the final layer. Your choice will depend on your budget. The rubber roofing, which is applied using a heat process, is recommended, however it is relatively expensive. Consult a roofer in your area for other choices.

A cold process tar roof is the cheapest and easiest and can always have a rubber roof installed over it later.

When you begin, bring the roofing out over the rubber roofing used to cover the seam between structure and dirt (discussed Fig. 69b) and out over the first 2'-0" of the metal gutter (figure 74b).

Regardless of the type of roofing you use, always begin at the back or north of the structure and overlap the seams 4" to 6" (Fig. 63b).

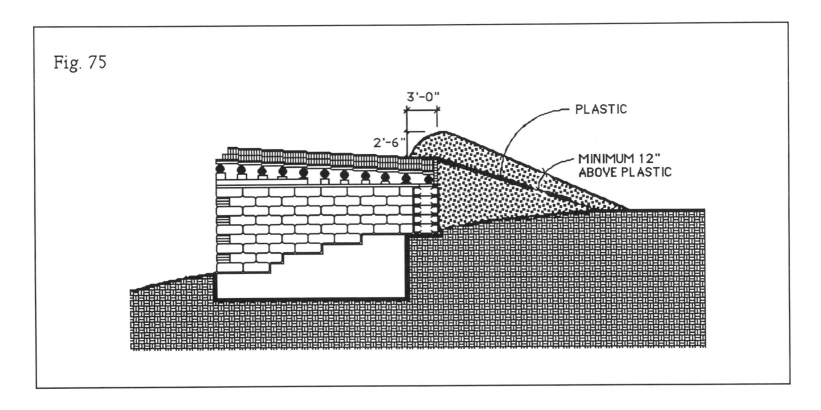

Fig. 75

3'-0"

2'-6"

PLASTIC

MINIMUM 12"
ABOVE PLASTIC

THE SECOND BURIAL

Now, you must form the dirt parapet. Simply berm up over the roof to a height of about 2'-6". This will overlap the roof structure about 3'-0". Continue the berm out to cover the plastic with a minimum of 12" of earth compressed with the backhoe. (Fig. 75)

Taper the berm down toward the canal, leaving about 1'-6" of sheet metal showing. (Fig. 76)

You now have a weather proof "U". It is very important to note that the greenhouse and other detailing should not be started until the "U" is "captured and "dried in" to the extent illustrated here. A common mistake is not weatherproofing the "U" before going on to other details. This method of construction requires immediate roofing and site shaping around "U"s, as illustrated in fig. 76, to divert surface water.

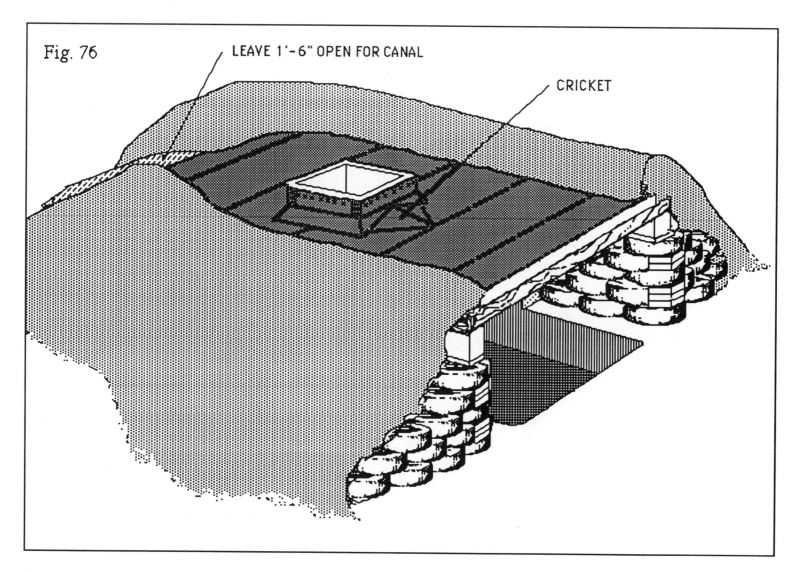

Fig. 76

LEAVE 1'-6" OPEN FOR CANAL

CRICKET

A captured "U".

7. THE GREENHOUSE

HOW TO BUILD THE GREENHOUSE-HALLWAY-HEATING DUCT

The greenhouse - hallway - heating duct is mostly carpentry work involving relatively common carpentry skills to build the window framework on top of a tire foundation. This chapter takes you step by step through the construction and detailing of this part of the "U module".

Beginning of Greenhouse.

Finished Greenhouse - interior.

Finished Greenhouse - exterior.

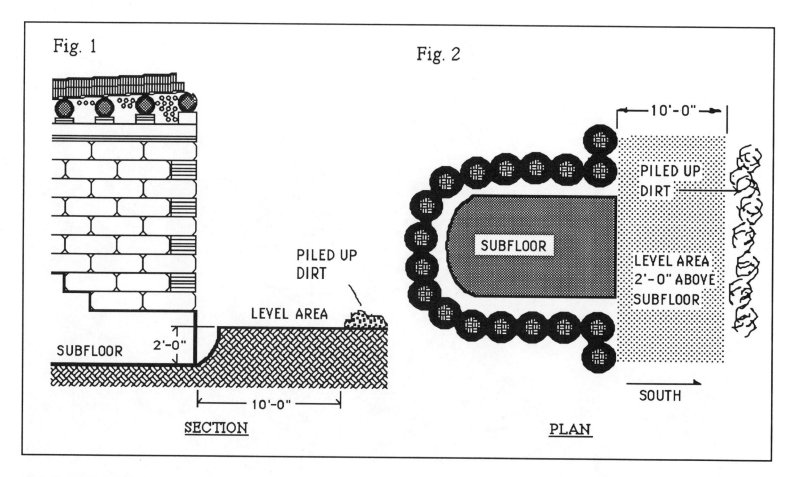

Fig. 1

Fig. 2

PILED UP
DIRT

LEVEL AREA

SUBFLOOR

2'-0"

10'-0"

SECTION

10'-0"

PILED UP
DIRT

SUBFLOOR

LEVEL AREA
2'-0" ABOVE
SUBFLOOR

SOUTH

PLAN

EXCAVATION

The first step in building the greenhouse is to layout the tire foundation for it. Preparation for this tire work involves a second excavation where a level area is created for about 10'-0" south of the "U". This level area is usually about 2'-0" above the sub floor. The subfloor is the level of the dirt excavated inside the "U". In preparation for pounding the tires, loose dirt should be piled up east to west along the south side of the leveled area (Fig. 1 & 2).

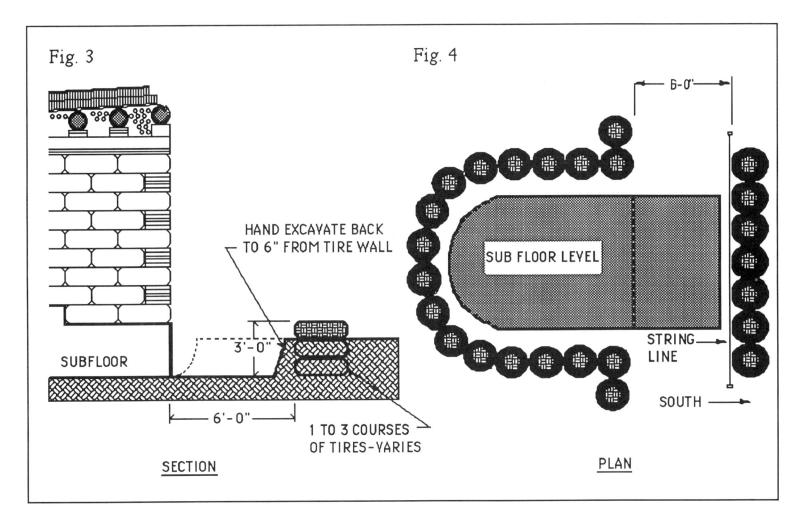

Fig. 3

Fig. 4

HAND EXCAVATE BACK
TO 6" FROM TIRE WALL

SUBFLOOR

3'-0"

6'-0"

1 TO 3 COURSES
OF TIRES-VARIES

SECTION

6-0'

SUB FLOOR LEVEL

STRING
LINE

SOUTH

PLAN

TIRE FOUNDATION

Now install a row of pounded tires placed 6'-0" to the south of the "U" (Fig. 3). This row will be one to four courses high depending on the existing terrain. Use a string, east to west, on the inside of the row of tires as a guide (Fig. 4). The top of the top course must be about 3'-0" above the subfloor (Fig. 3). It is very important that this top course of tires be perfectly level (see Fig. 14 & 15 Chap. 6). Now you can hand excavate the subfloor level back to within 6" of the tire foundation (Fig 3).

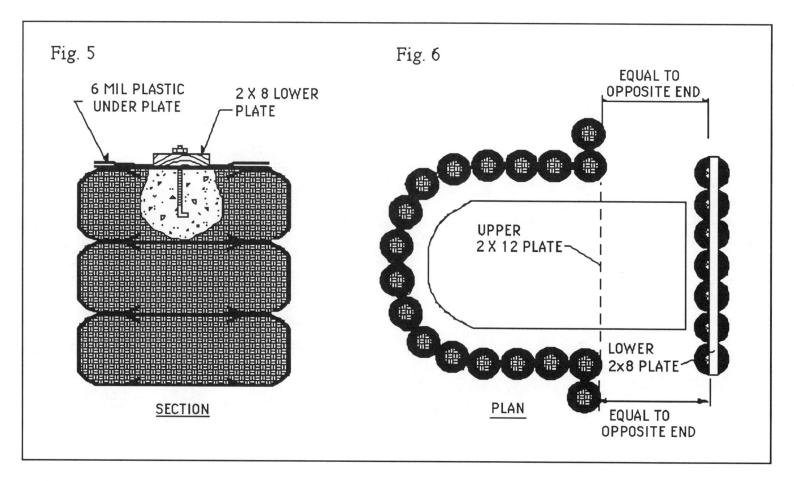

Fig. 5

6 MIL PLASTIC UNDER PLATE

2 X 8 LOWER PLATE

SECTION

Fig. 6

EQUAL TO OPPOSITE END

UPPER 2 X 12 PLATE

LOWER 2x8 PLATE

PLAN

EQUAL TO OPPOSITE END

WOOD PLATES

Now you are ready to install the upper and lower wood plates that receive the carpentry for the front face of the greenhouse. This process requires some fairly conventional carpentry skills. We suggest you consult a carpenter for this phase. It is very important that these plates be level and parallel to each

other. The lower wood plate is a pressure treated 2x8 (Fig. 5) installed the same as the 2x12's on the top of the tire wall of the "U". Anchor bolts occur in every other tire (See Figures 35 and 36 Chap. 6). Put down two layers of 6 mil. plastic over the tires first.

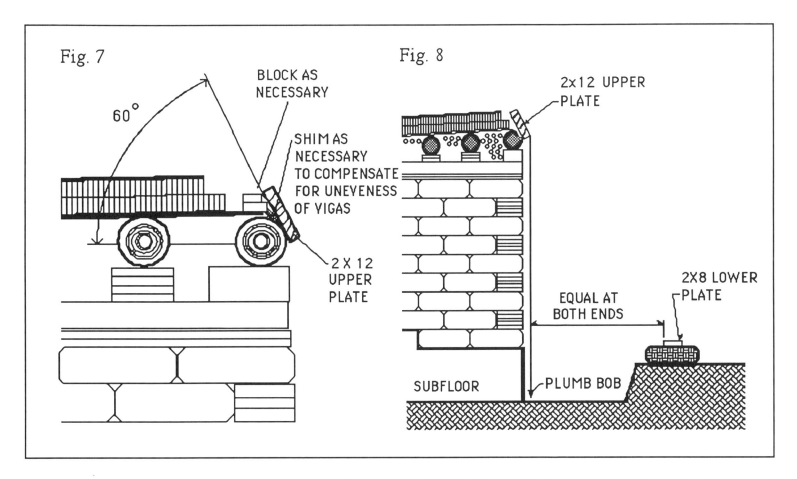

Fig. 7

60°

BLOCK AS NECESSARY

SHIM AS NECESSARY TO COMPENSATE FOR UNEVENESS OF VIGAS

2 X 12 UPPER PLATE

Fig. 8

2x12 UPPER PLATE

2X8 LOWER PLATE

EQUAL AT BOTH ENDS

SUBFLOOR

PLUMB BOB

The top plate is a 2x12 installed on the front viga or beam at a *60° angle to the horizontal (Fig 7). The board is simply nailed to the beam with 16cc nails. It must be perfectly level and parallel to the lower 2x8 plate. To achieve this, drop a plumb bob off both ends and measure over to the lower 2x8 plate on the tires (Fig. 8). Minor adjustments can be made with shims between the beam and the 2x12 plate (Fig 7). Place 2x4 blocking behind the

2x12 plate to help support and anchor the top of it. Nail the blocking into the deck and the 2x12 plate into the blocking. Be careful not to punch nails through the decking since they may be visible below.

* This angle is perpendicular to the lowest winter sun for your area. If the low winter sun is coming at 30° this angle is 60°. Check the angle of the sun at the winter solstice for your latitude. See chap. 2.

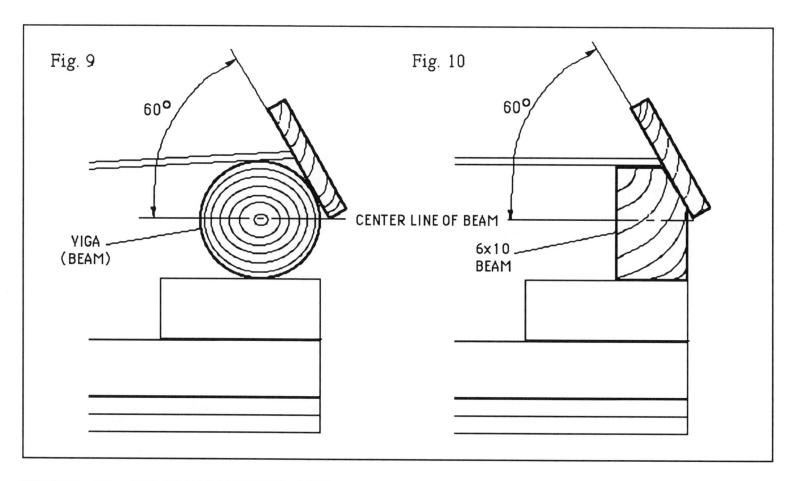

Fig. 9

60°

VIGA
(BEAM)

Fig. 10

60°

CENTER LINE OF BEAM

6x10
BEAM

UPPER PLATE VARIATIONS AND LOCATION

In cases where round vigas (beams) are not available square timbers are often used. This requires the appropriate angle (60° in this example) to be cut off at the corner of the beam to receive the 2x12 plate. In both cases notice that the 2x12 is placed with the bottom corner at the approximate center of the beam. This allows the ceiling decking to stop or butt

into the beam and also allows for other roof detailing later. Have a builder size your beams for you. In most cases 6x10 roof beams are used. The size of the beam is related to how far it has to span and what loads it has to carry relative to snow, additional stories, etc.

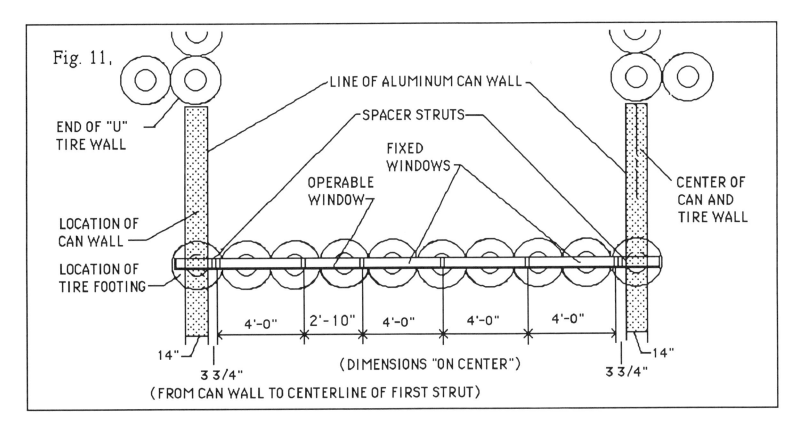

Fig. 11,

END OF "U" TIRE WALL

LINE OF ALUMINUM CAN WALL

SPACER STRUTS

FIXED WINDOWS

OPERABLE WINDOW

CENTER OF CAN AND TIRE WALL

LOCATION OF CAN WALL

LOCATION OF TIRE FOOTING

4'-0" 2'-10" 4'-0" 4'-0" 4'-0"

14"

3 3/4"

(DIMENSIONS "ON CENTER")

14"

3 3/4"

(FROM CAN WALL TO CENTERLINE OF FIRST STRUT)

GLAZING LAYOUT

You are now ready to lay out the front face on the wood sill plate. The end walls of the greenhouse (which are made of aluminum cans) must be located on the plate first. These walls are 14" wide and are centered on the tire walls of the "U". Locate these can walls and project them to the lower wood plate. Next allow for two spacer struts on each end. These take up 1 1/2" each. so allow for a 3" space on each end next to the can wall. The first structural strut will go next to the spacer struts. Each strut is 1 1/2" wide. Structural struts are located relative to the center of the strut so the center of the first strut must be established. This is done by measuring over 3/4" from the spacer struts. **You now have the center of the first strut established 3 3/4" from the can wall.** Strut dimensions for fixed glass are 4'-0" on center and operables call for 2'- 10" on center. You can now layout as many of each as you want. Only one operable window per "U" is needed. Stock glass sizes are much cheaper than custom sizes.The 4"-0" dimension allows

137

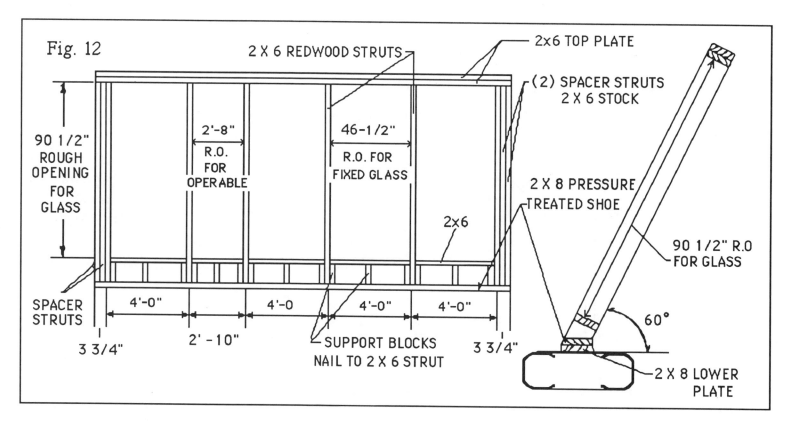

Fig. 12

2 X 6 REDWOOD STRUTS

2x6 TOP PLATE

(2) SPACER STRUTS
2 X 6 STOCK

90 1/2" ROUGH OPENING FOR GLASS

2'-8"
R.O. FOR OPERABLE

46-1/2"
R.O. FOR FIXED GLASS

2 X 8 PRESSURE TREATED SHOE

90 1/2" R.O FOR GLASS

2x6

SPACER STRUTS

4'-0"   4'-0   4'-0"   4'-0"

60°

3 3/4"   2'-10"   SUPPORT BLOCKS NAIL TO 2 X 6 STRUT   3 3/4"

2 X 8 LOWER PLATE

for a stock 46"x 90" glass size available all over the country. Struts should be placed with this in mind wherever possible. Three easily accessible stock glass sizes are 34 x 90, 46 x 90, and 58 x 90. Rough openings must be 1/2" larger each way.

FRAMING THE FRONT FACE

The front face is now framed much like a regular frame wall. A framing carpenter should be consulted here. The wall is framed flat on the ground as a unit out of redwood 2x6 stock. The pressure treated 2x8 is attached to a 60° angle cut on the bottom of the strut. For this example the angle is 60° (see chap. 2 for your angle). This shoe will then be nailed flat on to the 2x8 plate. Notice the support blocks (from 2x6 stock) under all rough openings. Use galvanized nails for all connections in framing the front face. **The critical point in framing the front face is to have square openings for the glass.**

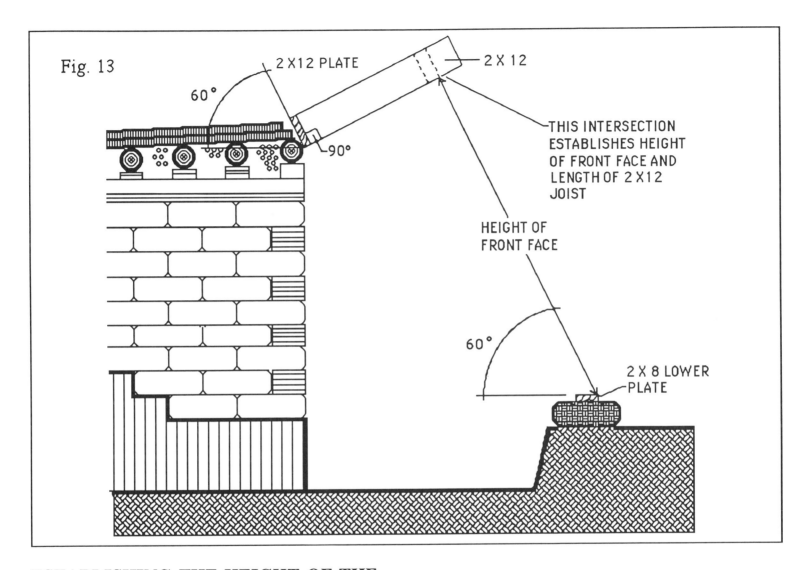

Fig. 13

2 X 12 PLATE

2 X 12

60°

90°

THIS INTERSECTION ESTABLISHES HEIGHT OF FRONT FACE AND LENGTH OF 2 X 12 JOIST

HEIGHT OF FRONT FACE

60°

2 X 8 LOWER PLATE

ESTABLISHING THE HEIGHT OF THE FRONT FACE

The dimension height of the front face frame varies with your specific situation. To establish it simply project a 2x12 straight out from (at 90 degrees to) the upper 2x12 plate.

Measure up from the outside edge of the lower plate at 60°. Where these meet is the measurement for the height of the front face frame wall, and the length of the 2x12 joists.

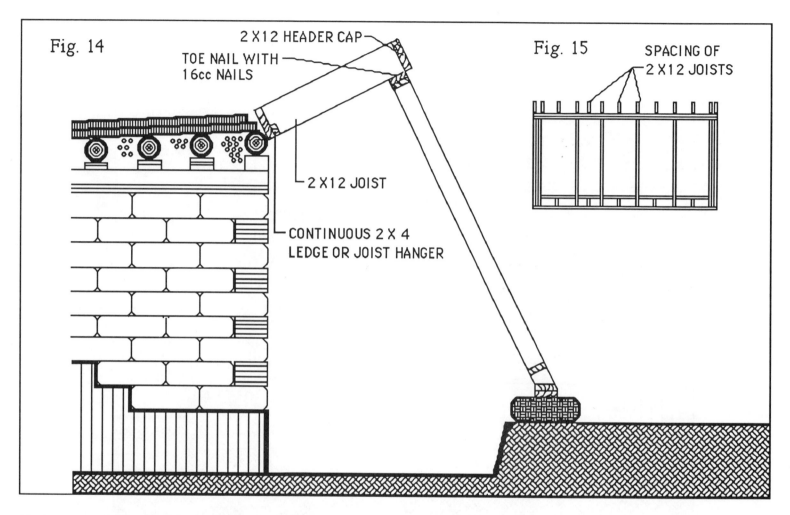

Fig. 14
2 X 12 HEADER CAP
TOE NAIL WITH 16cc NAILS
2 X 12 JOIST
CONTINUOUS 2 X 4 LEDGE OR JOIST HANGER

Fig. 15
SPACING OF 2 X 12 JOISTS

INSTALLING THE FRONT FACE

The 2x12 joists are notched to rest on a 2x4 ledge nailed directly to the upper 2x12 plate. Typical metal joist hangers are also an alternative to this ledge. The other end of the 2x12 joists rest on the top of the framed front face wall with a toe-nailed connection using 16cc nails. Joist hangers can also be used upside down here for a better connection. The 2x12 joists occur directly above each vertical 2x6 framing strut and are in the middle of each rough opening (Fig. 15). Now a 2x12 header cap can be nailed across the top of the front face.

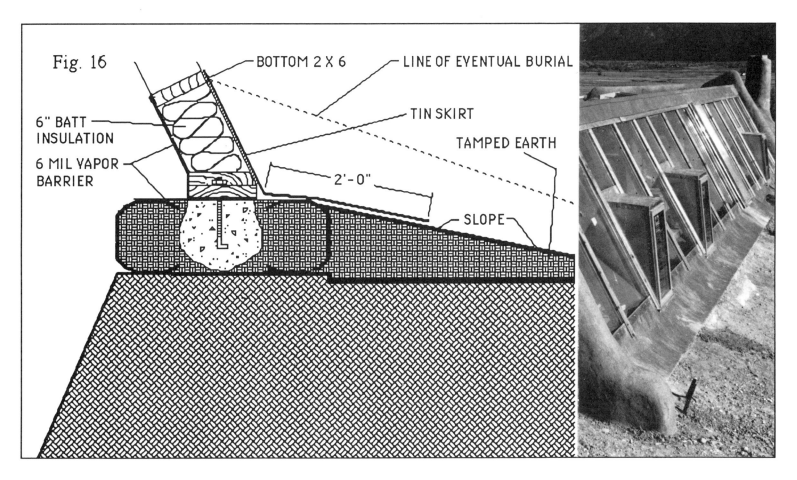

Fig. 16

BOTTOM 2 X 6 — LINE OF EVENTUAL BURIAL

6" BATT INSULATION

6 MIL VAPOR BARRIER

TIN SKIRT

TAMPED EARTH

2'-0"

SLOPE

TIN SKIRT

After the front face framing has been installed, a tin sheet is nailed on from the bottom horizontal 2x6 down and out, sloping away from the building about 2'-0". Earth must be back filled and tamped to create a slope away from the building for this tin to lay on. This is 28 gauge sheet metal usually from a 3'-0" x 50' roll. It is painted with liquid tar on the underneath side before installation. After installation it is painted on the top side. The tar is to prevent the galvanized sheet metal from deteriorating. The eventual burial will cover all of this sheet metal. Next install 6" batt insulation under the bottom 2x6 and staple a 6 mil vapor barrier over the inside cavity formed by the tin and the wooden sections under the window frames (Fig. 16).

141

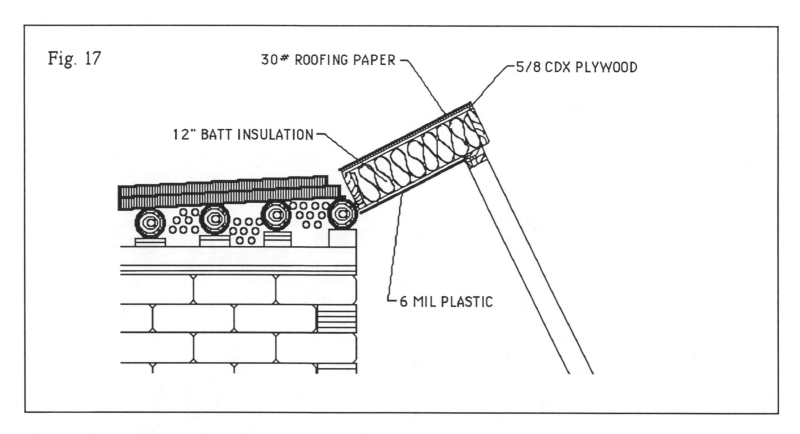

Fig. 17

30# ROOFING PAPER

5/8 CDX PLYWOOD

12" BATT INSULATION

6 MIL PLASTIC

DECKING AND INSULATING ROOF

Staple a layer of 6 mil plastic vapor barrier on the under side of the 2x12 joists. Next lay in 12" of fiber glass batt insulation from the top. The pieces should be neatly cut to fit in the spaces. This is your insulation. Make it fit tightly, but keep it fluffy. The fluffiness is what makes it work. The top of the 2x12's can now be decked with 5/8" CDX plywood installed with 8cc nails.

The plywood should be immediately protected by stapling on a layer of 30# roofing paper.

The insulated cavity of the greenhouse roof can be used to run electrical wiring. So, before you close up this area below consult your electrician.

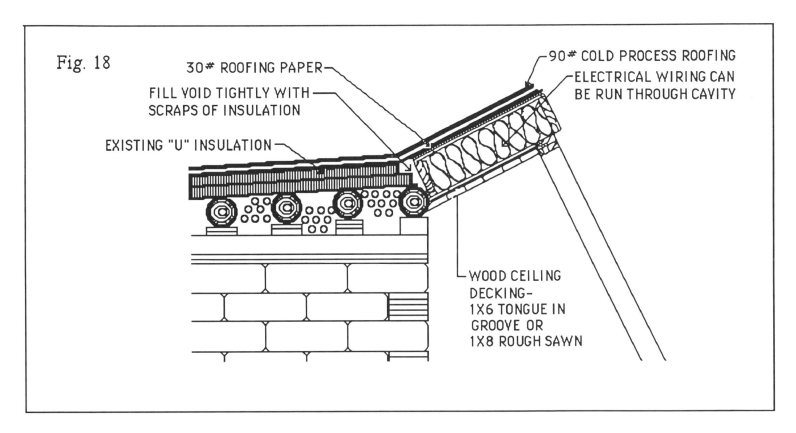

Fig. 18

30# ROOFING PAPER

FILL VOID TIGHTLY WITH SCRAPS OF INSULATION

EXISTING "U" INSULATION

90# COLD PROCESS ROOFING

ELECTRICAL WIRING CAN BE RUN THROUGH CAVITY

WOOD CEILING DECKING- 1X6 TONGUE IN GROOVE OR 1X8 ROUGH SAWN

ROOFING

Now the void between the new greenhouse roof and the existing insulated "U" roof can be filled with scraps of 4" thick urathane insulation (R-30 per 4" sheet for a total of R-60). Make this a tight, neat job since sloppy gaps in the insulation allow your warm air to leak out. You are now ready to roll out more 30# roofing over this newly filled patch and install a cold process 90# roof or a rubber roof, which can be installed by a roofer. Wood ceiling decks can also be installed now. Any 1x6 dimension decking can be used.

143

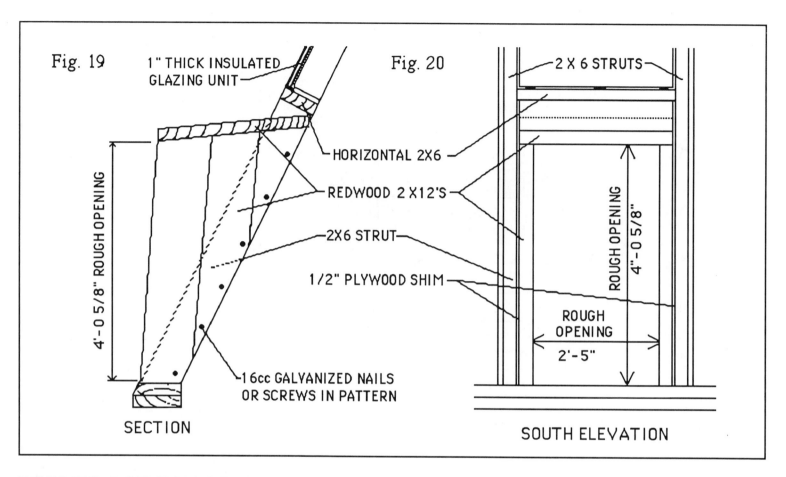

Fig. 19   1" THICK INSULATED GLAZING UNIT

Fig. 20   2 X 6 STRUTS

4'-0 5/8" ROUGH OPENING

HORIZONTAL 2X6

REDWOOD 2 X12'S

2X6 STRUT

1/2" PLYWOOD SHIM

16cc GALVANIZED NAILS OR SCREWS IN PATTERN

ROUGH OPENING 4"-0 5/8"

ROUGH OPENING 2'-5"

SECTION

SOUTH ELEVATION

DORMER BOX FOR OPERABLE WINDOW

The dormer box for the operable window is sized for a Hurd metal clad casement window. It is simply a box made of redwood 2x12's built into the existing framing as shown above. A horizontal 2x6 is installed above it as the bottom sill for a fixed piece of glass. This upper opening is then set up for glazing in the the same way as for the 46 1/2" x 90 1/2"

openings described on the following pages. The Hurd window is #2343 with a rough opening of 4'-0 5/8" x 2'-5" (Fig. 20). Note the 1/2" plywood shim between the 2x12 dormer box and the 2x6 strut (Figs. 20 and 22). This is necessary to provide a good fit for the glazing covers discussed on the following pages.

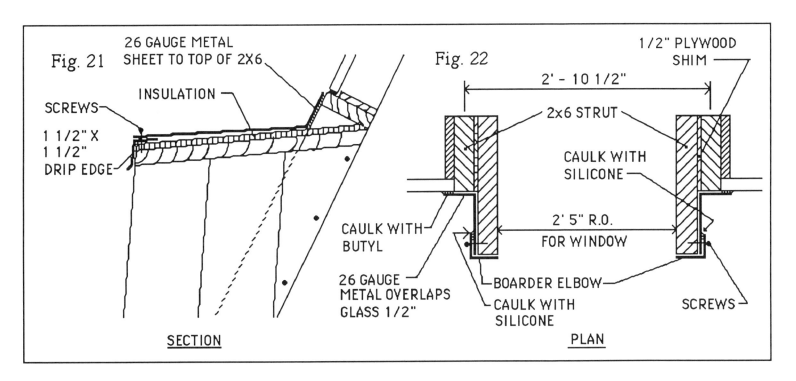

Fig. 21
SCREWS
1 1/2" X 1 1/2"
DRIP EDGE
26 GAUGE METAL SHEET TO TOP OF 2X6
INSULATION
CAULK WITH BUTYL
26 GAUGE METAL OVERLAPS GLASS 1/2"
SECTION

Fig. 22
1/2" PLYWOOD SHIM
2' - 10 1/2"
2x6 STRUT
CAULK WITH SILICONE
2' 5" R.O. FOR WINDOW
BOARDER ELBOW
CAULK WITH SILICONE
SCREWS
PLAN

INSULATING AND SHEETING THE WINDOW DORMER

The dormer box should first be wrapped and stapled with a layer of 6 mil plastic. Next, the top is insulated with 1" foam (R-7 or equal) rigid insulation (Fig. 21). Now the sides are sheathed with 26 gauge sheet metal. The flashing should overlap the glass 1/2" as shown (Fig. 22). Caulk this joint with clear butyl caulk between glass and metal. A border elbow of 26 gauge flashing is now installed over the side sheathing. Caulk where this elbow overlaps the side sheathing as shown (Fig. 22) with silicone caulk. Screw this elbow on as shown. Next a 1

1/2" x 1 1/2" drip edge goes on the front top edge of the box over the insulation (Fig. 21). Now sheath the top with 26 gauge metal as shown (Fig. 21). This sheath laps down over the east and west side of the dormer 1 1/2" and is screwed on there. Note that clear butyl caulk is sometimes called for and clear silicone caulk is sometimes called for. This is because silicone caulk causes a reaction with the seal on some glazing units. For this reason avoid all contact between glazing units and silicone caulk.

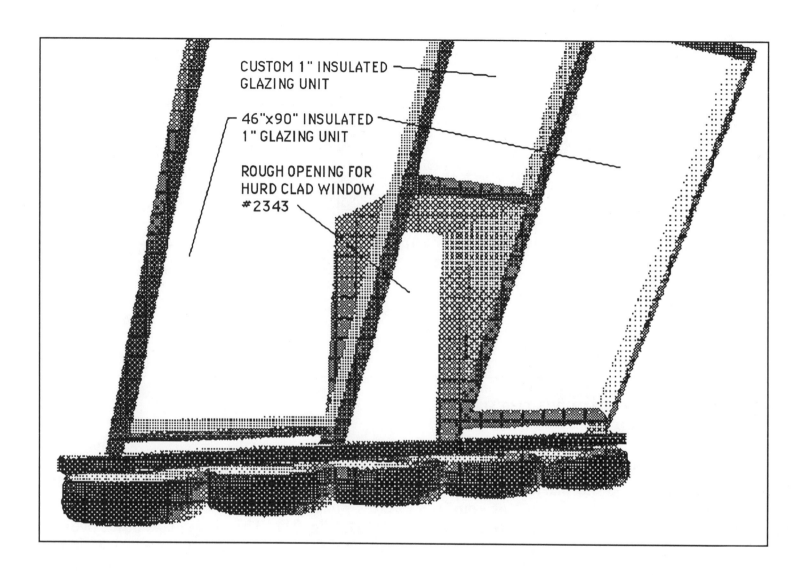

CUSTOM 1" INSULATED
GLAZING UNIT

46"x90" INSULATED
1" GLAZING UNIT

ROUGH OPENING FOR
HURD CLAD WINDOW
#2343

Inside view of dormer box.

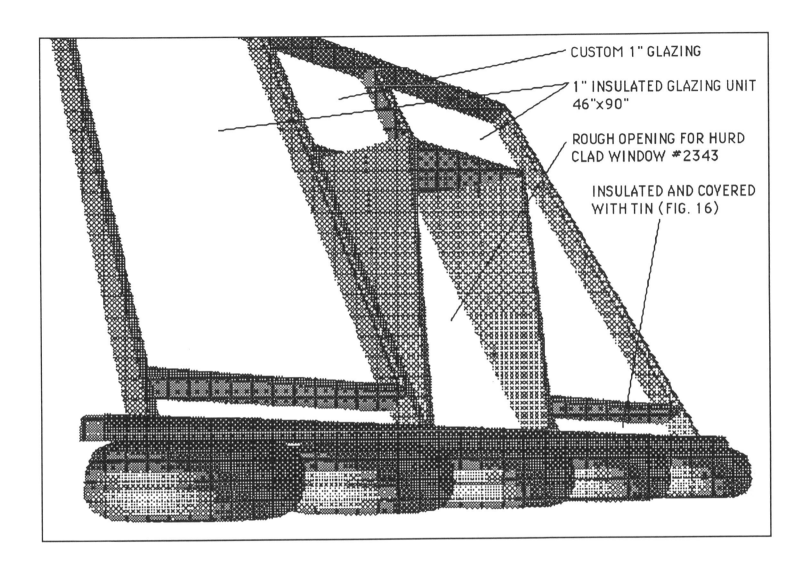

CUSTOM 1" GLAZING

1" INSULATED GLAZING UNIT
46"x90"

ROUGH OPENING FOR HURD
CLAD WINDOW #2343

INSULATED AND COVERED
WITH TIN (FIG. 16)

Outside view of dormer box.

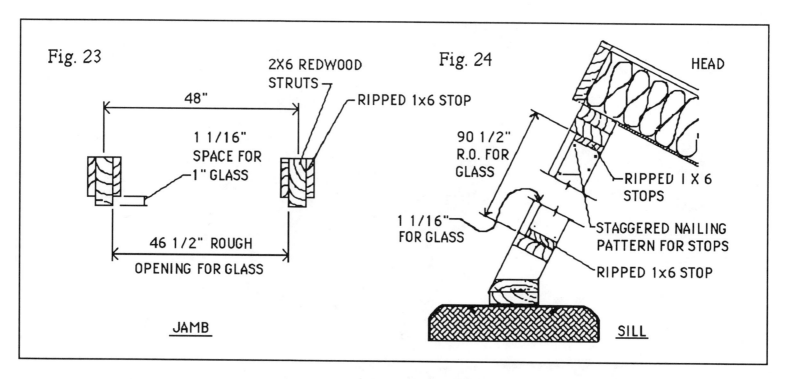

Fig. 23

2X6 REDWOOD STRUTS

RIPPED 1x6 STOP

48"

1 1/16" SPACE FOR 1" GLASS

46 1/2" ROUGH OPENING FOR GLASS

JAMB

Fig. 24

HEAD

90 1/2" R.O. FOR GLASS

RIPPED I X 6 STOPS

STAGGERED NAILING PATTERN FOR STOPS

1 1/16" FOR GLASS

RIPPED 1x6 STOP

SILL

GLAZING

The 46" x 90" standard insulated glazing units can now be installed. These are stock glass units, 1" thick, sold all over the U.S.A. See your local glass dealer. The rough opening for this 46" x 90" glass is already built into your front face framing. It is 46 1/2" x 90 1/2". The front face framing must be square to allow this glass to fit with 1/4" tolerance on all sides, thus the 46 1/2" x 90 1/2" rough opening. The

redwood stops for this glazing unit must be installed first. They are made from redwood 1 x 6 stock ripped down to the appropriate size to allow a very accurate 1 1/16" space for the 1" thick glass to fit into (Fig. 23). These stops occur all the way around the rough opening (Figs. 23 & 24). They are nailed into the 2x6 strut with 6cc galvanized finish nails with a staggered nailing pattern (Fig. 24).

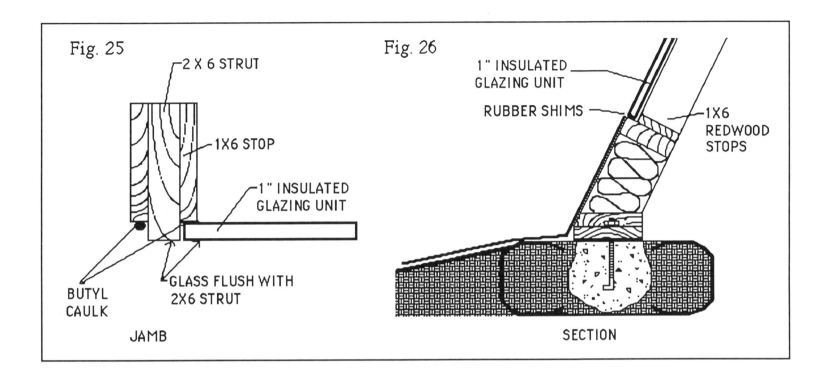

Fig. 25

2 X 6 STRUT

1X6 STOP

1" INSULATED GLAZING UNIT

BUTYL CAULK

GLASS FLUSH WITH 2X6 STRUT

JAMB

Fig. 26

1" INSULATED GLAZING UNIT

RUBBER SHIMS

1X6 REDWOOD STOPS

SECTION

GLAZING CONT.

The stops must now be caulked with clear butyl caulk (Fig. 25) just before the glass is installed. The glass must sit on rubber shims which come with the glass (Fig 26). Your local glass dealer should be consulted for this procedure. In most cases they install the glass upon delivery. The glass is 1" thick. The caulk takes up about 1/16". This results in the glass being perfectly flush with the 2x6 strut (Fig.25).

These insulated glazing units should cost between $110 and $120. Be sure that you get tempered, regular glass. The new special formula glass types on the market retard solar gain. It would not be advisable to use these if you have a serious winter.

149

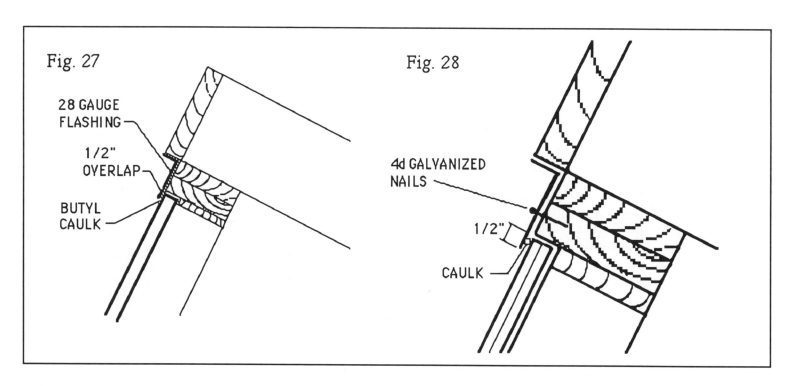

Fig. 27

28 GAUGE FLASHING

1/2" OVERLAP

BUTYL CAULK

Fig. 28

4d GALVANIZED NAILS

1/2"

CAULK

TOP FLASHING

Preparation for the top glazing board involves flashing the top of the windows with 28 gauge sheet metal flashing as shown (Fig. 27). 28 gauge sheet metal flashing comes in 50 foot rolls in almost any width. Get the width you need and cut it into a manageable length (8 to 10 ft.) and make the 90 degree bend over a straight edge. These pieces can also be purchased pre-bent from a sheet metal shop. These pieces are then tacked in place with 4cc galvanized nails as shown (Fig. 28). Overlap the joints as these pieces are installed. First caulk the top 1/4" of the glass with clear butyl caulk. Next, install the

flashing with 4cc galvanized nails. The lower part of the flashing must overlap the glass about 1/2". As it is nailed down, the caulk will ooze out. It can be trimmed later. Lengths of flashing should be tacked up and positioned first and then permanently nailed from the middle out towards the ends. This will avoid a crooked installation of the flashing.

Note that it is a good idea to do all metal work on a hot day so that the metal is hot and fully expanded, otherwise, when you do get a hot day the metal will expand in place and buckle.

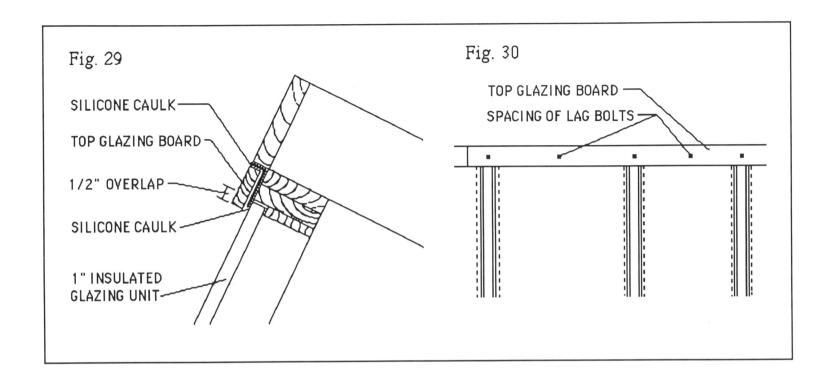

Fig. 29

SILICONE CAULK

TOP GLAZING BOARD

1/2" OVERLAP

SILICONE CAULK

1" INSULATED
GLAZING UNIT

Fig. 30

TOP GLAZING BOARD

SPACING OF LAG BOLTS

TOP GLAZING BOARD

The top glazing board is ripped from a redwood or pressure treated 2x6. It is about 4" wide and must overlap the glass about 1/2" like the flashing. It is installed with 5/16 x 4" lag bolts. Predrill it with 5/16" holes for the lags spaced as shown (Fig. 30). Hold it in place and predrill the structure with 3/16" holes as pilot holes for the lag bolts.

Apply silicone caulking on the bottom underneath side and top as shown (Fig. 29) and install it. Lags with washers occur above each strut and in the middle of each strut (Fig. 30). Fill the lag holes with silicone caulk as you install the lags.

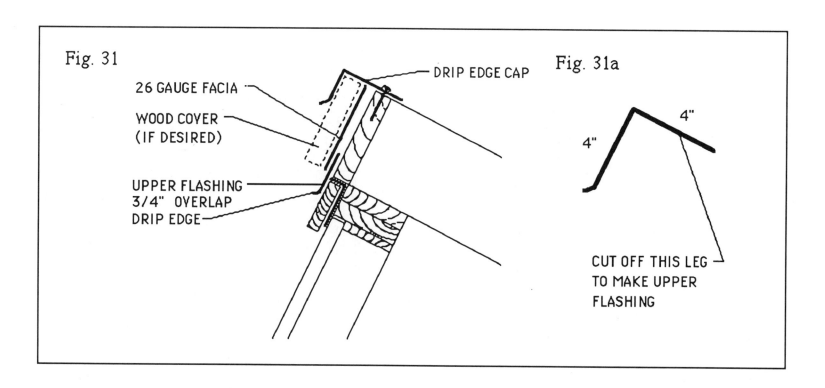

Fig. 31

26 GAUGE FACIA

WOOD COVER
(IF DESIRED)

UPPER FLASHING
3/4" OVERLAP
DRIP EDGE

DRIP EDGE CAP

Fig. 31a

4"

4"

CUT OFF THIS LEG
TO MAKE UPPER
FLASHING

Now, the upper flashing can be installed. It overhangs the glazing board 3/4". It is made by cutting off one leg of a 4x4 standard drip- edge flashing (Fig. 31a). The piece with the drip edge is then nailed into place as shown (Fig. 31). Next a 26 gauge metal facia piece can be nailed on with a wood finish facia cover as desired. A drip edge cap is now installed with galvanized roofing nails, capping the finished wood facia and the roofing. Install all flashing in manageable lengths tacked first then nailed from the center out as described before on page 147.

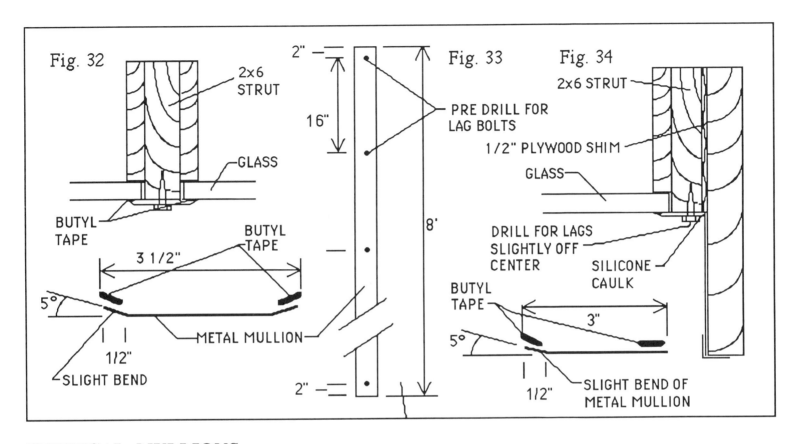

Fig. 32

2x6 STRUT

GLASS

BUTYL TAPE

BUTYL TAPE

3 1/2"

5°

1/2"

SLIGHT BEND

METAL MULLION

2"

16"

PRE DRILL FOR LAG BOLTS

8'

2"

Fig. 33

Fig. 34

2x6 STRUT

1/2" PLYWOOD SHIM

GLASS

DRILL FOR LAGS SLIGHTLY OFF CENTER

SILICONE CAULK

BUTYL TAPE

3"

5°

1/2"

SLIGHT BEND OF METAL MULLION

VERTICAL MULLIONS

There are two vertical mullion conditions. One is between two pieces of fixed glass (Fig 32) and one is between fixed glass and an operable window box (Fig. 34). Both require 18 gauge metal strips fabricated in a sheet metal shop. The length is determined by measuring from the top glazing board down to the bottom of the front face. The width is shown above. The slight bends illustrated above are very important as they create a better seal when the metal mullions are tightened down. Pre-drill the metal mullions for 5/16" x 3 1/2" lags every 16" starting 2".from the top. Hold the metal mullion up and predrill the strut with 3/16" holes as pilots for the lag bolts. Drill in the center for Fig. 32 and slightly off-center for Fig 34. This is to insure that the lags will hit the center of the appropriate strut. Install butyl tape (from your local glass dealer) as shown on the metal

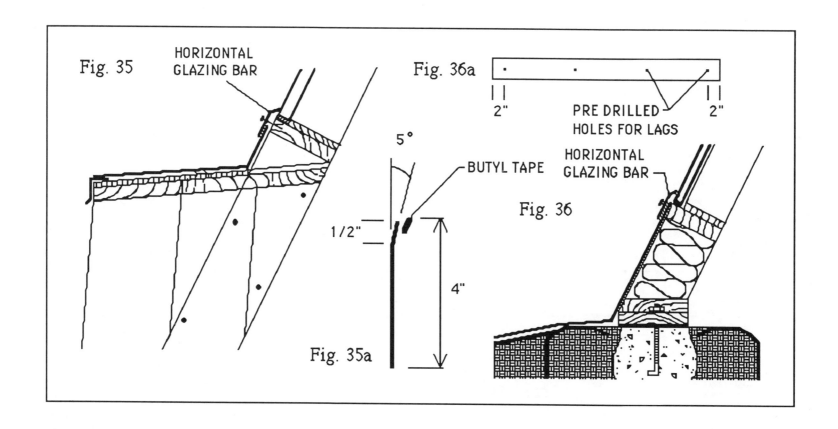

Fig. 35

HORIZONTAL GLAZING BAR

Fig. 36a

2" PRE DRILLED HOLES FOR LAGS 2"

5°

BUTYL TAPE

HORIZONTAL GLAZING BAR

Fig. 36

1/2"

4"

Fig. 35a

HORIZONTAL BOTTOM GLAZING BAR

mullion and lag screw it to the struts. Run a bead of silicon caulk down against the metal sheeting on the dormer box (Fig. 34). There are some glazing systems on the market that are prefabricated to work in much the same way as this method. Consult your local glass dealer for more information.

The bottom glazing bar occur at the bottom of the large fixed glass units (Fig. 36) and at the bottom of the small fixed glass units above the dormer (Fig. 35). They are made of 18 gauge sheet metal fabricated in a sheet metal shop. Width is 4" with a 5 degree bend (Fig. 35a) and length is measured between vertical mullions. They are installed with butyl tape and 5/16" x 3 1/2" lags much the same as the vertical mullions. Spacing is as shown in Fig. 36a for all openings.

154

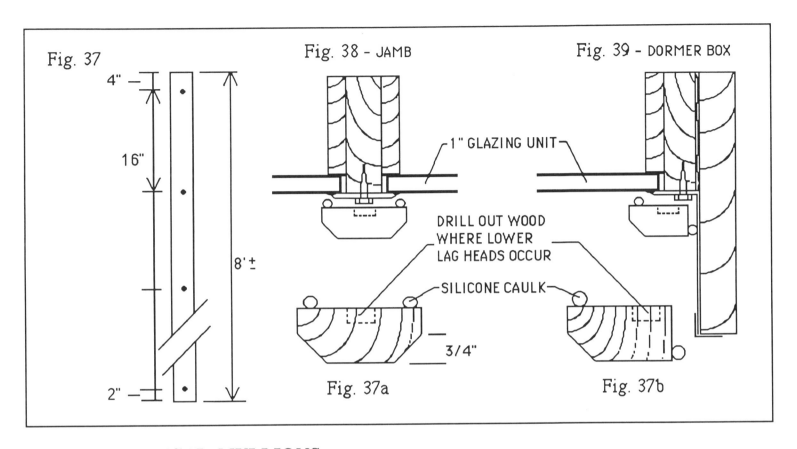

Fig. 37

4"

16"

8' ±

2"

Fig. 38 - JAMB

1" GLAZING UNIT

DRILL OUT WOOD
WHERE LOWER
LAG HEADS OCCUR

SILICONE CAULK

3/4"

Fig. 37a

Fig. 39 - DORMER BOX

Fig. 37b

FACING VERTICAL MULLIONS

The metal vertical mullions can now be rubbed with *vinegar and painted or faced with pressure treated 2x4's with the corners ripped off as shown in (Fig. 37 and 37a). The back side of the 2x4 mullion covers will be drilled out to accommodate the lag bolt heads already installed. Pre-drill the 2x4's for 5/16 x 4" lags. Pre-drill thru the metal mullion with a 5/16" bit and into the wood strut with a 3/16" bit to receive the lag screws. Shift the same lag pattern (16" apart) down 4" this time (Fig. 37) so that you do not hit the lags already in place. Run a bead of silicone down both sides of the wood mullion cover and screw it down with lags. The wood mullion cover against the window box is similar (Fig. 38 and 39).

*Galvanized sheet metal must be thoroughly washed with vinegar to prepare it for exterior metal paint, otherwise the paint will peel.

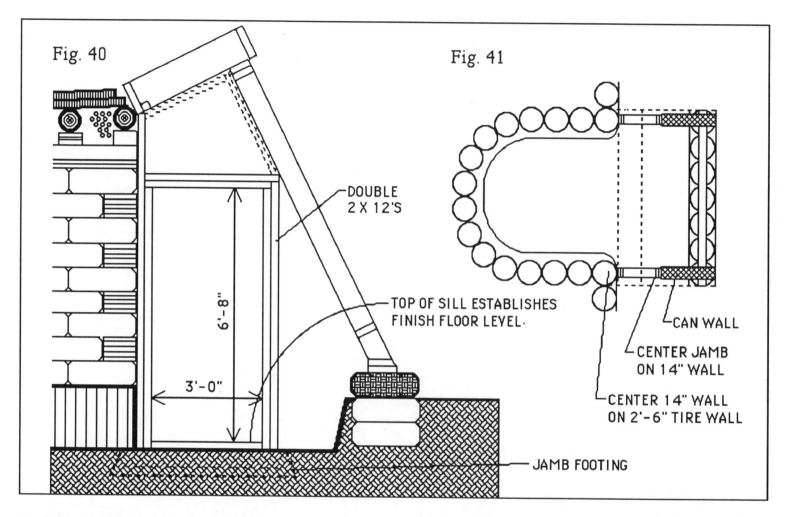

Fig. 40

Fig. 41

DOUBLE
2 X 12'S

6'-8"

3'-0"

TOP OF SILL ESTABLISHES
FINISH FLOOR LEVEL.

CAN WALL

CENTER JAMB
ON 14" WALL

CENTER 14" WALL
ON 2'-6" TIRE WALL

JAMB FOOTING

INSTALLING DOOR JAMB

The door jamb is made from 2x12 pine stock. Both sides are double 2x12's as shown (Fig. 40) with the side against the tires extending all the way up. The jambs are made to door size 3'-0" x 6'-8" and installed on the center of the 14" can wall on either end of the greenhouse (Fig. 41). The can wall (discussed on the following pages)

is 14" wide and centered in the tire wall of the "U". The door jamb sets on an 18" deep concrete footing with (2) 1/2" rebar. The top of the door sill establishes finish floor level. The bottom of the door sill is treated with wood preservative and "porcupined" with 16cc nails (Fig. 42a). This involves driving 20 or 30 16cc nails in about 1" at various angles. This is then set onto the wet mound (2" or 3" higher than

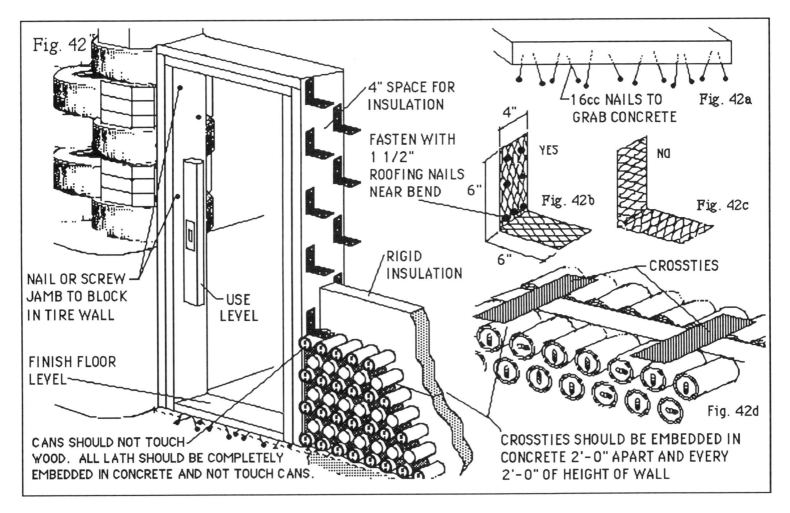

Fig. 42

4" SPACE FOR INSULATION

FASTEN WITH 1 1/2" ROOFING NAILS NEAR BEND

16cc NAILS TO GRAB CONCRETE   Fig. 42a

4"

6"   YES   NO

Fig. 42b   Fig. 42c

6"

RIGID INSULATION

CROSSTIES

NAIL OR SCREW JAMB TO BLOCK IN TIRE WALL

USE LEVEL

FINISH FLOOR LEVEL

Fig. 42d

CANS SHOULD NOT TOUCH WOOD. ALL LATH SHOULD BE COMPLETELY EMBEDDED IN CONCRETE AND NOT TOUCH CANS.

CROSSTIES SHOULD BE EMBEDDED IN CONCRETE 2'-0" APART AND EVERY 2'-0" OF HEIGHT OF WALL

finish) of the concrete footing so that the door box sinks in and down. This gives you room for plumbing and leveling. Screw and or spike the door jamb to the end blocking of the tire wall. This jamb must be installed level and plumb. Allow concrete to set up. Lath tabs are now installed on the door jamb to receive the can work. They are installed every 16" on both edges of the jamb in a staggered pattern (Fig.

42). They tie the can masonary to the door jamb. Tabs are cut from expanded metal lath. They are dimensioned as shown in Fig. 42 b and c, and are nailed on with 1 1/2" roofing nails as shown. Make sure the "diamond" pattern in the metal lath is running the way it is shown in Fig. 42b, since the other way allows the lath to expand like an accordion and renders it

157

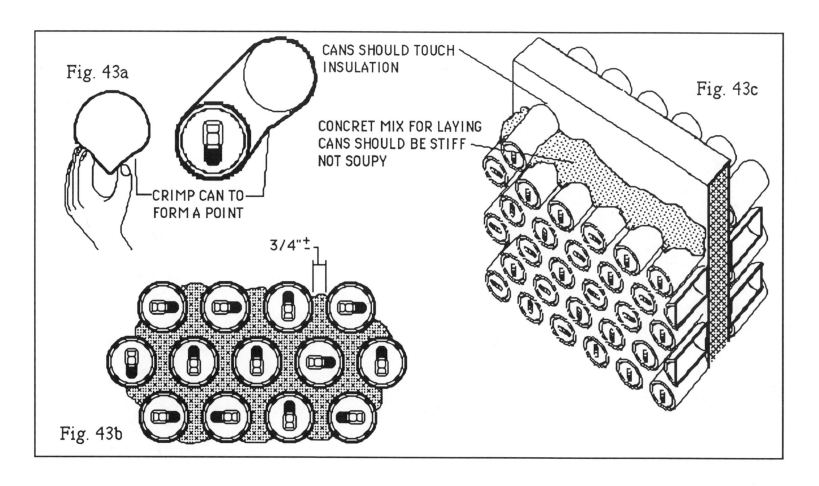

Fig. 43a

CANS SHOULD TOUCH
INSULATION

CONCRET MIX FOR LAYING
CANS SHOULD BE STIFF
NOT SOUPY

Fig. 43c

CRIMP CAN TO
FORM A POINT

3/4"±

Fig. 43b

LAYING ALUMINUM CANS

worthless as a masonry tie. Place the lath 4" apart horizontally in order to accomodate 4" of foam insulation (R-30) placed in between the double can wall. The insulation is cut and positioned tightly against the door jamb first (Fig. 42) and then plumbed using a level. This acts as a guide for laying cans. Use 2'-0" high sections of insulation at a time so that crossties made of lath can be embedded every 2'-0" between walls (Fig 42d).

You are now ready to lay an insulated aluminum can wall. Cans are layed with a stiff (not soupy) mix of 1 part portland cement to 3 parts sand. Cans should never touch. They are layed 3/4" apart. The cement is the strength of the wall so if the cans touch there is no strength. Cement is placed in a little ridge right along the middle of the previous row of cans. Each individual can is then crimped

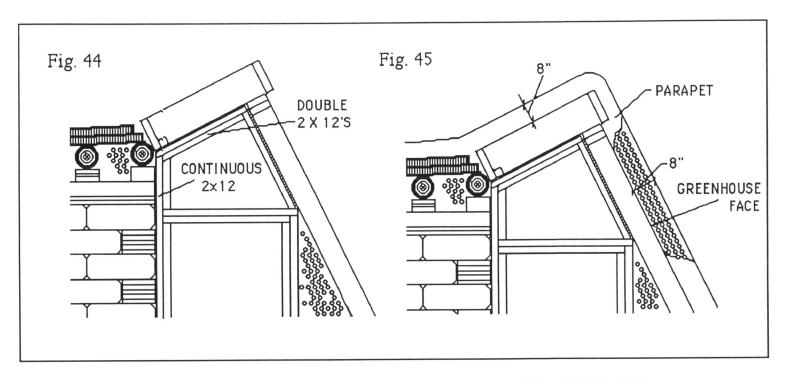

Fig. 44

Fig. 45

DOUBLE
2 X 12'S

CONTINUOUS
2x12

8"

PARAPET

8"

GREENHOUSE
FACE

UPPER FIXED WINDOW

(Fig. 43a) to form a "V" or point to push into the mortar. Keep cans against the insulation - it is your guide. If the mortar is stiff enough you can lay 2 courses on one side of the insulation and then 2 courses on the other side and switch back and forth until you have gone 5 or 6 courses high. If the mortar is too soupy you will only get 2 courses high before it will start sagging. Constantly get back and look at your can work and check it with a level. Can walls, like any other wall must be installed level and plumb. Always lay the mouth piece of the cans to the outside. These act as a natural lath to receive plaster later.

The fixed glass window over the door can now be built of 2x12's and installed on top of the door jamb. Notice it is doubled 2x12's on the top and sides. The box is simply nailed to the top of the door jamb and to the continuous extended 2x12 on the tire wall side of the door jamb. Now take the can work 8" past the greenhouse face and 8" above the roof. This is a parapet wall. After it becomes an exterior wall (above and beyond the interior of the building) it is no longer necessary to keep using the insulation in the middle. You can simply fill with cement and cans between the two rows of cans.

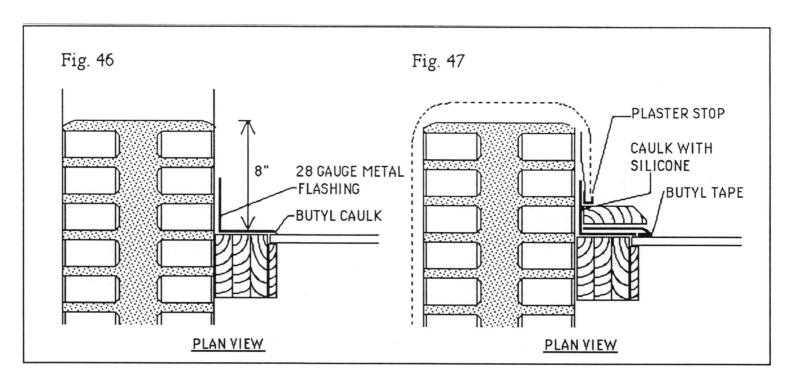

Fig. 46 Fig. 47

8" 28 GAUGE METAL
FLASHING

BUTYL CAULK

PLASTER STOP

CAULK WITH
SILICONE

BUTYL TAPE

PLAN VIEW PLAN VIEW

PARAPET DETAIL

An "L" of 28 gauge metal flashing is now installed against the parapet over the spacer struts (Fig. 46) and 1/2" onto the glass with butyl caulk between flashing and glass. Now install an 18 gauge pre-bent sheet metal mullion with 5° bend as shown in Fig. 47. The width of this piece will be about 5 1/2". Measure your own condition and see. It is installed with 5/16" x 3 1/2" lag bolts and butyl tape in the same way as on Fig. 34 page 150.

Next install a wood facing made from a 2x6. Caulk with silicone between the wood and the metal flashing (Fig. 47). This is similar to Fig. 39 page 152. A piece of plaster stop must now be installed over the metal flashing. It can be purchased in any building supply store. It must be nailed into the can/cement wall with 16cc nails. Nail into the space between the can and the cement. If you nail into the can it will not hold. If you nail into the cement the nail will bend. Slip the nail in between the can and cement. Drive as many as you need to hold the plaster stop in place. You are now ready to plaster and stucco. These methods are covered in Chapter 9 - Finishes.

160

8. ASSIMILATION OF MODULES AND DETAILS

THE DETAILS INVOLVED IN ASSIMILATION OF "U" MODULES

Now that you know how to build a "U" module and how to add the green house hallway on to it, you are ready to learn the details necessary to assemble more than one "U". This information, together with a few miscellaneous structural and mechanical details, will provide enough information for you to be able to build your own "Earthship".

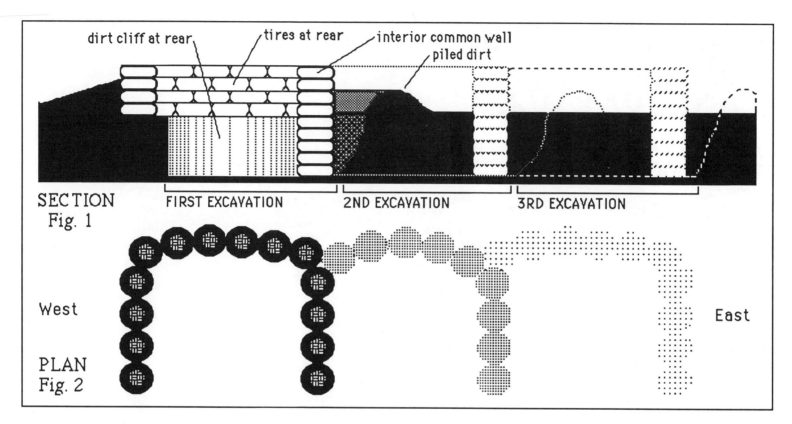

dirt cliff at rear   tires at rear   interior common wall
                                       piled dirt

SECTION
Fig. 1   FIRST EXCAVATION   2ND EXCAVATION   3RD EXCAVATION

West   East

PLAN
Fig. 2

JOINING "U's"

Building more than one "U" involves a different initial excavation than a single "U". The east/west structural section above (Fig. 1) illustrates that each excavation is taken far enough to fully accommodate the interior common wall. This is so that the common wall can go all the way down to floor level. This is necessary since it is excavated on both sides.

The second excavation would then accommodate the next "U" and the next common wall. It is advisable to excavate in steps (one "U" at a time) as shown (Fig. 2). This allows piled dirt to be accessible for tire pounding and also keeps the project in simple steps and operations that are easy for the novice builder to deal with.

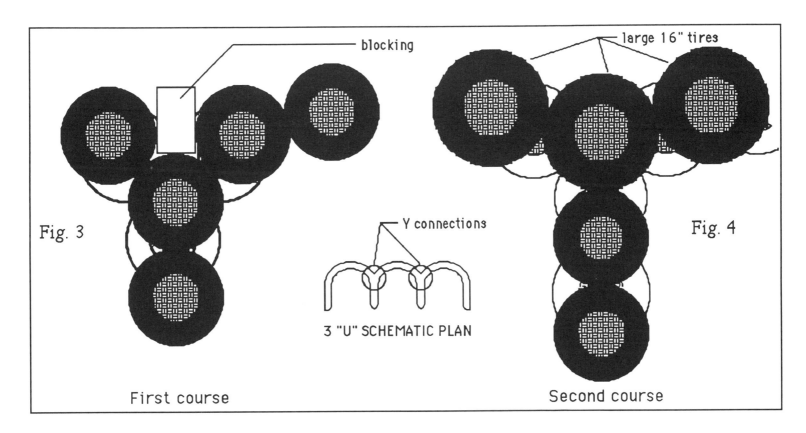

Fig. 3

First course

blocking

Y connections

3 "U" SCHEMATIC PLAN

large 16" tires

Fig. 4

Second course

Y-Connections

Building more than one "U" also involves a Y connection not encountered before. The diagrams above show the alternate coursing patterns necessary to accommodate this joint. Blocking (Fig. 3) is installed to allow alternate courses of tires to always overlap each other in staggered coursings. This staggered coursing provides the structural integrity of the wall. It is important never to have two tires directly on top of each other in these joints.

On the alternate course over the blocking (Fig. 4) a large #16 tire would be needed to provide the necessary overlaps. The important thing to remember in a "Y" joint is to create overlaps in alternate courses however you can – with larger tires, with blocking, etc. The purpose being to "knit" all three walls together.

163

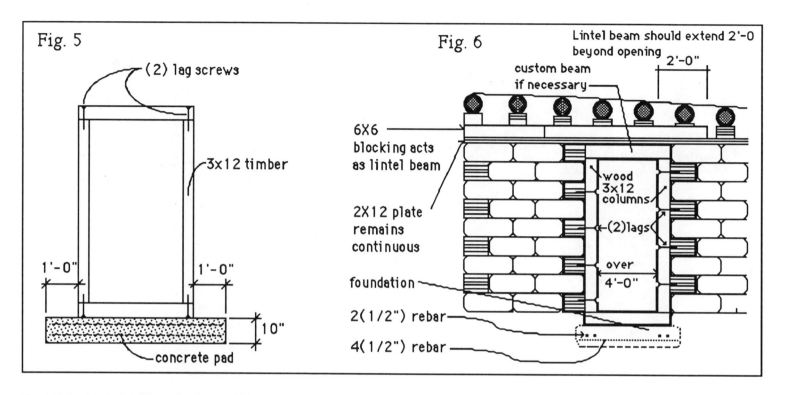

Fig. 5

(2) lag screws

3x12 timber

1'-0"   1'-0"

10"

concrete pad

Fig. 6

Lintel beam should extend 2'-0 beyond opening

2'-0"

custom beam if necessary

6X6 blocking acts as lintel beam

wood 3x12 columns

2X12 plate remains continuous

(2)lags

over 4'-0"

foundation

2(1/2") rebar

4(1/2") rebar

WALL BREAKTHROUGH

It is best not to break through a tire wall into another "U" for economical and thermal reasons. However when a breakthrough in a tire wall is necessary the main consideration is not to break the structural continuity of the wall. **The double 2x12 plate should never be interrupted.** The opening should be built out of rough sawn 3x12 timber or an equivalent thickness of laminated dimension lumber (Fig. 5). This opening box should then be placed in position on a 2'-0" concrete pad as shown.

This pad should have (4) 1/2" rebar for its full length. Tires and blocking are then laid to the box on either side. It is best to locate this box by laying out the ground course of tires so it will relate to actual tire coursing. The timber box should be lag screwed to the 1/2 blocks as the wall goes up. If possible, the 6x6 shim should be extended to form a lintel beam over the opening. If this is not possible, the top 3x12 of the box should be doubled to form a beam.

164

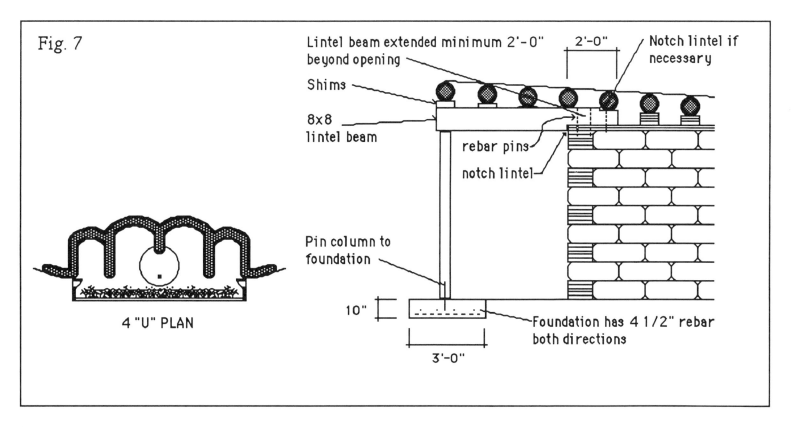

Fig. 7

Lintel beam extended minimum 2'-0" beyond opening

Shims

8x8 lintel beam

2'-0"

Notch lintel if necessary

rebar pins

notch lintel

Pin column to foundation

10"

3'-0"

Foundation has 4 1/2" rebar both directions

4 "U" PLAN

SHORTENED "U" WALL

Often it is desirable to let one "U" space flow into another by shortening one wall in between two "U's". This simply involves a column to receive the 2x12 plates and using the shim blocking as a beam to span the opening. In this case the shim beam would want to be an 8x8 to provide more strength. If your span is longer an 8x10 would be needed. Get some advice for the size of this beam. Let the beam extend 2'-0" beyond the opening. This beam will be notched over the 2x12 plates and pinned to the

plates in six places (Fig. 7). This will join it to the plate for continuity. Allow for a concrete foundation under the column. This is usually 3'-0" x 3'-0" square, 10" thick, with (4) 1/2" rebar each way. Consult a local builder for any concrete foundations as they will need to be typical to requirements for your area. The column can be pinned to the foundation with a 1/2" rebar pin set in the concrete foundation and extending up 5-1/2" into the column. The column is simply drilled with a loose sloppy hole 6" deep to slip over this pin.

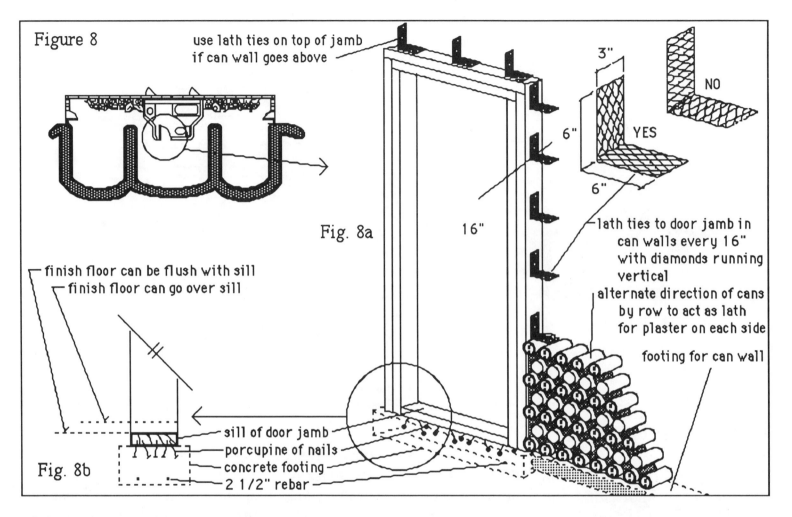

Figure 8

use lath ties on top of jamb
if can wall goes above

Fig. 8a

3"

6"   YES

NO

6"

16"

lath ties to door jamb in
can walls every 16"
with diamonds running
vertical

alternate direction of cans
by row to act as lath
for plaster on each side

footing for can wall

finish floor can be flush with sill
finish floor can go over sill

sill of door jamb
porcupine of nails
concrete footing
2 1/2" rebar

Fig. 8b

INTERIOR DOOR JAMBS IN CAN WALLS

Bathroom and closet walls are made of aluminum cans layed in cement mortar. Specifications of how to lay cans have already been discussed on pages 155 & 156. Door jambs in these walls are made of 2x6 stock and are always doubled on the sides and top (Fig.

8a). They are always porcupined on the bottom (Fig. 8b). The porcupine technique has been discussed on page 154. The sill of all jambs can be recessed to allow floor materials to go over the sill. Laying cans in single walls must be done with a level used horizontally and vertically. You can only go about four courses in a "hit" and then wait a couple of hours for the mortar to set up before going

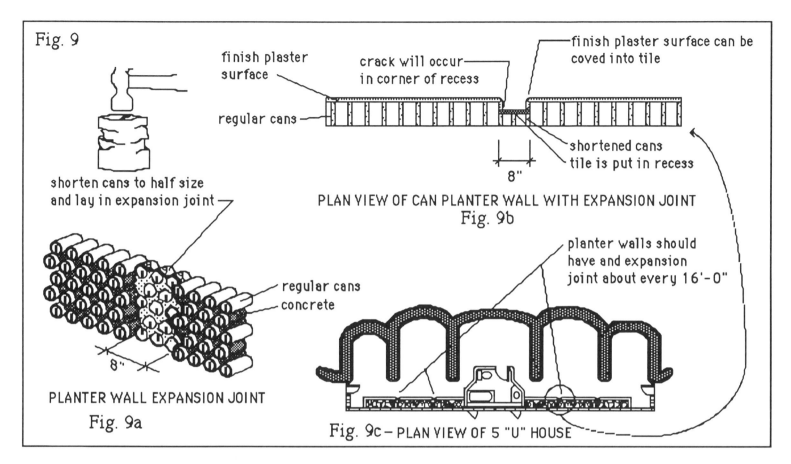

Fig. 9

finish plaster surface

shorten cans to half size and lay in expansion joint

regular cans
concrete

8"

PLANTER WALL EXPANSION JOINT

Fig. 9a

finish plaster surface

crack will occur in corner of recess

finish plaster surface can be coved into tile

regular cans

shortened cans

tile is put in recess

8"

PLAN VIEW OF CAN PLANTER WALL WITH EXPANSION JOINT
Fig. 9b

planter walls should have and expansion joint about every 16'-0"

Fig. 9c – PLAN VIEW OF 5 "U" HOUSE

higher. Metal lath, as explained on page 154, should be used where ever can masonry walls touch another material. This includes all jambs, ceilings, tire walls etc. Metal lath ties can be screwed to tire walls for tying in the can wall.

PLANTER WALLS

Planter walls are built with aluminum cans laid as described before. Lay them with the mouth pieces out to allow an irregular surface to hold whatever finish plaster is applied. They are usually 2'-0" high and should not go over 16'-0" in length without an expansion joint. Expansion joints are made with shortened cans. Tap them with a hammer (Fig. 9) and lay an 8" space with shortened cans (Fig. 9a). This will cause the expansion crack to occur in the corner of the thinner space (Fig. 9b). This recess space is usually filled with tile.

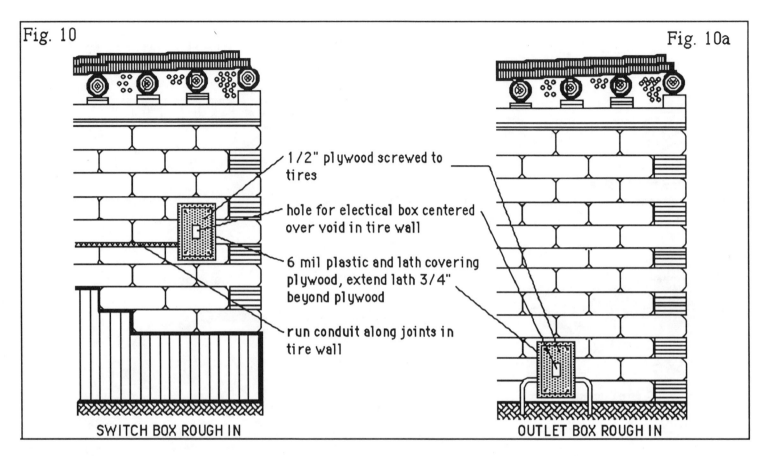

Fig. 10

Fig. 10a

1/2" plywood screwed to tires

hole for electical box centered over void in tire wall

6 mil plastic and lath covering plywood, extend lath 3/4" beyond plywood

run conduit along joints in tire wall

SWITCH BOX ROUGH IN

OUTLET BOX ROUGH IN

ELECTRICAL ROUGH IN - TIRE WALL

Electrical boxes for plugs and switches can be mounted on plywood plates and screwed to tires as shown in Fig. 10 & Fig. 10a. This establishes the plane of the mud plaster (or other plaster) wall at the same time. Plasters will be explained in chapter 10. Be sure to locate the plywood plate over a void between two tires. This allows room for the box itself

behind the plywood plate. The electrical box is then anchored to the plywood plate with conventional means. Wires can be run along channels between tires in conduit sized to code requirements. The plywood plate is covered with 6 mil plastic and metal lath extending 3/4" around the plate to provide a surface for the plaster to overlap onto the tire wall and thus prevent a crack in the plaster immediately around the plate.

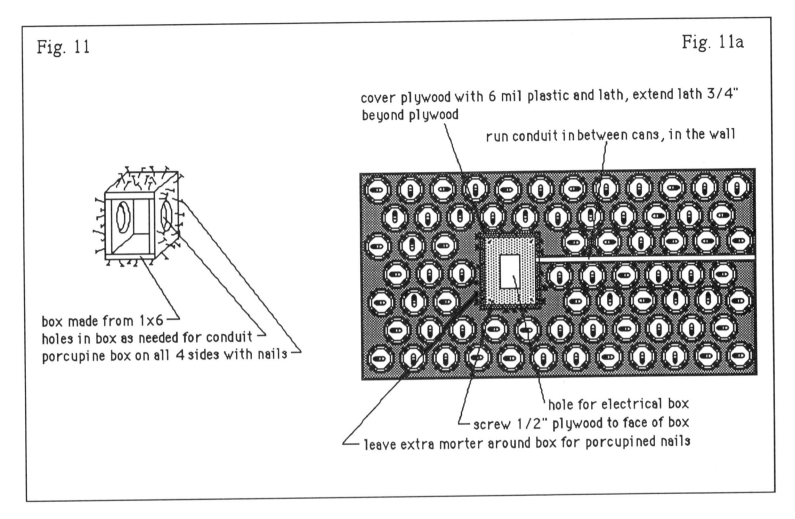

Fig. 11

Fig. 11a

cover plywood with 6 mil plastic and lath, extend lath 3/4" beyond plywood

run conduit in between cans, in the wall

box made from 1x6
holes in box as needed for conduit
porcupine box on all 4 sides with nails

hole for electrical box
screw 1/2" plywood to face of box
leave extra morter around box for porcupined nails

ELECTRICAL ROUGH IN - CAN WALL

Wherever electrical boxes are required in can walls a wood box made from 1x6 stock and porcupined (Fig. 11) must be provided to lay into the can work. Wires are then run in the can work as it goes up to feed the boxes. Again wires can be in conduit or layed directly into the can work as code allows. A 1/2" plywood plate is screwed into the 1x6 boxes to provide conventional anchoring for the electrical boxes. Again this plywood plate must be covered with 6 mil plastic and metal lath extending 3/4" all the way around to prevent a crack in the plaster immediately around the plywood plate (Fig. 11a).

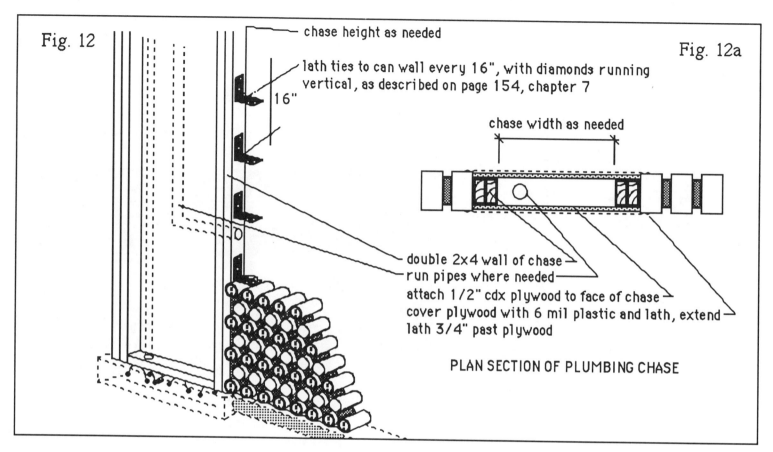

Fig. 12

Fig. 12a

chase height as needed

lath ties to can wall every 16", with diamonds running
vertical, as described on page 154, chapter 7

16"

chase width as needed

double 2x4 wall of chase
run pipes where needed
attach 1/2" cdx plywood to face of chase
cover plywood with 6 mil plastic and lath, extend
lath 3/4" past plywood

PLAN SECTION OF PLUMBING CHASE

PLUMBING CHASES

Plumbing vent and water pipes are located in 2x4 frame chases in much the same way as conventional frame houses. These chases are built into the can walls similar to door jambs (Fig. 12). They are made of 2x4 stock doubled on the sides with lath masonry ties every 16". They can be as wide or as tall as the condition calls for (Fig. 12a). Can masonry walls are then layed up to

and around these chases as required. The chases are then covered with 1/2" CDX plywood, 6 mil plastic and metal lath extending 3/4" around the plywood to prevent a crack between the plywood and the can wall. Plumbing usually occurs in can walls. If your plan calls for plumbing against a tire wall simply build a 2x4 chase against the tire wall. Tire walls are never interrupted for plumbing.

170

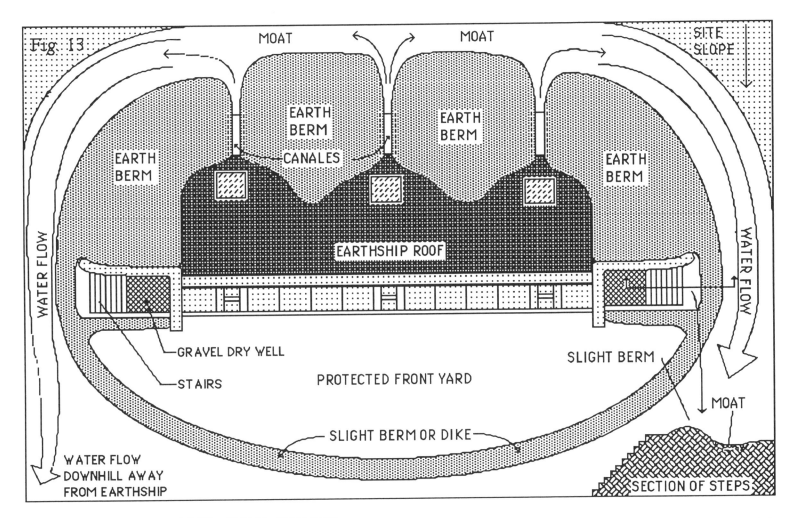

Fig. 13

MOAT — MOAT — SITE SLOPE

EARTH BERM — EARTH BERM — EARTH BERM — EARTH BERM

EARTH BERM

CANALES

WATER FLOW

WATER FLOW

EARTHSHIP ROOF

GRAVEL DRY WELL

STAIRS

PROTECTED FRONT YARD

SLIGHT BERM

MOAT

SLIGHT BERM OR DIKE

WATER FLOW DOWNHILL AWAY FROM EARTHSHIP

SECTION OF STEPS

FINAL BURIAL AND SITE WORK

Immediately after your building is roughed out the site shaping must be done to create proper surface water movement and drainage. Above is a typical drainage plan for a slightly sloped site. Water is taken around (east and west) the building via slight dishes or "moats" on the surface of the earth (Fig. 13)(also see page 40, ch. two). Canalies drain roof water into this dish. The steps going down into the building have a slight berm between them and the moat to keep water from running down the steps (Figs. 13b and 14). In this case all water is running south. **All earth should slope away from building.** A slight berm or "dike" on the south side keeps water from coming back in towards the building.

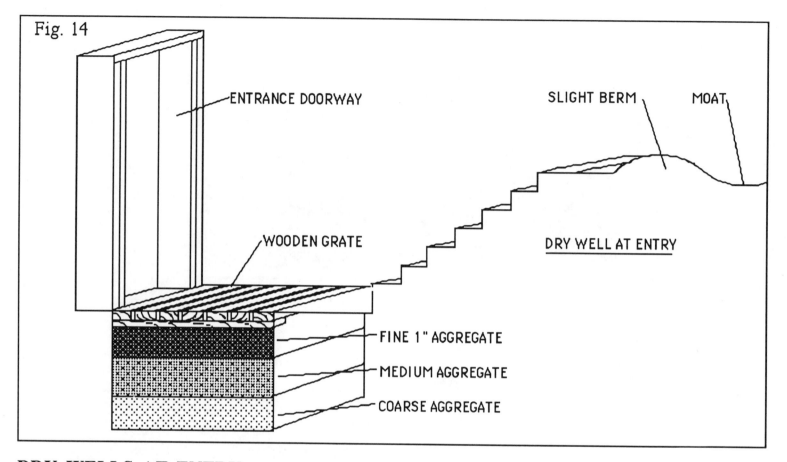

Fig. 14

ENTRANCE DOORWAY

SLIGHT BERM   MOAT

WOODEN GRATE

DRY WELL AT ENTRY

FINE 1" AGGREGATE

MEDIUM AGGREGATE

COARSE AGGREGATE

DRY WELLS AT ENTRY

If your site shaping is done properly the only water that will collect at the bottom of the stairs going down into the building is the water that rains on the steps themselves. This is handled with a dry well. This involves a 3'-6" deep pit right in front of the door filled with large rock on the bottom, finer rock in the middle and very fine (1") aggregate on the top.

A wood grate can be built over the gravel if desired. This collects what little run-off is caught by the steps and takes it below floor level of the house.

172

9. FINISHES

THE FORMULAS AND TECHNIQUES FOR VARIOUS FINISHES

The finishing techniques involve some do-it-yourself methods and some professional plasterer methods. The do-it-yourself methods are presented step-by-step with referrals to professional plaster contractors when applicable.

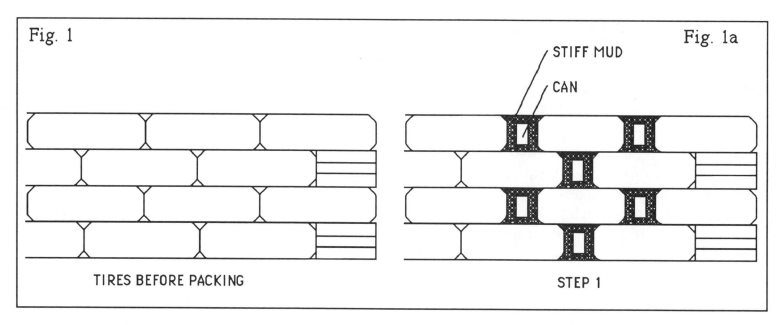

Fig. 1

Fig. 1a

STIFF MUD

CAN

TIRES BEFORE PACKING

STEP 1

PACKING TIRES - STEP 1

Packing of the voids between the tires can begin very soon after the tires are laid. Step 1 is simply to throw a big double handful of stuff-mud in the void between the two tires and then stick an aluminum can in the mud. The can acts as a spacer to reduce the amount of mud needed and to facilitate its' drying.

This job can be very easy or very hard depending upon the consistancy of the mud. The mud is mixed with half dirt from the site and half concrete-sand (course) and four large, double-handfuls of chopped straw per average electric concrete mixer load. This is equivalent to about one wheelbarrow load. Mix the sand,

dirt and water in the mixer until it is soupy, then add straw until it gets so thick that it will hardly fall around in the mixer.

Wet the tires and throw on the mud.

The straw for this job is simply bailed straw run through a hammer mill. It comes out in 1" long straw fibers. Check your local feed or grain store for someone with a hammer mill. A leaf shredder will also work for chopping up the straw.

If the mud is too loose and runny this job will be next to impossible - **YOU NEED STIFF MUD.**

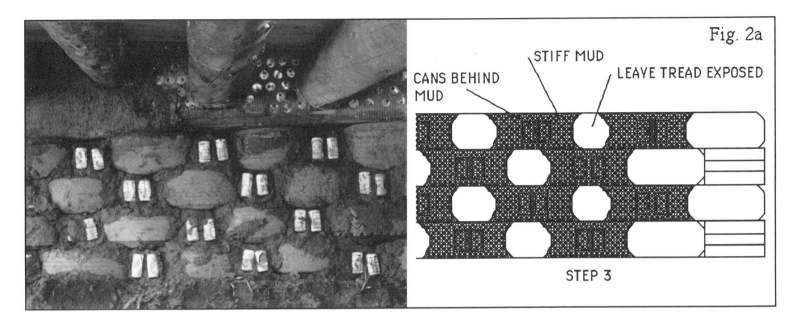

Fig. 2a

CANS BEHIND MUD

STIFF MUD

LEAVE TREAD EXPOSED

STEP 3

PACKING TIRES - STEP 2 + 3

First allow Step One to dry. New mud should never be applied over wet mud, but always wet the surface of dry mud when applying new mud. Misting the dry mud with a hose works well. Now use the same consistancy of stiff-mud as in step one. Slam two more double-handfulls of stiff mud into the voids you have left over from step 1. Cover the aluminum cans with mud and then stick on two more cans. (Fig. 2a)

Allow this to dry and with your hands push on more stiff mud (this may take two coats) until you bring the mud-filled voids out to the surface of the tire treads. You should end up with a mud wall with little sections of tire tread showing through (Fig. 2a). This wall should now be almost all in the same plane.

Electrical wiring rough-in should go in between Step One and Step Two.

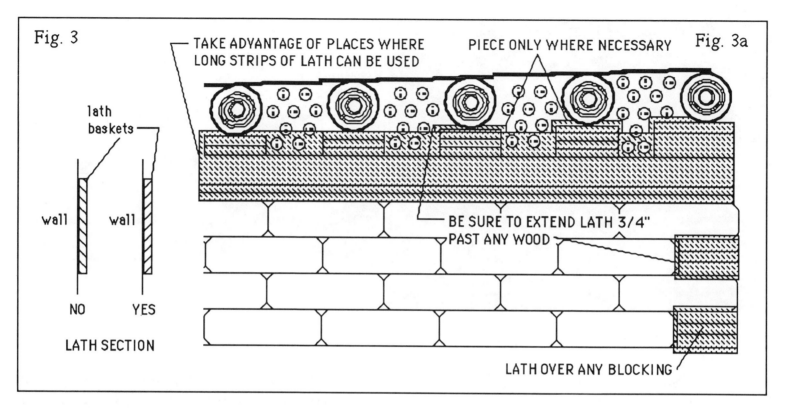

Fig. 3

TAKE ADVANTAGE OF PLACES WHERE
LONG STRIPS OF LATH CAN BE USED

PIECE ONLY WHERE NECESSARY

Fig. 3a

lath
baskets

wall   wall

NO   YES

LATH SECTION

BE SURE TO EXTEND LATH 3/4"
PAST ANY WOOD

LATH OVER ANY BLOCKING

PREPARATION FOR SCRATCH COAT

The shelf above the tire walls where the blocking shims and can infill is should now be prepared for scratch mud. The cans should have been laid with mouth ends out. This provides a natural lath for receiving the scratch plaster. The wood should all be covered with 6 mil plastic stapled over it. Over this, nail on metal lath with 1 1/2" roofing nails. If you look closely, the holes in

the metal lath are at an angle. One way they create little "baskets" that hold plaster. The other way angles down and allows the plaster to slide off. Angle the "baskets" up whenever possible (see lath section above) and the plaster will stick to the lath much better. Remember to allow the lath to overhang around the wood. Lath should always overlap joints between two different materials.

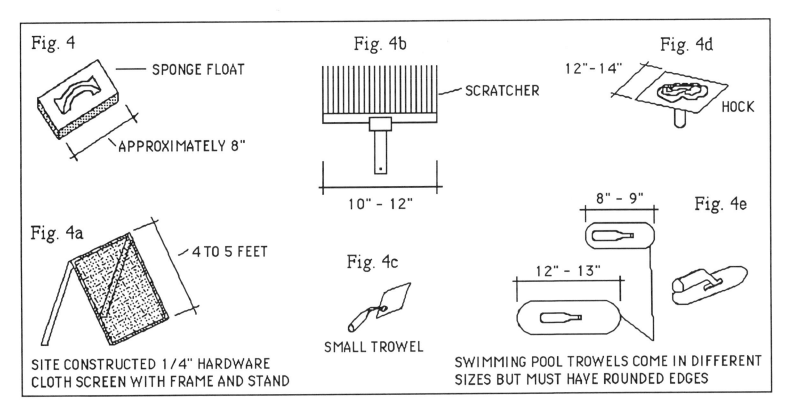

Fig. 4 — SPONGE FLOAT — APPROXIMATELY 8"

Fig. 4a — 4 TO 5 FEET — SITE CONSTRUCTED 1/4" HARDWARE CLOTH SCREEN WITH FRAME AND STAND

Fig. 4b — SCRATCHER — 10" – 12"

Fig. 4c — SMALL TROWEL

Fig. 4d — 12" – 14" — HOCK

Fig. 4e — 8" – 9" — 12" – 13" — SWIMMING POOL TROWELS COME IN DIFFERENT SIZES BUT MUST HAVE ROUNDED EDGES

SCRATCH COAT

Now that all surfaces are prepared, you are ready to apply the scratch coat of mud. This coat is applied with swimming pool trowels that have rounded ends (Fig. 4e). It is also good to have a hock (Fig. 4d) to hold the mud. The mix is still half dirt from the site and half sand. However, the dirt must now be sifted through a 1/4" screen (Fig. 4a) and the sand must be plaster sand. Still mix a soup with these proportions and add chopped straw until it gets thick. This mix is not as stiff as the fill-packing mud. It must be able to be applied and spread with the trowel.

Sometimes two scratch coats are needed to get the shape one desires for the wall. Make sure the first coat is dry before applying the second. Never apply new mud over wet mud. Scratch the mud horizontally with a scratcher (Fig. 4b) after it is applied and is still wet. This makes the surface rough enough to receive the final coat. Make sure all surfaces are scratched while they are wet before moving on to finish mud.

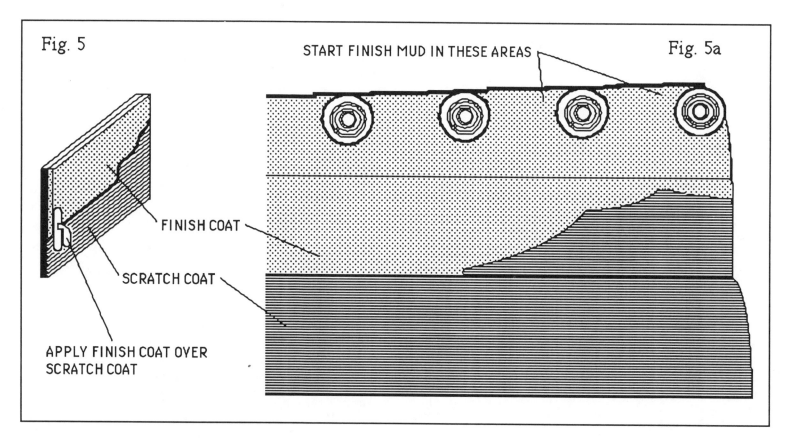

Fig. 5

Fig. 5a

START FINISH MUD IN THESE AREAS

FINISH COAT

SCRATCH COAT

APPLY FINISH COAT OVER SCRATCH COAT

FINISH COAT MUD

Finish mud is a different proportion of sand and dirt. The proportion is usually two sands (plaster sand) to one dirt (sifted) with the same amount of straw. However, this varies relative to the clay content of your site-dirt. Several 3'-0" square test patches should be done with varied amounts of fine plaster sand in the mix starting with two sand to one dirt. You are looking for a finish that has no cracks. When you obtain the formula that works, you are ready to do an entire wall.

It is best to start with the high areas around the beams. These are small, more obscure areas with which to learn the nature of the mud. First, wet the wall thoroughly with a fine spray from a hose, then trowel on the mud using a small trowel in small areas. After you obtain the shape you want on the wall, you can get a smooth surface by spraying the mud with a plant-mist bottle. Spray (to make the suface slightly wet) and trowel until you get a smooth surface. Do this over and over, smoothing the mud with very controlled, regular strokes of the trowel. Spraying the surface with the mist brings out the fine grain and allows you to work the surface until you achieve the look that you want. Never apply finish mud more than 1/2" thick since it will crack. Never let the finish mud dry in direct sunlight. Put a tarp over the windows if necessary to provide shade. If you are not going to paint the mud, you must "design where you place the seams" (where you start and stop a mudding session) since the seams will be visible. Plan out a wall section to mud so that the seam will be in a corner or hidden by something.

ALTERNATE FINISHES

Finish mud plaster can be painted with any latex , enamel, or epoxy paint. Cracks can be spackled and painted. Painting makes the mud more durable and refines the finish, however, it can also reduce the amount of sunlight absorbed by the wall.

There is a product available through builder's supply stores called "Structolite". It is a hard plaster that can be applied over scratch mud. It provides a more durable surface than mud plaster, however, it would most likely require a professional plasterer to apply.

Stucco companies now have many different acrylic products that come in any color and can be painted, troweled, or sprayed on.

Consult your local building supply store. All of these products can be applied over Finished Mud. The idea here would be to get the shape you want with mud and then use an acrylic product for the finish.

179

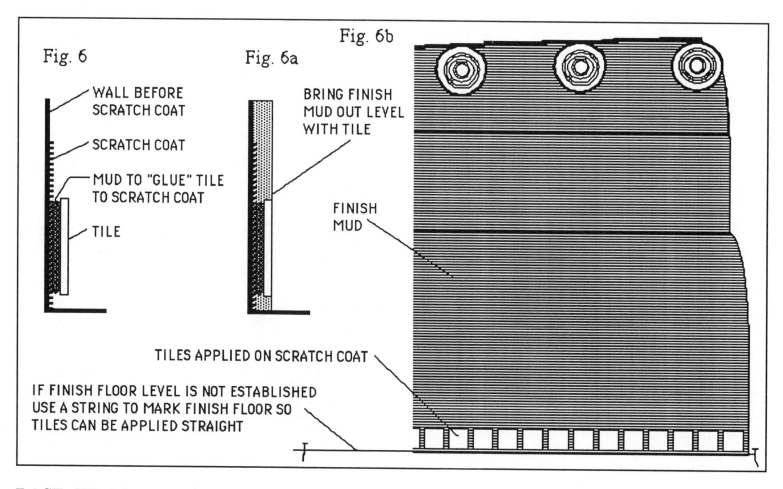

Fig. 6

WALL BEFORE SCRATCH COAT

SCRATCH COAT

MUD TO "GLUE" TILE TO SCRATCH COAT

TILE

Fig. 6a

BRING FINISH MUD OUT LEVEL WITH TILE

FINISH MUD

Fig. 6b

TILES APPLIED ON SCRATCH COAT

IF FINISH FLOOR LEVEL IS NOT ESTABLISHED USE A STRING TO MARK FINISH FLOOR SO TILES CAN BE APPLIED STRAIGHT

BASE TILES

After you get your scratch coat on, it is time to decide whether or not you want to have tiles at the base of your walls. This is a good idea since it acts as a baseboard and protects against mopping, brooming, and vacuuming, which all tend to scratch up the base of the wall finish. Tiles are installed by establishing a finish floor level with a string, unless you already have the floor installed, and "gluing" the tiles on the wall with a mud-mix. Soak the tiles in water and wet the wall surface, then apply mud to the back of the tile and press it on the wall (Fig. 6). Space the tiles about a fingers thickness apart. Finish mud plaster can now be brought out to the face of the tile (Fig. 6a + b).

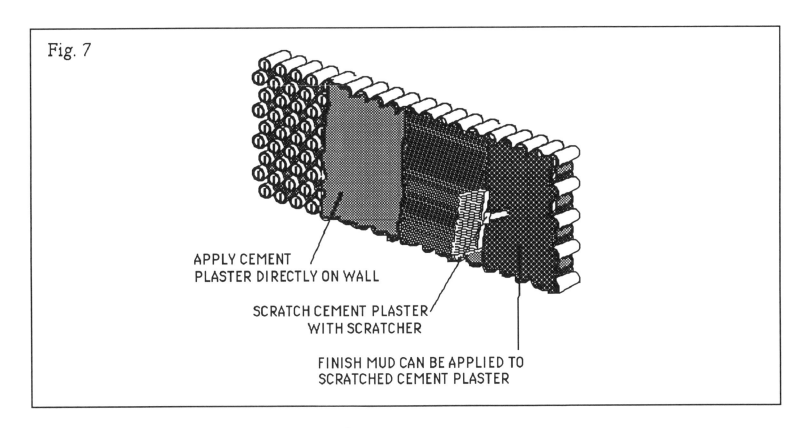

Fig. 7

APPLY CEMENT
PLASTER DIRECTLY ON WALL

SCRATCH CEMENT PLASTER
WITH SCRATCHER

FINISH MUD CAN BE APPLIED TO
SCRATCHED CEMENT PLASTER

PLASTERING ALUMINUM CAN WALLS

Aluminum Can Walls are laid with the mouth opening pointing out. (Fig. 7 above and 43a, page 155) This creates a natural lath surface for the plaster. When aluminum can walls are finished on both sides (as with a partition wall) then alternate the direction of the mouth openings as you build the wall (Fig. 8a page 162). This allows for the "lath surface" on both sides and provides for a good plaster connection on both sides of the wall.

The can walls are scratch-plastered with cement plaster in order to add strength to the wall since the cement IS the strength of the wall. A mix of one part Portland cement to three parts plaster sand is used. Wet the wall and apply the plaster with a swimming pool trowel, then scratch it horizontally with a scratcher (Fig. 7). Finish mud can be applied over this cement-scratch coat if you wish to match the finish of the tire walls.

If you are finishing the wall with something other than mud, (i.e. stucco) if the wall is in a bathroom or is an exterior wall, then the next step after cement-scratch coat is to apply a "floated-brown coat". This is simply another coat of the same mix (one part Portland to three parts sand - though, some people add a 1/2 part of masonary cement to the formula). This coat is for shaping the wall, thus, after it is troweled on, it is "floated" with a sponge float (Fig. 4, page 177). This is a standard building technique and any plaster contractor can help you with it. All plaster of any kind should be allowed to dry out of direct sunlight in order to avoid cracking due to quick drying.

After the brown coat is applied, conventional stucco, Structolite, or any hard plaster can be applied. Consult a plaster contractor if you do not want a mud finish.

Internal mud finishes are not limited to the southwest. They are quite durable - especially with paint - and can be easily applied by the average do-it-yourselfer. Different regions of the country require some experimentation with the proper formula.

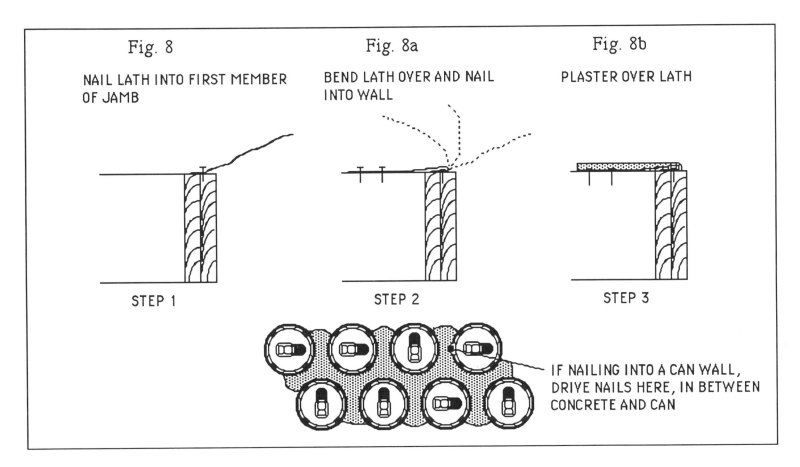

Fig. 8
NAIL LATH INTO FIRST MEMBER OF JAMB
STEP 1

Fig. 8a
BEND LATH OVER AND NAIL INTO WALL
STEP 2

Fig. 8b
PLASTER OVER LATH
STEP 3

IF NAILING INTO A CAN WALL, DRIVE NAILS HERE, IN BETWEEN CONCRETE AND CAN

PLASTER PREPARATION AROUND DOOR JAMBS

Any mud plaster or cement plaster that comes in contact with a window or door jamb must have a "bull-nose" metal-lath detail applied in order to "tie-down" the plaster to the wood. Since, otherwise, it will simply crack and fall off around the woodwork. The bull-nose detail is done by nailing four to five inch wide strips of expanded metal lath to the corner of the outside jamb member (Fig. 8), then bending it back over the wood against the adjacent material - cans or tires (Fig. 8a and 8b). The overlapping flap must then be nailed into the other material. If the adjacent material is a can wall, use 16 cc nails and nail in between the cans and the concrete. Nails won't hold in cans and they won't go into concrete, but they will hold if they are driven in between the two. This detail is often forgotten, but it is a very important detail in finishing your building. Any wood, window, or door-jamb must have a bull-nose lath detail.

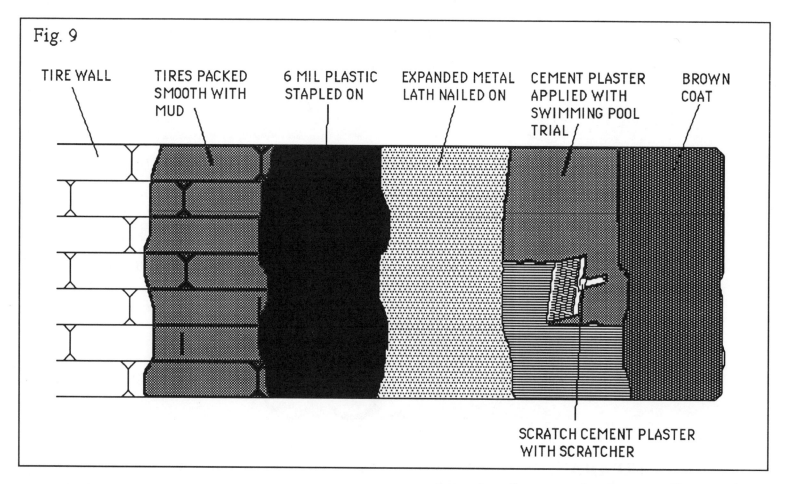

Fig. 9

TIRE WALL
TIRES PACKED SMOOTH WITH MUD
6 MIL PLASTIC STAPLED ON
EXPANDED METAL LATH NAILED ON
CEMENT PLASTER APPLIED WITH SWIMMING POOL TRIAL
BROWN COAT
SCRATCH CEMENT PLASTER WITH SCRATCHER

EXTERIOR PLASTER

Anytime wing walls on the exterior are packed out to a smooth plane with mud (Pages 174-175), they should be covered with 6 mil plastic that is stapled on. This is then covered with expanded metal lath, baskets up (Fig. 3, page 176). Aluminum can parapets have their own "built-in" lath. Any other odd details or materials should have metal lath installed in

preparation for scratch plaster. Conventional scratch plaster can then be applied, one part Portland to three parts plaster sand.

Exterior plaster takes much abuse due to weather changes. For this reason, small synthetic fibers are added to this mix. There are different brand names for these fibers. Usually about two handfuls per wheelbarrow load is enough. The fibers are known as "structural concrete fibers" and can be bought at your local builders supply store or concrete company.

After the scratch plaster has cured, a "floated brown coat" is applied in order to achieve the desired shape and provide a surface for stucco. This is a conventional technique and therefore a professional plasterer can be consulted. The fibers should also be included in the brown-coat mix. Sometimes plastic cement is used instead of Portland cement. It is more expensive, but it helps prevent the formation of cracks. See your builders' supply store or professional plasterer.

Conventional stucco or one of the new acrylic stucco products can be applied over the brown coat. The brown coat can have many additional applications if you do not obtain the shape you want right away. Just don't put it on too thick since it is better to build up through many layers. Consult a local plasterer for stucco products and applications in your area.

186

10. OWNER'S MANUAL

HOW TO OPERATE YOUR "EARTHSHIP"

In that Earthships are a new concept in living techniques as well as construction, some specialized knowledge regarding operation and maintenance of an Earthship is required. This chapter will help you derive the most comfort and performance from your Earthship.

TEMPERATURE

Too Hot

If you are too hot, it could be from air temperature, direct sun or both. If direct sun is involved, see the shading section. To cool the air temperature down, you must create a "chimney" for hot air to leave and an inlet for fresh, cooler air to come in. Often, the air movement itself has a cooling effect. This, in a subtle way works like a windchill factor. All "U"s should have an operable skylight. Simply open the skylight in the "U" that is too hot, and open the nearest front face window and/or door to that "U". This creates the chimney and the inlet and breeze. Each "U" has the potential for individual temperature control this way.

If your Earthship is on two or more levels, the entire building can be cooled by opening fully the highest skylight in the highest room and the lowest windows or doors in the lowest level. This creates a chimney effect and gentle breeze throughout the whole vessel. Any combination of venting individual rooms and/or the whole building will have an effect. If the air is crisp and cool outside, you will find that it doesn't take much before you will close your skylights, as you will have exchanged all the air in the space for fresh, crisp air very quickly. If the outside air itself is warm, you may keep the "chimney effect" operational all day long. In this case, the gentle breeze is a factor of the comfort level.

Obviously, weather conditions and local climate are factors of venting, however, it is typical for Earthships to have some venting (even if the windows are just slightly cracked open) almost all year round. Cloudy winter days and winter nights are the only times venting is not typical. For the most part, fresh air is always drifting through the vessel. The tremendous thermal mass allows winter venting since we are not as concerned with heating air as conventional heating systems are. We are living next to a giant warm "body" - the body of the Earthship. Air movement helps keep pests (bugs and white flies) to a minimum and people healthy.

Too Cold

Obviously, if you are too cold, you must close all vents, windows and doors. In winter months, or cloudy weather it is always good to close the vessel up if you are not at home. This allows heat to be stored in the house while you are gone. When you come home, the air will feel stuffy. Simply create a "chimney" effect as described above for a brief time (10 minutes) and you will have changed all the stuffy air. **Do not vent in the winter while you are not home.** This keeps the mass from storing heat. In the winter, always keep the individual spaces unvented (closed up) if you are not in them. The more heat they are allowed to store, the longer they will be warm without sun or auxilliary heat. The point here is that you must be aware that **you can over-do venting in the winter** and retard your collection of heat storage in your mass. Winter venting should be employed only when comfort or air quality demands. The rest of the time you should be storing heat whenever possible.

In extremely cold climates, with many cloudy days, insulated shades may be necessary. All east and west windows should have insulated shades anyway. The south sloping windows are designed to have insulated shades installed between the struts as shown in Fig 1. These insulated shades are available through Solar Survival Architecture (SSA).

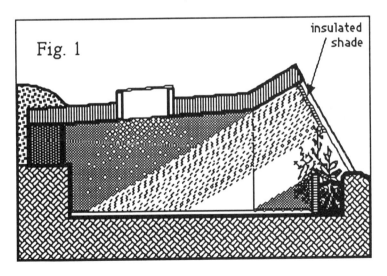

Fig. 1

insulated shade

The shades are closed at night, if needed, to retard heat loss. Earthships have been in operation in extremes as low as -30° fahrenheit, and these shades have not been necessary. However, it is conceivable that there are some conditions where they would be needed.

If control of venting and/or insulated shades does not provide the comfort level you want, a small amount of back-up heat is necessary. This condition would be more likely in high ceiling areas or areas where a large amount of east or west glass has been used. A fire place, small wood stove, small ventless gas heater, or warm floor system is recommended here. Earthships are so massive and well insulated that a very small input of heat from any source goes a long way.

Bathrooms that are not directly on the solar face often require a blast of heat after a shower. This can be achieved with instant electric heaters with fins or small gas units. Wherever the possibility of back-up heat exists, it should be roughed in first with electric wiring and gas lines. Add the actual heating unit only if you find that you need it. Very small amounts of heat go a long way in Earthships. Most Earthships have and need nothing but a fireplace for back-up heat.

SUNLIGHT

Too Much

The Earthships are designed so that the sun does not come into the living spaces in the summer (Fig. 2), while it floods them in the winter (Fig. 3).

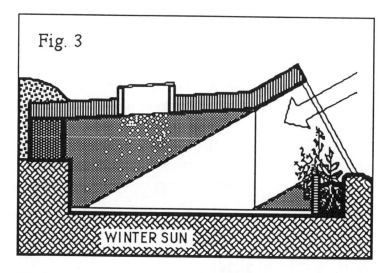

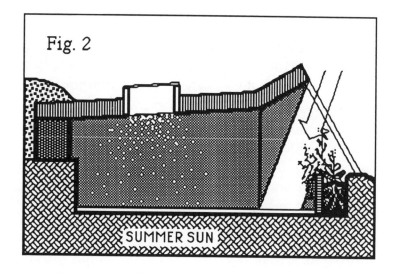

Summer sun doesn't go any further than the greenhouse hallways. If you have developed any seating areas in the greenhouse hallway, you may want to shade them in the summer. Shading is also necessary occasionally in the winter when the sun enters the living spaces. There are two specific ways to deal with shading in the Earthship.

The first way is done with drop shades or drapes (Fig. 4). **This method can totally shade the "U" while still allowing the Greenhouse Hallway to heat up and collect heat.** It is the most economical and

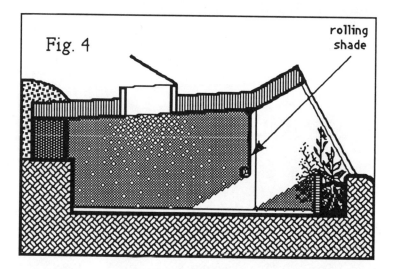

easy way to have some sun control. It is rarely used in the summer, since the sun doesn't come in any further than the greenhouse hallway. Any type of roll-up shade or drape will work. Roll-up shades have the advantage of not being dropped all the way down, thus allowing winter sun to still heat the floor while you are in shade.

SHADING ON THE FRONT FACE

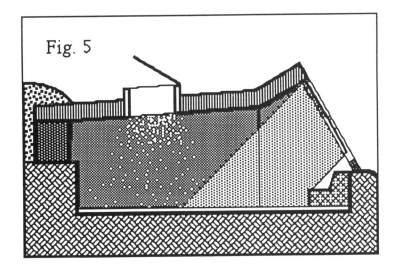

Fig. 5

Front face shading is only recommended if you have built seating areas instead of a planter under the glass (Fig. 5). There are times when this will be a delightful place to be and times when the sun here is too much. To have some control over this situation, you would need a

struts, and will slide up and down on the guide rails, thus keeping them against the front face. SSA is a dealer for a very lightweight shade that will work here. They come in white and a variety of colors. The disadvantage of this type of shading is that it cuts off **all** sun to the area - hallway included - so that you are cutting off your heat absorption by fully shading against the glass. Therefore, this type of shading should be used sparingly in the winter - perhaps by only letting it down two or three feet when in use (Fig. 6).

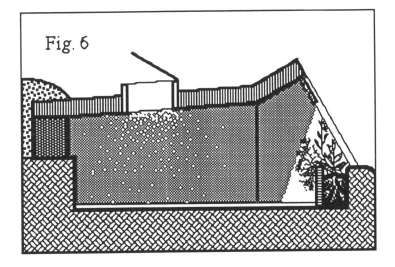

Fig. 6

This lets the sun into the greenhouse hallway and floor, but shades the bulk of the "U".

front face shade. There are many shades available that will fit between the 60° sloped

NOT ENOUGH SUN

An advantage of front face shading up against the glass is that in extremely cold climates with very little sun, these types of shades could be let down at night to insulate the south windows from heat loss. In areas where there is a lot of sun, this is not necessary due to the tremendous gain and storage capacity of the Earthship, however it is an advisable device in <u>cold cloudy</u> climates.

The bottom line with shading is to know what you are trying to do with it and what the consequences are, so that you can select the proper method.

PLANTS

The greenhouse hallway heating duct is the major place for planting because it gets full light all the time. Another very good place for plants is between the "U" and the hallway (Fig. 7a and 7b). This area gets full sun most of the time. Planters in this area can be open on the bottom to tap into uncontained earth.

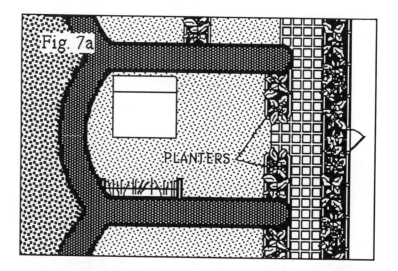

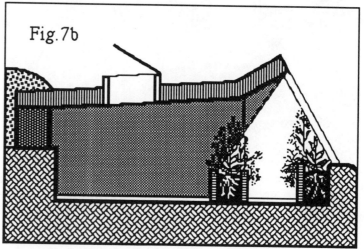

Here the plants can act as a partition to give some shade and/or privacy to the "U".

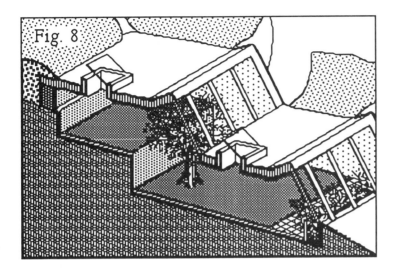

Fig. 8

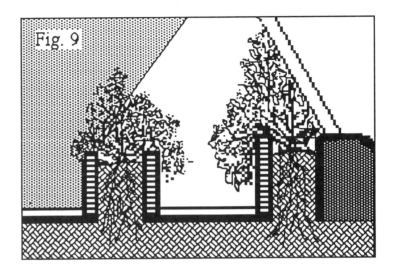

Fig. 9

In some step arrangements of "U"s, two story spaces are created which allow trees to grow (Fig. 8). The Earthships are thus designed for maximum living with plants. The reasons for this are for food, beauty, oxygen/CO_2 exchange between people and plants, and for convenience. It is very easy to tend a garden if it is on the way to your bedroom.

Living with plants to the extent we are talking about in an Earthship does require some understanding of the nature of plants themselves. There are many opinions and theories about how plants should be cared for. The instructions in this section are those of the author, based on 15 years of <u>living with</u> large amounts of plants.

Planters on single level Earthships go directly to the ground.

That is, the planter has no bottom (Fig. 9). Planters that are on upper levels of a stepped arrangement are contained, drained and have a rock and gravel bottom to facilitate drainage (Fig. 10).

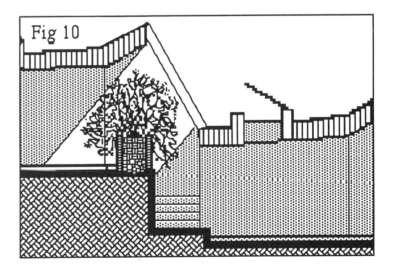

Fig 10

Planters are filled with topsoil from the site up to the last 6 inches. The last 6" is topsoil from

193

the site mixed with sand, vermiculite and peat moss. Any soil that is used over and over has to be fed. Household grey water should be directed or caught and poured into planters whenever possible. This is a "natural" way to feed your soil with your own by-products. All plants love dirty bath water and the food particles in the kitchen sink water. Mild soaps like Ivory Liquid, when diluted, are actually good for plants in that they help to immunize plants against pests. Grey water systems will be discussed in depth in Earthship Volume II.

There are some plants that require almost no care, grow fast and are very hardy. These are the best plants to "establish" your green areas with. You can come back later and clear out areas for more delicate plants that require more time and care. The hardy plants will practically take over and there are very few bugs that will harm them. Even later, when you plant more delicate plants or food producing plants, which are more vulnerable to bugs, it is best to leave "patches" (sometimes as much as half the area) for these hardy plants since a large area of delicate plants is easy prey for bugs. When there are strong hardy plants on either side of delicate plants, vulnerability is somewhat reduced.

These hardy plants are:

Wandering Jew - There are many varieties ranging from green to purple leaves. All have blooms. All need almost no care and they simply take over. Bugs never bother the Wandering Jew and plants can be started from a trimming stuck directly in the soil. Keep it very wet until it takes hold - about one week.

Geraniums - There are many varieties, all of which have beautiful blooms in many colors. They spread rapidly and bloom often. They get no bugs and fill planters with foliage up to 3' high. They can be started with a clipping stuck directly into wet soil - keep it wet until it takes hold and starts growing.

Bulb plants like Amaryllis, lilies, iris, etc. all do very well with no care.

Grapes - Grapevines take over and vine up the windows providing shade in the summer. They are cut back all the way in the winter and have very few problems. They also provide grapes!

Aloe vera - Aloe is a good plant to have around for medicinal purposes (see a medicinal plant book). It spreads, needs little or no care and gets no bugs.

Any succulents - Succulents can take the sun and grow rapidly in the Earthship environment.

All of the above plants are easy to obtain, easy to start and are resistant to bugs. They will establish your green areas. After you fill your green areas, you can come back and clear out certain areas to plant more vulnerable plants that require more care. You will have too much to care for until you slowly program plants into your life. It is strongly recommended that you start with plants that require little care and slowly integrate plant care into your life. It is very depressing to have a greenhouse full of sick, screaming dying plants that you have no time to care for. This experience will dampen the whole idea of living with plants. Start with an easy situation and work into more variety. Large amounts of plants can take much time, work, and money to care for - more than you may realize.

BUGS

Most food-producing plants are vulnerable to various pests. Common pests are white flies, aphids, and pill-box bugs. There are other insects that appear around large planted areas that aren't necessarily pests. The idea is to keep pests to a minimum, and simply allow some insects to exist with the plants. To try and create a sterile environment is not healthy for plants or humans, and is a very expensive, time-consuming, loosing battle. Plants will have some bugs since this is natural. Ideally, the greenhouse area should get much fresh air, and have some bees and butterflies passing through.

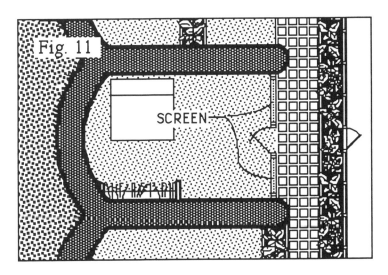

Fig. 11

SCREEN

If bugs completely scare you, some "U"s could be closed off or screened off from the growing areas (Figs. 11 and 12).

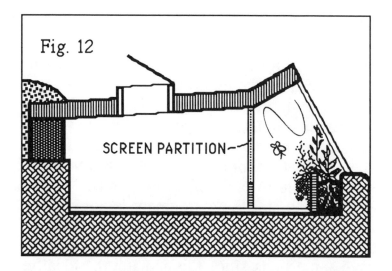

Fig. 12

SCREEN PARTITION

The point is that plants require some insects for pollination and policing for harmful insects. For instance, lady bugs are often turned loose in greenhouses for the purpose of eating aphids. If you want to live with plants, you must accept some bugs. One of the most common mistakes made in living with plants is the struggle for a sterile (no bug) environment. **The solution to the bug problem is control, not annihilation.** Many methods can help control bugs. One easy way is to mist vulnerable plants often with water that has a few drops of Ivory Liquid in it. Anything yellow with something sticky on it will attract and catch white flies. Lady bugs eat aphids. Misting with water that has tobacco soaked in it causes many pests to run. Don't try to get rid of all of them. Just don't let them take over. This will keep you from frustration. This is another reason to start with "bug free" hardy plants as discussed

above, and gradually work into the more vulnerable food producing and flowering plants. One of the best defenses against pests is strength. Strong plants have their own resistance. Grey water is one of the best ways to make plants strong. The more watering you can do with grey water, the happier and healthier your plants will be. There are many ways to capture and distribute grey water. These will be discussed in Earthship Volume II.

FOOD PRODUCING PLANTS

Food production is a major reason for living with plants. To be able to stagger crops and harvest a little at a time (as opposed to massive harvests, canning, etc. of a conventional garden) is a luxury and a convenience available to Earthship owners. Easier plants to start with are tomatoes, zucchini, romaine lettuce, and bell peppers. All can get bugs, but if the bugs are kept to a minimum, via the techniques mentioned previously, you can get much produce that is far better in quality than any store bought produce - organic or not. Almost any vegetable, herb-citrus product, or root crop can be grown inside. Serious production would definitely demand grey water use.

Conventional glass does allow plants to produce; however, in areas of serious food production, the plastic and acrylic glazing products produce a diffused light with more of the ultraviolet light that plants like. Serious food production is more successful under Lascolite or a similar product. (See your local solar supply store for obtaining Lascolite or similar products). If you can live without a view in certain areas (you can't see through Lascolite), Lascolite glazing would be recommended for optimum food production. Regular glass glazing units could be installed every third window to get the best of both worlds for intense production areas. Or, another method is to make the bottom 2'-0" of glazing Lascolite (or equal) and then make the top 6'-0" out of regular glass (Fig. 13). This requires a little more detailing but gives you the best of both worlds. Some people also like the added privacy this gives.

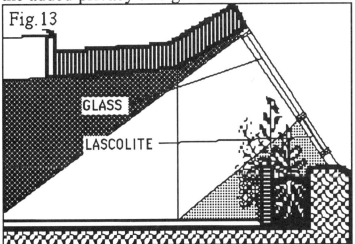

Fig. 13

GLASS

LASCOLITE

Living with plants is much like living with other people, i.e. a family. You must relate to their needs as well as your own and try to integrate the two. You can't ask plants to adapt totally to your world if you want them to produce. This is how we get some of the inedible foods we find in stores. Plants like grey water, some bugs, fresh air, strong friends, (neighboring bug resistant plants) and, in serious production areas, a plastic (Lascolite or equal) type of glazing.

Food crops produce longer inside an Earthship, but they do have to be ripped out and replanted as they get old. Some tomatoes produce for as long as a year if they are happy. Plants should be considered and provided for just as another "member of the family." Pets have this status - why not food producing plants?

MAINTENANCE

Any building or vessel requires maintenance. Since Earthships are mostly covered with earth on the north, east, and west, maintenance is basically limited to the south face which is mostly glass. Whatever wood you use on the south face should be oiled once a year for longer life.

Site drainage should be inspected and reinforced annually. **Make sure surface water is always rapidly running away from your vessel.**

Interior mud finishes can be touched up once a year. Many Earthship owners will opt for acrylic or hard plaster finishes over the mud fill on the tire walls. These finishes do provide more durability than natural mud or painted mud. However, cracks, movements, or changes do appear over time (as they will in any building due to settling), and so the more modern products require more expensive and involved methods of patching and in some cases, require entire walls to be replastered. Mud finishes, however, even if they are painted, can simply be patch-mudded and/or spackled and repainted. Mud finishes allow easy maintenance executed by the owner. This obviously has advantages if you are a do-it-yourself type of person. The point is that there will be some cracks, scores, and in some areas around wood detailing, movement in the finish plaster no matter what material you use. How much relates to how well your detailing and plastering techniques were executed. Mud, while not as durable, is easier to patch and maintain than other products. The result is you may have to police your mud plaster once a year yourself as opposed to having someone every two or three years professionally retouch and/or redo your hard plaster or acrylic walls. Most major expansion and contraction (thermal movement) in a massive Earthship will occur within the first three years. The bottom line is to expect some plaster cracks during this time. They will diminish as the Earthship finds it's thermal cycles and seats itself into the seasons of your site. We are talking about one day of mud patching once a year for the first three years in an average sized house.

Other than systems operation, which will be outlined in Earthship Volume II, this is all you need to know to operate your Earthship.

Bon Voyage!

11. EXISTING EARTHSHIPS

THE PROTOTYPES

Photographs (finished and during construction) and plans of existing Earthships are presented here. Costs range from $20.00 per square foot to $90.00 per square foot. Sizes range from 600 square feet to 10,000 square feet to an 80 unit destination lodge. A wide spectrum of uses of the concept are illustrated here.

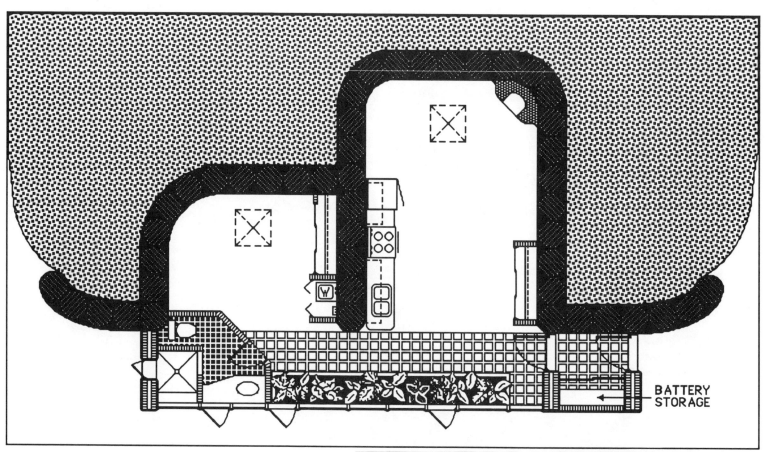

Owner: Pat Habicht
Taos, New Mexico
675 square feet
Owner worked on job
Cost- $45.00 per square foot
Job managed by Joe Hoar

BATTERY STORAGE

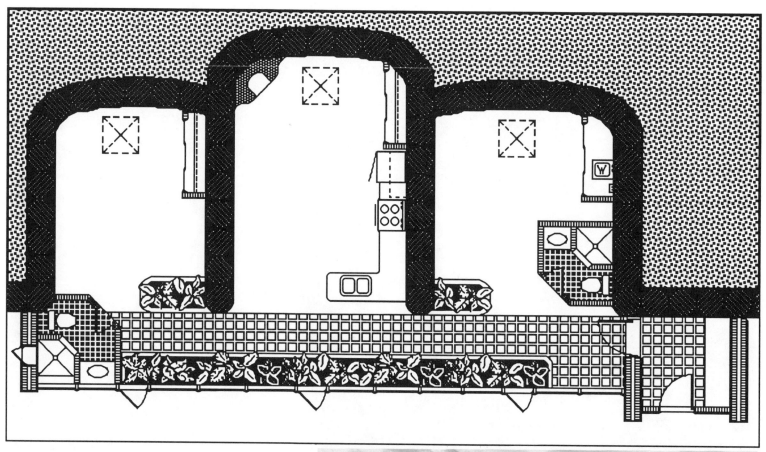

Owner: Steve Trujillo
Taos, New Mexico
1250 square feet
Owner-builder
Cost- $50.00 per square foot
Job managed by Justin Simpson

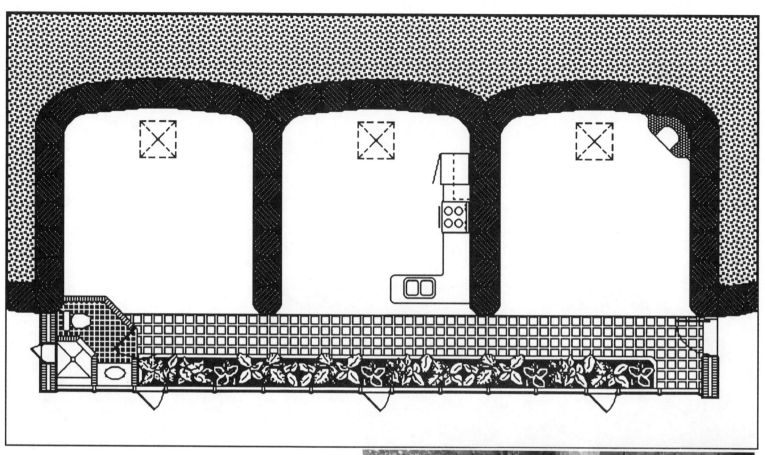

Owners: Me'l Christensen
and Sam Bascom
Taos, New Mexico
1000 square feet
Owners built project
Cost- $30.00 per square foot
Job managed by owners

205

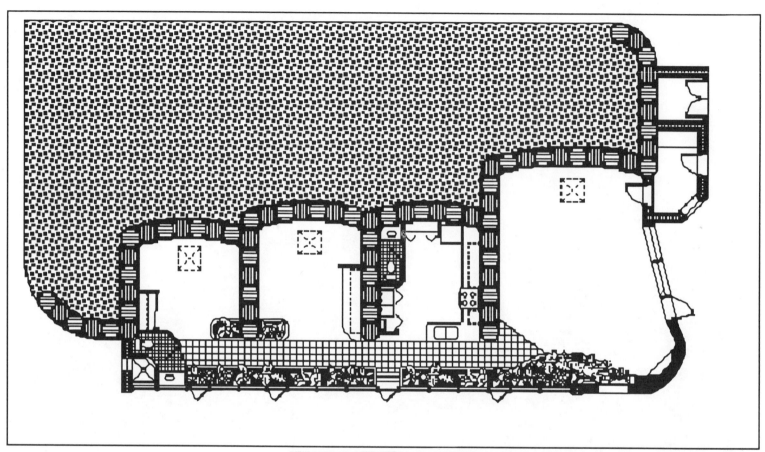

Owner: Pat Habicht
Taos, New Mexico
1600 square feet
Owner worked on job
Cost- $50.00 per square foot
Job managed by Peter Kolshorn

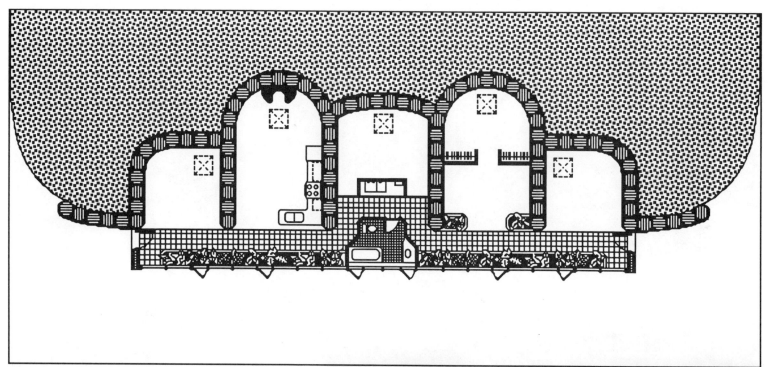

Owners: Michael Reynolds
and Chris Simpson
Taos, New Mexico
1600 square feet
Owners built project
Cost-$20.00 per square foot
Job managed by Michael Reynolds

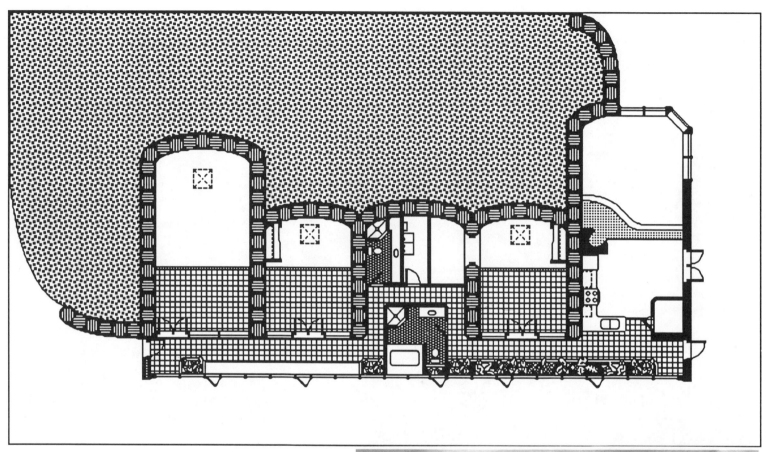

Owners: Carolyn Lake and Joy Franklin
Taos, New Mexico
2800 square feet
Owners worked on job
Cost-$55.00 per square foot
Job managed by Joe Hoar

211

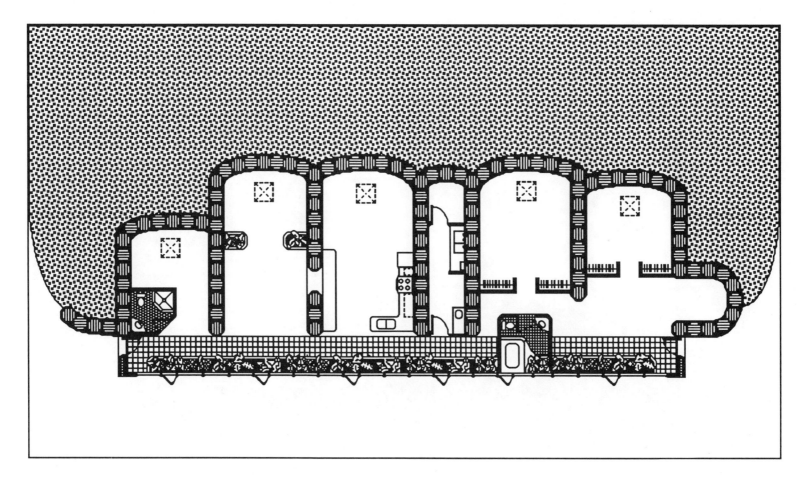

Owners: Susan and Eric Henley
Albuquerque, New Mexico
2600 square feet
Owners worked on job
Cost-$60.00 per square foot
Job managed by William Stoddard
Construction Company and Dan Reardon

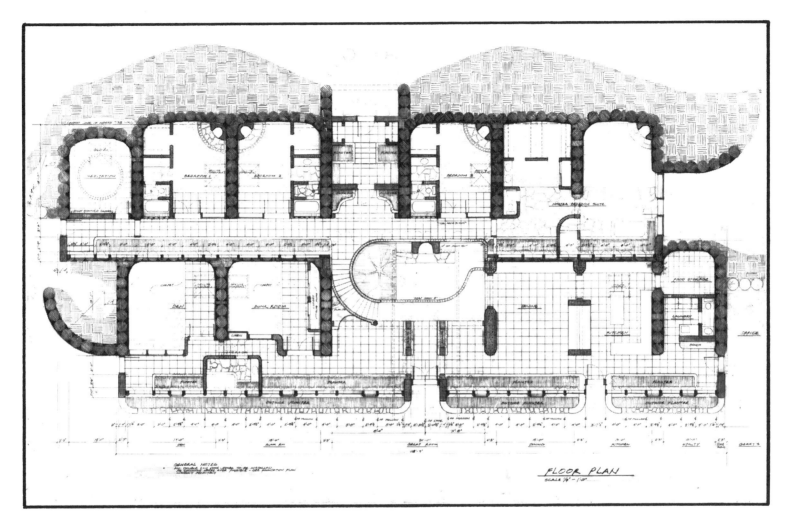

Owners: Dennis and Gerry Weaver
Ridgway, Colorado
7000 square feet plus garage
Owners worked on job
Cost-$90.00 per square foot
Built by Allison Construction Company

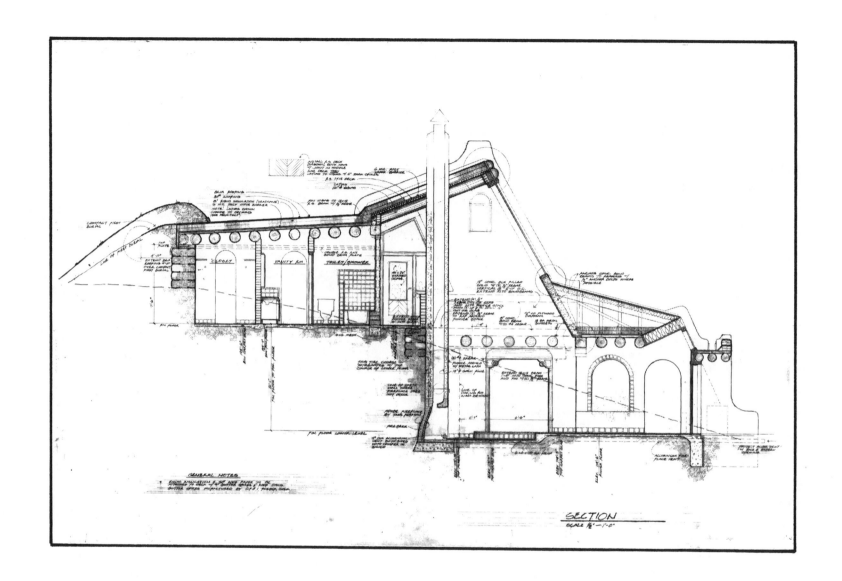

Weaver Section

214

Weaver Construction

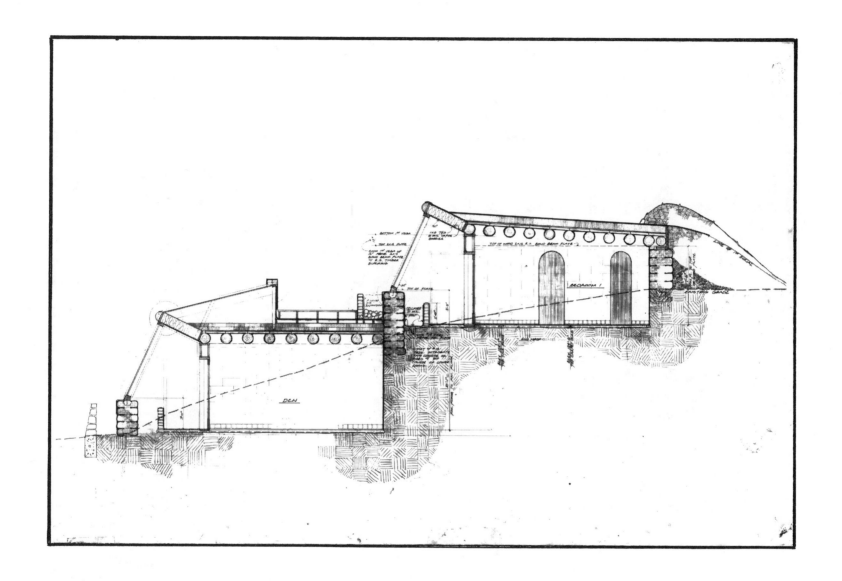

Weaver Section

Weaver Tire Wall on Rock Cliff

Weaver West End

Weaver Overview

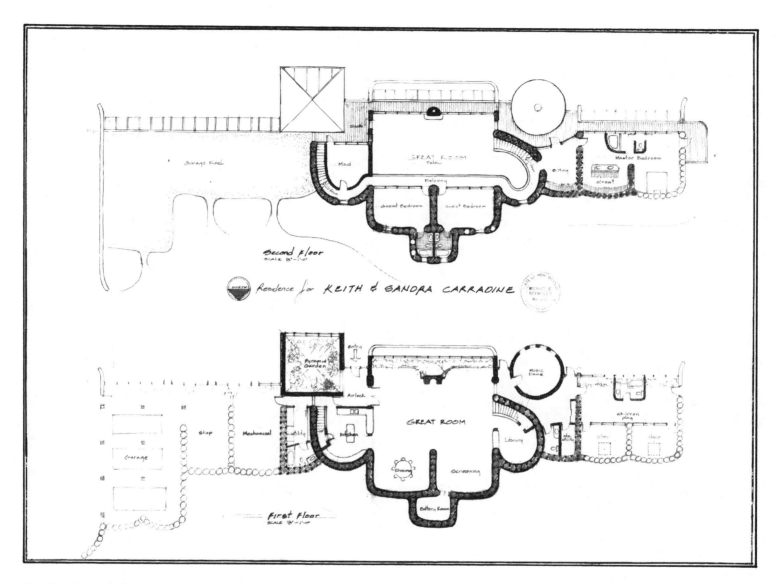

Preliminary Design
Keith and Sandra Carradine
Telluride, Colorado

OVERVIEW STUDY

EARTHSHIP for KEITH & SANDRA CARRADINE

STUDY of EAST ENTRY

Preliminary Design
Keith and Sandra Carradine
Telluride, Colorado

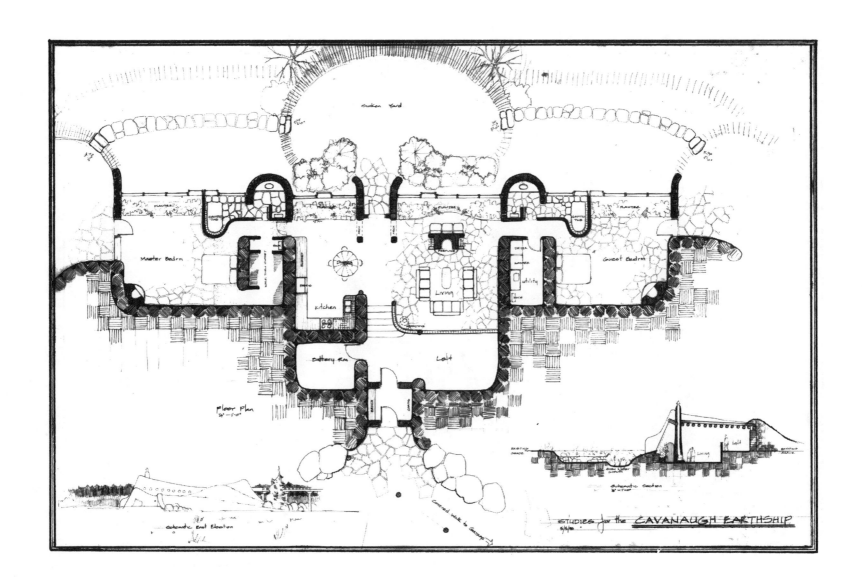

Preliminary Design
Tom and Peggy Cavanaugh
Ridgway, Colorado

Preliminary Design
Tom and Peggy Cavanaugh
Ridgway, Colorado

Preliminary Design
Destination Lodge
Ridgway, USA
Ridgway, Colorado

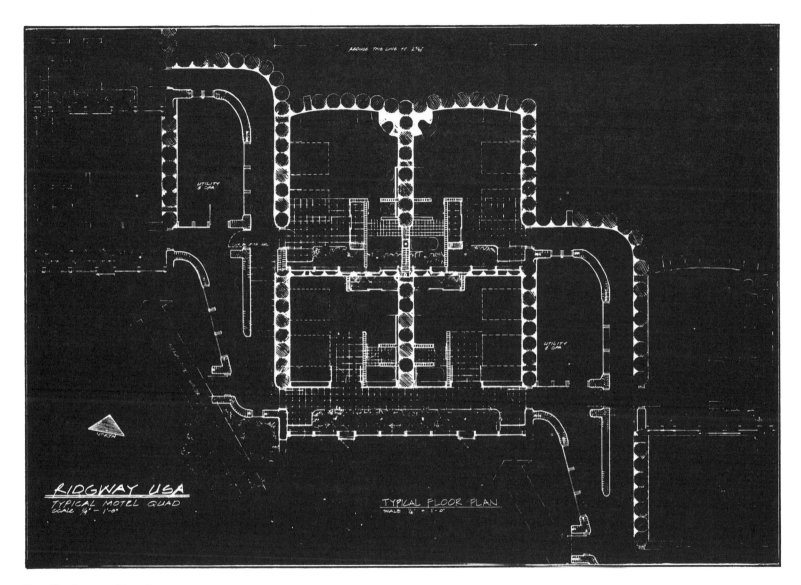

RIDGWAY USA
TYPICAL MOTEL QUAD
SCALE 1/4" = 1'-0"

TYPICAL FLOOR PLAN
SCALE 1/4" = 1'-0"

Preliminary Design
Destination Lodge
Ridgway, USA
Ridgway, Colorado

226

EPILOGUE

Having been involved in building homes and other structures out of tires for 20 years, I get very excited when I see the giant tire piles that exist in almost every populated area. Knowing how easy and inexpensive it is to construct energy efficient homes from these tires, I begin to see the tire dumps **as a solution to other problems** (housing, energy, employment), **not a problem in themselves.** These tire dumps are potential communities, towns, and even cities of Earthships. We have unknowingly been mass-producing and stockpiling ideal building materials for the future. The time has come to begin using them.

A major factor in establishing the proper frame of mind for "voyaging" in an Earthship is that an **Earthship is not a house.** A house as we know it is an out-of-date concept, no longer appropriate for human life on Earth. With this understanding, we will not be trying to make an Earthship into a house. An Earthship is a vessel to take care of us in the world of tomorrow, when population and global abuse will be realities to reckon with. This tomorrow is coming fast. We will be more concerned with self-sufficient comfort and food production than with "style" and "tradition".

When one buys a mobile home, one accepts certain factors about mobile home that allow it to be different than a house, because it is a given that it is mobile. When one buys an Earthship, there are certain factors relative to performance that one must accept as givens to allow it to be a vessel that will "sail on the seas of tomorrow" where common housing will surely sink. The point is that human dogma is the only thing between us and a harmonious future on the Earth.

Michael E. Reynolds

CONSULTATION – SCHOOL – ARCHITECTURAL SERVICES

There are many levels on which the concepts and techniques put forth in this book can be applied. It is the aim of this book to guide people through the use of this concept with as little outside help as possible. However, there will undoubtedly be questions and additional expertise needed in many cases.

SOLAR SURVIVAL ARCHITECTURE holds a contractor's license and an architectural license under the name of Michael E. Reynolds. We offer minimal consultation all the way to full architectural services, and in some cases we actually do the construction.

We also have regularly scheduled seminars and an ongoing school to teach these methods and concepts to home owners, builders, and architects. Please contact us if we can help take you farther on your voyage.

Earthship Volume Two will be available in late winter of 1991. It will include how to build fireplaces, skylights, stairs, doors, cabinets, greywater systems, solar electrical systems, mud relief sculpture, domes and vaults, and more.

REBEL

let the world fall away
i am not boundaried by
your boxy repetition
i am not living under your fashion magazine
my bullets are hidden for later
i have deceived you
i have no microwave ha ha
i have not eaten for 8 days
my children are illegal aliens
my american car has no engine
i wear boots with formal wear
i don't care i just don't care

let the world fall away
to snowfalls of dust
and institutions of clutter
demanding dirty dishes and laundry
leave it all along the asphalt
there is lots of jungle left
the birds are blue and green
trees are truer than television
the sky holds a million sparks
for each of us

we are withering in our darkness
under electric light
our bleached sheets and blankets
will never be clean
we will not survive
until we set ourselves free

— anonymous, 1982